Hispanic Marketing:
A Cultural Perspective

Felipe Korzenny
Betty Ann Korzenny

ELSEVIER
BUTTERWORTH
HEINEMANN

AMSTERDAM • BOSTON • HEIDELBERG • LONDON
NEW YORK • OXFORD • PARIS • SAN DIEGO
SAN FRANCISCO • SINGAPORE • SYDNEY • TOKYO

Elsevier Butterworth–Heinemann
30 Corporate Drive, Suite 400, Burlington, MA 01803, USA
Linacre House, Jordan Hill, Oxford OX2 8DP, UK

Library of Congress Cataloging-in-Publication Data
Korzenny, Felipe.
    Hispanic marketing : a cultural perspective / Felipe Korzenny, Betty Ann
Korzenny.
        p. cm.
    Includes bibliographical references and index.
    ISBN 0-7506-7903-4 (pbk. : alk. paper)   1. Hispanic American consumers.
2. Consumer behavior—United States.   3. Target marketing—United States.
I. Korzenny, Betty Ann, 1933–   II. Title.
    HF5415.33.U6K67   2005
    658.8′0089′68073—dc22
                                                                2005008903

British Library Cataloguing-in-Publication Data
A catalogue record for this book is available from the British Library.

ISBN 13: 978-0-7506-7903-9
ISBN 10: 0-7506-7903-4

For information on all Elsevier Butterworth–Heinemann publications
visit our Web site at www.books.elsevier.com

Printed in China

05 06 07 08 09 10   10 9 8 7 6 5 4 3 2 1

Advance Praise for *Hispanic Marketing*

"This book is a must-read not only for those engaged in ethnic marketing, but for all marketing professionals. *Hispanic Marketing* provides true insight into the Hispanic market and compelling rationale for addressing Hispanic consumers as part of any organized approach to marketing in the U.S. overall. This market segment is far too large, far too affluent, and growing far too quickly to be ignored—and yet it is much too rich and distinct as a culture to be communicated to superficially. Felipe and Betty Ann Korzenny provide us with salient information, and more importantly, tools and an approach, to unlock the full potential of the Hispanic consumer. This book is truly a breakthrough in enabling a comprehensive and meaningful understanding of this market."

—**Michael Durance**, Vice President & General Manager, Telecommunication Systems Division, Communications Information Group, Toshiba America Information Systems, Inc.

"Account planners contemplating how they might grow a brand with the Hispanic consumer will zoom up the learning curve with a read of this book. Planners will also find a very useful guide for the next steps they need to take to collect the category and brand specific insights they need to forge a strong emotional brand connection with Hispanic consumers. And they will be inspired by the many case studies discussed throughout the book. Marketers approaching Hispanic marketing with vexing questions of language dialect usage, translations, research paradoxes, and even what to call this market, will find well-informed guidance on these matters. They will also come away with a good basic understanding of how to bring their brand messages to the marketplace, with a great primer on Hispanic media in the U.S."

—**Denise Fedewa**, Senior Vice President, Planning Director, Leo Burnett, USA

"As a marketer, and as a Hispanic I found the book enlightening and educational. In an environment where there is so much information about the demographics and psychographics of the U.S. Hispanic market, the authors offer a much deeper understanding of how to be successful in marketing to Hispanics by going beyond stereotypes and generalizations, developing new models and approaches and doing this via a wealth of case studies and a "how to" approach that any marketer or agency will find helpful."

—**Ernesto Levy**, Associate Marketing Director, Procter & Gamble— Household Needs Division

"The Hispanic market is at once one of the most attractive, yet most misunderstood consumer segments in America. Thankfully, Felipe and Betty Ann Korzenny bring years of career wisdom, built on work with America's top marketers, to dispel long-held cultural myths and stereotypes and to focus on the key cultural drivers for this consumer. It is an invaluable resource for anyone involved in marketing to Hispanics."

—**Dan Nance**, President & CEO, Casanova Pendrill

"The Korzennys have accomplished a complex feat in their new book, *Hispanic Marketing*. Somehow this powerful and important work satisfies the

needs of anyone and everyone that has an interest in the evolution, realities, theories, craft, art and science of U.S. Hispanic marketing. Additionally, it serves to provide insight into the societal and cultural aspects of the U.S. Latino experience. Top-level marketers will appreciate the specific action-oriented recommendations and key marketing implications that accompany each chapter. Advertising agency executives from integrated marketing disciplines will value the Korzennys' depth of experience and objectivity in presenting the many sides to the many stories that make up a day-in-the-life of the multi-dimensional U.S. Hispanic consumer. But this is also a wonderful book for non-industry readers to embrace because of the story it tells about the vibrant history and significant future of Latinos in the rich culturally-blended story that is unique to life in the United States."
—**Rochelle Newman-Carrasco**, CEO, Enlace Communications

"During many years of working in Hispanic marketing I have never seen anything that so clearly describes and understands the complex dynamics of the New America! The Korzennys have built their reputation over many years as the best multicultural minds of our business. I have entrusted them with many projects in our 10-year relationship and have always relied on their expert advice. This work allows me to confirm once again that they are the leaders of thought I always knew and will continue to lead insight development within the Hispanic market as they shape the minds of generations to come."
—**Juan Carlos Olivar**, Customer Marketing Manager, The Coca-Cola Company

"The Korzennys understand the Latino market deeply and thoroughly. Reading their book is like sitting in one of their seminars and being enthralled by their insights and depth of knowledge. Their writing is especially powerful in that it demonstrates hands-on knowledge of consumers, marketers, and Latino advertising agencies. The Korzennys provide actionable answers to frequently-asked questions and guidance on how to manage the obstacles in developing effective marketing programs."
—**Hector Orcí**, CEO/Co-Chair, La Agencia de Orcí & Asociados

"There is no more important segment of the American consumer marketplace of tomorrow than Hispanics, and there is no more important book to read about marketing to Hispanics than this one. Every page delivers an insight worth knowing. Most marketers get it wrong when it comes to Hispanics, leaving an enormous opportunity for first movers who do it right. This book shows the way to get there first. I've put it on the Yankelovich short list of must-read books."
—**J. Walker Smith**, Ph.D., President, Yankelovich Partners, Inc.

"An in-depth understanding of the Hispanic community's cultural pillars and biases is the foundation for sound Hispanic marketing. The Korzennys' book provides that and more. It offers a rich and much-needed perspective for anyone trying to target U.S. Hispanics by making the crucial linkage between culture and marketing strategies."
—**David Wellisch**, Vice President and General Manager, AOL Latino

Dedication

This book is dedicated to the approximately 45 million Hispanics in the United States in 2005. They are shaping not only the future of marketing, but the culture of this great country. We have worked with many of them over the past 30 years. They have patiently answered our many questions and taught us the inner workings of culture. That knowledge enables human connection at a deeper level, which is what good marketing is all about.

Contents

2

3

4

5

**The Processes of Enculturation, Acculturation,
and Assimilation** 128

6

7

8

9

Acknowledgments

This book has been a shared endeavor that started a long time ago. We began our work with U.S. Hispanics in the late 1970s. Many people influenced us along the way and we are thankful to them. Bradley Greenberg and Michael and Judy Burgoon, then at Michigan State University, were instrumental in our involvement in the elaboration of the book *Mexican Americans and the Mass Media*. This was a seminal piece in the early 1980s because that study detailed how Hispanics used the media as compared with non-Hispanics at a time when very little was known about Hispanic consumers.

Also in the early 1980s, Brett Blackwell stimulated our first commercial involvement in Hispanic marketing. He saw a future in that nascent market and he was right. Many people placed their trust in our ability to understand the market in those early years. Some of those individuals who were clients and now are also friends include Mike Durance, now with Toshiba America; Emmanuel Cargill, now with Grand Marnier USA; Greg and Eva May, now with Español Marketing and Communications; Dan Nance, now with Casanova Pendrill; and many others who got us started in an in-depth immersion in the U.S. Hispanic market.

Our former company, Hispanic & Asian Marketing Communication Research, had talent that enriched our and the industry's knowledge of U.S. Hispanics. Some H&AMCR colleagues we want to thank individually include Adrien Lopez Lanusse, Suzanne Irizarry, Sandra M.J. Wong, Jennifer Mitchell, Carolina Echeverria, Lucia Fuentes Skinner, Ricardo Flores, Eulalio Segovia, and Horacio Segal. Our merger with Cheskin in 1999 brought many other people we learned from and they all deserve our gratitude. We want to thank individually our former Cheskin partners Christopher Ireland, Davis Masten, and Darrel Rhea. Two other Cheskin colleagues made contributions to the last chapter of this book: Stephen Palacios and Maria Flores Letelier.

The hundreds of clients and suppliers that helped us conduct thousands of observations of Hispanic consumer behavior are too many to mention individually but they should know we have not forgotten one of them.

In the elaboration of this book we had the support of several generous friends and colleagues. First of all, we could not have done this work without the trust and support of John Mayo, Gary Heald, Lawrence Abele, Stephen McDowell, and other colleagues at Florida State University. Several students directly contributed to this book: Erika Lea Watters, Maria Gracia Inglessis, Monique Mahler, and Yarma Velásquez. Many other students have served as sounding boards for much of what has been stated here.

Many of the professional and trade organizations that offer educational seminars on the U.S. Hispanic market have provided the opportunity over the past few years to develop some of the material for this book. These organizations include the Strategic Research Institute, The Association of Hispanic Advertising Agencies (AHAA), Yankelovich, the International Quality and Productivity Center, the World Research Group, the Hispanic Association for Corporate Responsibility, the National Hispanic Corporate Council, Florida International University, Expo Comida Latina, the International Dairy Deli Bakery Association, the International Boston Seafood Show, the Florida Public Relations Association, Marcus Evans, the National Kitchen and Bath Association, the Midwest Hispanic Marketing Conference, and many others. Rupa Ranganathan of the Strategic Research Institute deserves our special acknowledgement for her continued dedication to the trade and to the stimulation of thinking about Hispanic marketing.

The following individuals and their companies contributed case studies, ideas, narratives, and examples that made this book a richer source of knowledge. We want to thank them publicly because, despite their very busy schedules, they made the effort to tell their stories of the Hispanic market for the reader:

- Jeff Balter, Time Warner Cable Houston
- Montse Barrena, Grupo Gallegos
- Ernest Bromley, Bromley Communications
- Sharon Brunot-Espeziale, Lapíz Integrated Hispanic Marketing
- Ray Celaya, Allstate
- Carlos Córdoba, Acento Advertising
- Melanie Cyr, MendozaDillon
- Karla Fernández Parker, K. Fernandez & Associates
- Annette Fonte, Unilever
- Marco Garsed, Bromley Communications
- Jason Hagemann, Unilever

- Katherine Key, The San Jose Group
- Dolores Kunda, Lapíz Integrated Marketing
- Eva May, Español Marketing & Communications
- Cesar Melgoza, Geoscape
- Benito Martínez Creel, Acento Advertising
- Jessica Massay, Bromley Communications
- J. Moncada, Bromley Communications
- Rochelle Newman-Carrasco, Enlace Communications
- Hector Orcí, La Agencia de Orcí
- Ingrid Otero-Smart, MendozaDillon
- León Potasinski, La Agencia de Orcí
- Richard Ross, Marbo, Inc.
- David Wellisch, AOL Latino
- Jennifer Woods, The San Jose Group

Others who should be thanked for the advancement of our knowledge of Hispanic marketing include Loretta Adams, Isabel Valdes, Gary Berman, Richard Tobin, Deborah Gonderil, Peter Dickson, Gerardo Marin, Amado Padilla, Felix Gutierrez, Federico Subervi Vélez, Robert Suro, Carlos Santiago, Jorge Schement, Louis Nevaer, and Marilyn Halter. We apologize for omitting many others who deserve recognition.

At Elsevier/Butterworth-Heinemann, we have a great debt of gratitude to Jane MacDonald for her trust and support, to Dennis McGonagle for managing this book project, and to Sarah Hajduk for production supervision. Their efforts and continued attention have made this effort possible and a pleasure to work on.

Then, of course, we need to finally acknowledge those close to us who have patiently endured our inattention while writing. These include our kids and grandkids: Rachel, Ben, Mark, Hiro, Alex, Chris, David, Anna, David Jr., John, Jessica, Andrew, Ceci, Daniela, and Andrea. They encouraged us and we always strive to make them proud of us. There are also some other four-legged creatures that have put up with our neglect and they remain loyal and continue to nourish us: thank you Sugar, Spice, Dulce, Canela, Micio, and Boomer.

Introduction

The fundamental goal of this book is to provide professionals that cater to the Hispanic market with conceptual tools to do their jobs. The focus throughout the book is to increase cultural understanding of the Hispanic market as an essential element of a marketing toolkit. We believe that marketing success in any culture is predicated on reaching the emotional core of the consumer. For this reason, this book aims to empower marketers to lift the cultural veil obscuring their view of Hispanic consumers and the commonalities that bind them.

This book is not about citing statistics regarding the Hispanic market, although these descriptive statistics are necessary and will be included. Each of the chapters is a section of an overall collage depicting the Hispanic market. Each has been the subject of public presentations and lectures to marketing professionals. The evaluations received from the marketers who attend these presentations are always positive. The main reason for their appreciation is that no one has yet approached the study of the U.S. Hispanic market from a cultural perspective for the purposes of marketing.

There are over 70 advertising agencies in the United States that now cater exclusively, or with great emphasis, to the growing U.S. Hispanic market who are members of AHAA (the Association of Hispanic Advertising Agencies; www.ahaa.org). In addition, there are many more agencies that claim they have Hispanic expertise in-house, or that at some point or another have helped their clients in reaching this market. Conservatively, there are about 500 major U.S. companies now specifically targeting U.S. Hispanics.

The U.S. Hispanic market increased in visibility to major corporations when the 2000 U.S. Census declared that there were 35.3 million Hispanics in the United States at that point. In addition to the growing number of Hispanics in the United States, the buying power attributed to this group was endorsed by the industry at approximately $500 billion per year. Only five years later, the population figure has been revised to an estimate of over 40 million Hispanics with a purchasing power of over $700 billion per year by the Selig Center. This official population figure of U.S. Hispanics is surely an undercount. It does not take into consideration an estimated 8.5 million undocumented U.S. Hispanics. These are Hispanics who most likely would not be receptive to filling out census and other government forms. A conservative estimate of the total Hispanic population of the United States without counting Puerto Rico should be over 45 million people. At that size, the U.S. Hispanic population is the largest Hispanic population in the world with the exception of Mexico, which currently has over 100 million.

All these factors have contributed to the increased attention of U.S. corporations to the Hispanic market. Still the number of qualified individuals who understand the market is small, and many who are in positions to cater to the market have not found appropriate channels to learn more about its intricacies. The creation of appropriate training and education programs to develop such marketing resources as account planners knowledgeable about the Hispanic market is of critical importance for the future.

This book will describe and explain the principles of its subject matter mixed with marketing, advertising, public relations, and marketing communication examples that will help the marketer relate to the material pragmatically and conceptually. This is a book that integrates concepts and practical examples. It empowers the marketer to generalize and make decisions beyond the dogmatic wisdom that has characterized this discipline. It provides critical guidance as a tool for continual learning.

Chapter 1 of this book deals with the role of culture in cross-cultural marketing. You will find principles that will support you in conceptualizing marketing problems and questions when crossing cultural boundaries. The chapter clarifies the differences between subjective and objective culture, and explains how marketers need to take each into consideration to be effective in the Hispanic market. You also will be introduced to Psycho-Socio-Cultural analysis. This notion leads to an understanding of why marketing to a different cultural group requires further information and insight than marketing only to your own culture. Also, this chapter introduces you to the paradox of social class and culture. This paradox sheds light on the reasons why advertising and marketing that is directed to a seemingly uniform cultural group can fail if it does not take into consideration socio-economic class. Throughout this chapter you will find conceptual tools that help to define the elements that constitute a targetable culture from a marketing communication perspective. The chapter identifies and discusses the factors that delineate the Hispanic market as a culture.

Chapter 2 provides an overview of the Hispanic market from ethnic, demographic, geographic, historical, and socioeconomic perspectives. This chapter brings the market to life with its complexity and nuances. It explains the immigration patterns of Hispanics from diverse countries of origin. It presents the geographic dispersion of Hispanics in the United States and how that is currently changing to include cities never considered Hispanic centers before. It also gives a broad view of socioeconomic trends including social class, education, and family structure. Marketers need to obtain a holistic perspective in order to start making sense of the market and how it is configured. This chapter assesses the reality of the commonalities and differences that characterize the market. After studying this chapter, you will have an informed perspective on what you can and cannot expect from this market niche. Case studies illustrate the benefits of informed cultural understanding in Hispanic marketing.

Chapter 3 deals with the crucial subjects of Hispanic identity, labels, and how Hispanics think of themselves. The role of cultural identity in marketing is explored from a variety of perspectives. Marketers usually ask the question as to how they should address the market: as Hispanic, Latino, Chicano, or some other label. This chapter will constitute a research-based clarification of these issues and will provide informed direction as to the subjective cultural identity of Hispanics in the United States. This chapter not only discusses how identity concepts are linked to the labels of members of a cultural group, but also the measurement of Hispanic market characteristics related to identity. Two case studies show the effectiveness of marketing campaigns linked to elements of Hispanic identity.

Chapter 4 investigates the role of the language spoken by Hispanics in different contexts, be it Spanish or English. You will obtain an informed perspective on when the marketer should rely on Spanish, English, both, or even the "Spanglish" (code-switching) dialect. A key argument in this chapter is that the language used for the expression of emotion is likely to influence perceptions and thinking. If Spanish is the language of preference then it is likely that the worldview implied in this language will influence Hispanic consumer reactions to marketing communication. The growing importance of bilingual and English communication in the burgeoning Hispanic market is discussed. The issues of linguistic purism and pragmatism are central in this chapter since marketers continuously ponder the appropriateness of mixing the Spanish and English languages in their communications to the market. Translation problems are explored with practical suggestions for avoiding them. Furthermore, this chapter will identify the links between culture and language in order to build the argument that both are inextricably connected. Two case studies illustrate the power of language in connecting with consumer emotion for communication effectiveness.

Chapter 5 looks at acculturation, enculturation, and assimilation processes and their effect on Hispanic consumer perspectives. Marketers have been very concerned with issues related to the generational status of Hispanics and the extent to which assimilation will take place in the near future. Most marketers new to the Hispanic market argue that Hispanics will eventually assimilate like other national and ethnic groups have in the past and follow the old paradigm for assimilation—the melting pot. This chapter explains these concepts and argues that assimilation may not be the end state for Hispanics. The joint effect of acculturation processes and societal forces are creating a new model in which Hispanics are more likely to retain a bicultural and bilingual identity. These trends are also discussed in light of their implications for marketing and communication campaigns. Perhaps one of the most pragmatic concepts in this chapter is the idea of acculturation segmentation. Segmenting according to the degree to which individuals have acquired a second culture is crucial knowledge that marketers need in making strategic decisions. Examples of acculturation segmentation are provided based on the Yankelovich-Cheskin Hispanic segmentation model. Three case studies clarify how successful marketing campaigns take levels of acculturation and changes over time into consideration.

Chapter 6 explains the concepts of cultural archetypes and their application to marketing and communication campaigns. This chapter delves beyond surface issues in cultural marketing. The stereotype that the family is a key element that needs to be addressed in communicating with the Hispanic population has been abused to the extent that most advertisements directed to the U.S. Hispanic population portray a family. This overuse has produced a lack of differentiation in communicating with Hispanic audiences. This chapter argues that there are many other cultural dimensions and archetypes that need to be investigated in order to communicate effectively with Hispanic consumers. At the outset, this chapter differentiates between stereotypes, archetypes, and prototypes. It goes on to explore several less familiar archetypes that can be important sources of insights. For example, if a marketer of financial services knew the cultural meaning of money in Hispanic communities, he or she could find a better position for his or her services in this market. Another example of archetypes dealt with in this chapter is the notion of health and healthcare. Marketers in this category need to know how Hispanics think of life and death, health and illness, and other aspects that affect the degree to which Hispanics use, comply, and trust western medicine. The goal of this chapter is to enable you to formulate questions in your market inquiries that move beyond the surface of cultural manifestations to better connect with

Hispanic consumers. Four case studies illustrate how marketers who tapped into Hispanic cultural dimensions and archetypes forged effective, emotionally connected marketing campaigns.

Chapter 7 addresses the methods that need to be mastered by marketers in order to make sense of culturally diverse markets. This is the chapter for the "account planner" who is addressing the Hispanic community. The account planner is the ombudsperson of the consumer in advertising and marketing organizations. He or she is the person in charge of acquiring and interpreting valid market and communications data. Thus, this chapter will make the connection between the cultural knowledge derived from Chapter 6 with data collected from consumers. This chapter will enable you to make informed decisions about when to use or not use different qualitative and quantitative research designs. A sophisticated understanding of the how, when, what, and why of different approaches to gathering information is crucial for effective decision making. There are specific guidelines laid out in the chapter for making culturally informed marketing research decisions throughout the research process. This chapter infuses the theme of culture into the technicalities of creating meaningful research. Making use of culturally relevant research and informed analysis, the marketer can create effective campaigns that are emotionally linked to the Hispanic consumer. As in other chapters, examples will be provided.

Chapter 8 examines the U.S. Hispanic media environment and provides an orientation to its overall constitution and distribution. It will examine the evolution of Hispanic broadcasting, print, and the Internet. Here we illustrate the importance of integrating marketing and communication plans to effectively reach Hispanic consumers. This will not be a media inventory but a conceptual orientation to the role the media plays in Hispanic marketing. The chapter suggests a new way of thinking about media planning for the Hispanic market, a media-neutral approach based on media selection by each marketing objective. Such a versatile approach will allow marketers to consider the burgeoning array of media options as potential resources for the increasingly complex Hispanic market. This chapter will also provide insights regarding unconventional channels that promote the viral spread of messages about products and ideas. An example of these is Grassroots marketing, a relevant resource that strategists should employ to successfully reach the Hispanic market.

Chapter 9 looks at the evolution of Hispanic marketing in the United States from the impetus provided by the 1980 Census, declaring the "Decade of the Hispanic," to the surprising revelations of the 2000 enumeration. The market has almost quadrupled itself in just 20 years. This chapter will look at the evolution of ad agencies and marketing organizations from the pioneering period of the 1970s and prior, to the "Decade of the Hispanic" in the 1980s, to the "Take-off Years" of the 1990s, and finally to the 2000s' "Latin Boom." A group of six Hispanic marketing professionals give their perspectives on the development of the Hispanic market, and tell their personal stories of contributing to its growth over the past 20 years. The establishment of AHAA (the Association of Hispanic Advertising Agencies) in the mid 1990s constituted a visible marker in the history of the Hispanic market, and contributed to increased professionalism of Hispanic agency members. Despite all the achievements in Hispanic marketing, AHAA revealed significant under-spending on Hispanic marketing by large U.S. marketers.

Chapter 10 takes a futuristic look at the Hispanic market and its growing influence on the United States. The chapter explores future trends and planning that can benefit the Hispanic market as well as the United States as a whole. The chapter looks at breaking barriers faced by Hispanics—economic, geographic, and cultural—as a means to promote a better future for them, the countries they come from, and the United States in general. It also explores issues relating to border flows for labor and financial transactions. The chapter gives examples of emerging cross-border liaisons in which cities and whole towns in Mexico and other Latin American countries have cultural and economic ties to the United States that transcend physical and political borders. It discusses the attraction of *El Otro Lado* (the other side) of the border for Mexicans; how the constant influence, both economic and cultural, changes the lives of those who cross it, and provides marketing opportunities for products and services as well. The chapter discusses and provides examples of the impact of technology in promoting constant communication and business opportunities between Hispanics, their countries of origin, and the United States. The chapter concludes with a discussion of ethics in the Hispanic market and how they are served by a consumer-oriented, culturally informed marketing approach.

This book focuses on enabling marketers to gain a deeper understanding of Hispanic culture as a means for developing marketing campaigns, products, and services geared to the needs of Hispanic consumers. The final message of this chapter and of the book is that culturally guided consumer-oriented Hispanic marketing benefits Hispanics, their countries of origin, the overall U.S. market and economy, marketers, and the companies they serve. This approach leads to a future that is oriented toward growth beyond our imagination.

The Role of Culture in Cross-Cultural Marketing

The Importance of Culture in Marketing

Culture is a key that can unlock powerful marketing potential for professionals in their field. Yet, few marketers have incorporated the concept of culture in their day-to-day thinking and planning. Culture is an idea, a construct, a phenomenon, that many people in marketing talk about, but grasping the elements of culture to apply in all aspects of marketing has remained largely elusive. One of the main drawbacks has been that the meaning of the concept of culture is complex. It is easy to tell this by listening to the way people use the term: Culture can mean what educated people "have" when they talk about history, the opera, and museums. Or culture can mean foreign or radically different groups of people.

Culture is difficult to understand, particularly when humans are socialized in a homogeneous environment. Many cultures around the world are quite homogeneous. The Japanese tend to come from a specific ethnic group, tend to prefer not to intermarry, and make it very difficult for anyone not born from Japanese parents to become a citizen of Japan. The Japanese, then, share a great amount of accumulated experience among themselves. They can sometimes speak without words because situations speak for themselves and generate common understandings.

The Japanese are perhaps an extreme case of homogeneity. Many other nations around the world also have cultures that are homogeneous to some extent, but with the high level of mobility in contemporary society, generally there are diverse cultural influences within most societies.

The U.S. Anglo-Saxon-Germanic protestant dominant heritage has made for a relatively homogeneous centrally visible culture. It has a central set of beliefs, values, cognitions, behavior, and overall ways of living that are relatively consistent. The stamp of hard-working middle-class protestant America is everywhere in every town of the United States. Americans are known the world over for the productivity of their workers, and for the numerous and innovative products they manufacture, enjoy, and export. Yes, there is variability within the culture; however, anyone around the world can identify the American character and the American way of doing things in almost every commercial communication, product, and official message.

In addition to productivity, Americans in the United States tend to have a communication style that is identifiable and supported by a strong underlying value in the culture. In the United States there is a preference for heroes, spouses, politicians, bosses, and religious leaders to be straightforward and plain-spoken—to "tell it like it is." Some of the most respected and beloved cultural leaders have illustrated this norm: Clint Eastwood, John Wayne, Harrison Ford, Ronald Reagan, Abraham Lincoln, Harry Truman, Walter Winchell, Elizabeth Cady Stanton, Gloria Steinem, and Walter Cronkite to name a few. This is an aspect of American culture that has been revered at home, and sometimes caused misunderstanding and resentment in communication across cultures, not only with other countries but with diverse groups within the United States as well.

Homogeneity is an asset to American culture. It has created a craving for the glory of the ideas, style, and products of U.S. society. However, it is so valuable that many U.S. marketers, who are themselves generally part of the mainstream-homogeneous culture, have a very difficult time understanding that people from other cultures could be different. Even more surprising is the notion that a group of people within the United States who have become a very large and important market could be of a substantively different culture. That is the U.S. Hispanic market, the culture addressed in this book.

If every marketer who reads this book is stimulated to think about how the U.S. Hispanic market differs from mainstream America and has an increased orientation to establish better communication with it, then this book will have achieved its goal.

Culture

Culture is the baggage that human groups carry with themselves over history. A culture generally is understood to be the cluster of intangible and tangible aspects of life that groups of humans pass to each other from generation to generation. The reason why cultures have endured the passing of time is that they have provided survival value to founders of the cultures. For example, Jews and Muslims do not eat pork or seafood without scales because at a certain point in history, eating those organisms was very dangerous to human health. The custom endures to this day, even though the danger has greatly subsided. Elements of culture that had great survival value at some point in history continue to be important even after they lose their practical utility.[1]

Objective Culture

The tangible or objective aspects of culture are the most commonly known. Those are the artifacts and designs for living upon which cultural groups depend for everyday life. They include foods, buildings, attire, music, preferred colors, statues, urbanization, toys, and all the other aspects that an archeologist would be able to classify as forming part of a particular culture. An example of objective culture in a typically mainstream American cultural scenario might be a fall football game at a Big Ten university. A game with a profusion of home team colors, hotdogs and popcorn, cheerleaders bouncing up and down and making human pyramids, a mascot figure with an oversized fake head and upper body, the crowds doing "the wave," and the team heroes slamming blocks into the opponents and passing the pigskin for a touchdown. Examples that are more mundane include a little girl, eating sugar cereal alone at the breakfast table, looking at the cereal box designs and playing with Barbie, while her mom, briefcase in hand, urges the child to hurry because it is time for her to get to the office and for the child to be at school.

Examples of Hispanic Objective Culture

Hispanics of Mexican background are known to eat "Mexican food." In the United States, Mexican food typically is known to include items such as enchiladas, tacos, burritos, fajitas, and a few other items. Dishes not as well known in the United States include sopes, chalupas, arracheras, sabanas, mole, pozole, menudo, papatzules, cochinita pibil, and so on. Although Mexicans eat many foods not necessarily associated with Mexican food, those just listed tend to be characterized as being part of the heritage of the peoples of Mexico. Clearly, we should assume that there are many complexities even within one country, where regional cuisine can be quite different from one part of the country to the other.

Figure 1.1

Alebrije[a]

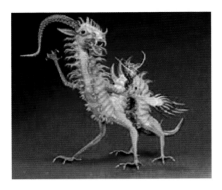

The typical "Spanish" look of many homes in Latin America—with stucco walls and Spanish tile roofs, painted white or in varied pastel colors—is clearly associated with Hispanic architecture. The internationally successful *alebrijes* (as seen in Figure 1.1) are fantasy figures that reflect the rich surrealistic imagination of Mexico and other Latin American countries.

The style of dress of the Mexican Tehuana, India Poblana, Andean Quechuas, and Aymaras, and so on, and the overall taste for style and colors differentiate Hispanics. Common trends in typical dresses include very colorful designs. More modern versions tend to be sexier than U.S. versions. The sense of femininity and masculinity found in Latin American dress styles tends to be markedly different from the United States. Men tend to dress more formally and women tend to dress so as to emphasize sexual attributes. Clearly, dress varies most markedly with socio-economic class and occupation.

These more evident objective aspects of culture symbolize the tip of the iceberg whose most substantive mass is subjective and below the surface. The submerged aspects of culture strongly influence how we perceive most aspects of life (see Figure 1.2).

Subjective Culture

The submerged part of the iceberg is the metaphor for the different aspects of the hidden or more subjective aspects of culture. Because most people share basic needs and values, many marketers tend to minimize cultural differences. They argue that overall, the same stimulus should have the same meaning for non-Hispanic consumers as for Hispanics.

[a] http://www.elbalero.gob.mx/kids/about/html/traditions/alebrije.html

Figure 1.2

Cultures are like icebergs

The differences become obvious after conducting research and checking for the accuracy of that assumption of similarity. For example, a beverage marketing professional had the impression that the famous rum Captain Morgan could have great potential among Hispanics. Hispanic male consumers, however, reported in the research that they were not just unfamiliar with the brand—they felt the imagery associated with Captain Morgan, the pirate, represented domination and exploitation. Clearly, an image that appears cool to Anglos can be interpreted in a totally different way by people with a different historical experience.

Wendy, the famous secretary in older commercials for Snapple, was found to be humorous and representative of the outspoken New York stereotype to Anglos. For Hispanics, however, Wendy was meaningless and irrelevant. This was because the cultural experience of Hispanics does not include this overweight woman with her brash New York accent.

Red Dog, a beer that was popular among non-Hispanics some time ago was advertised with ads portraying an actual male dog who was very assiduous in the pursuit of female dogs. The marketers in charge of that particular advertisement had a very difficult time believing that Hispanics could not relate to an ad for beer containing dogs as main characters. Unfortunately for the marketer, dogs do not enjoy the prestige and reputation with Hispanics as they do with Anglos. That is because the less affluent masses of Latin America have more basic priorities than caring for and feeding dogs. Further, Hispanics do not identify with dogs the way that young Anglos do. Thus, that Red Dog advertisement was not effective in conveying the appeal of the beer, and the marketers had to go back to the drawing board. If the team in charge had had a better understanding of the inner workings of the culture they could have anticipated that their ad did not translate as desired in the Hispanic mindset.

There are many subjective aspects of culture that can make critical differences in the effectiveness of advertising. They include beliefs about the world, attitudes, values, ways of interpreting and perceiving the world, and other mind constructs shared by the culture. These aspects tend to be deeply rooted in the psyche of Hispanic consumers and closely interconnected with their emotions. A lack of attention to these cultural aspects can mean the difference between a powerful ad, and either an ineffectual, or worse, an aversive ad for the intended Hispanic audience.

Beliefs

Beliefs about the nature of the world are particularly relevant in differentiating cultures. For example, Hispanics are more likely than Anglos to believe that nature and the supernatural control their lives. This is very much in contrast with the Protestant belief that humans can control the world around them. Although the majority of Hispanics would endorse the notion that destiny controls or influences their lives, generally Anglos would state that they believe they can shape their future and that destiny does not hold sway.

The marketer, then, needs to understand that advocating "being in control" with a particular product is likely to take a substantive amount of re-education and persuasion. Ideas like "you can plan for your retirement" are likely to be confronted with objections about the difficulty of sacrificing for an uncertain future. Why not enjoy today's life if the future is not in our hands? Saving is a sacrifice, and to sacrifice, one must hold the belief that one will reap the benefits of such sacrifice. Besides, tradition has influenced Hispanics to believe that their children are expected to take care of them in their old age. If the older folks took care of the kids for so many years, why could they not expect reciprocity?

Knowing these aspects of culture can prevent major snafus, save money, and assist marketers in concentrating on the issues that are more specific to a particular problem. There is no reason that marketers need to rediscover these issues over and over again. Acting on erroneous cultural assumptions is extraordinarily wasteful, and often can be avoided early in the conceptualization of advertising strategy.

The cultural foundation ought to be a prerequisite for anyone who is given a budget to serve a group of culturally distinct consumers.

Values and Attitudes

Attitudes and values are closely related to beliefs. If we believe that our children ought to support us in our old age, then we have a value for family cohesiveness, and a positive attitude toward family reciprocity. At the same time, we would devalue individualism or "each one is on his own in this world," and have a negative attitude toward products that replace family dependence. Table 1.1 provides examples of Hispanic beliefs that are associated with certain values and attitudes.

Interpretation and Perception

Interpretation and perception are similar. Perception is the addition of sensory input plus its interpretation. Thus, if Hispanics feel that dogs are lesser creatures, seeing a dog is interpreted based on that cultural baggage. The sensory input is the dog and the interpretation is that dogs are lowly beings. Perception, then, is the interpretation of the sensory input. The sensory input can be the exact same thing, but two or more people are likely to interpret it differently based on their past experience. Culture is based on a very large amount of past experience. Culture shapes how we interpret a great variety of items in the physical world of objects and in the social world of people.

Clearly, for the purposes of this book, perception has a most central role. The way in which members of different cultures interpret the same stimuli is one of the most common problems in marketing.

Table 1.1

Hispanic Beliefs, Values, and Attitudes	
Beliefs	**Values and Attitudes**
What my friends buy is good for me	Collectivism, the group is more important than the individual
Stay with a brand you know rather than switching around	Loyalty, fear of the unknown, risk avoidance
Please children by buying them what they want	Being a good mother, giving kids what she did not have growing up, compensating for a past of poverty
Live for today because tomorrow is uncertain	My life is in God's hands, fatalism, little control over the environment

Having credit in the United States is a very important asset and credit cards are seen as instruments of social mobility and well-being. But large numbers of Latin Americans have been educated to think that credit is shameful. Only those who cannot make it on their own have to rely on credit. Further, credit has many potentially negative consequences. Thus the same stimulus of a credit card can be interpreted in vastly different ways.

Culture, Fish, and Water

Part of the problem in marketing to Hispanics or any other culturally diverse group is that even members of those cultural groups have a difficult time articulating how they are different. Think of fish in the water, a part of their existence which is completely taken for granted. The water is a constant to the fish, like the air is for those of us who live outside the water. In the same way, culture is a constant for its members. It is hard for them to articulate how they are different because it's just the way people are. Only the trained individual can articulate the differences, which is why relying on someone to do cultural marketing just because he or she is Hispanic may be ill informed.

Our experiences color most aspects of life. A Hispanic born in the United States is likely to overemphasize the importance of the market segment that he or she represents if he or she is not well trained in scientific and cultural thinking. Increasingly, academia and business have been recognizing the importance of the study of culture in business. Some MBAs now pursue anthropological studies, and some anthropologists now pursue business training and opportunities.

The emergence of academic programs, like the Florida State University Center for the Study of Hispanic Marketing Communication and other programs and courses around the country, bring to the forefront the recognition of the study of marketing and culture. Some of these courses include the course taught by personnel of La Agencia de Orcí at the University of California Los Angeles Extension, and a course offered by Dr. Edward Rincon at Southern Methodist University. This book is about providing a perspective that delves in the intersection of marketing and culture.

Cultural Boundaries

What cultural difference makes enough of a difference to warrant attention in marketing? This is a very ambitious question, and is explored in this book. Initially, to establish basic knowledge, some overall principles will be discussed. Cultures do have commonalities and do overlap, and it is important to recognize this. Cultures are not unique enough such that members can unequivocally be classified as belonging to one culture or the other.

Part of the explanation for this has its roots in statistical thinking. There are several measures of central tendency. The mean or average is the addition of all scores in a distribution divided by the number of scores. The median is the value of the score precisely at the point below which and above which 50 percent of the cases fall. Finally, the mode is the most frequent score in a distribution. The mode, then, is the most intuitive measure of central tendency to characterize a culture. That is, it represents the most common set of individuals in a culture. Those people that are more like each other in a culture become the common denominator or the modal personality of the culture—they become the representatives of that culture. Others can be very different, and in many cases, more representative of another culture than of the culture in which they claim they are members.

This is possible because distributions, as cultures, overlap. The famous normal distribution or Gaussian curve is the graphical representation of most natural phenomena including things like weight, age, height, and so forth. Most natural phenomena distribute themselves normally with very few cases in the extremes and the majority of the cases toward the center, like in Figure 1.3. This can be the representation of one culture.

Further, Figure 1.4 illustrates the overlap of cultures.

As these figures show, there will be a relatively small number of individuals that will share more cultural aspects with others of another culture and thus will not be typical of their own culture. Individuals that are closer to the center of the distribution are more typical and they are more similar to those who occupy the mode—it is all relative.

Figure 1.3

Gaussian curve or normal distribution

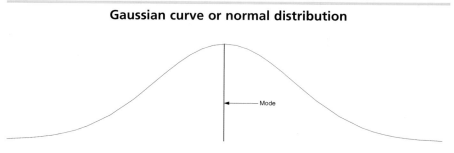

Figure 1.4

Cultures as overlapping normal distributions

Marketers "Angst"

The previous discussion helps explain why the boundaries of cultures are not as easy to delineate as we may want in managing marketing across cultures. A lack of firm delineation creates "angst" in most of us because we would love to grasp the nature of cultural bounds. This problem is not that different from the uncertainty that marketers typically face in dealing with market segments, but they are more used to that uncertainty than with cultural ambiguity.

In fact, one of the traits that helps marketers deal with this anxiety is the psychological trait known as *tolerance for ambiguity*. The more a marketer is able to tolerate blurred lines and to abstract essential elements, the better he or she can be in marketing to a different cultural group. This tolerance leads to the patience needed to unpeel the various levels of cultural nuance, and creates a powerful tool for successful cross-cultural marketing.

If the marketer looks for quick closure on important decisions, he or she is likely to make mistakes when dealing with another culture. The marketer needs to spend time analyzing quantitative and qualitative data in order to form a set of initial impressions. Then he or she needs to formulate hypotheses as to what different approaches would work best with Hispanics as compared with non-Hispanics. Testing these hypotheses becomes a critical exercise that takes involvement and work with members of the culture.

This anxiety is not abnormal—all feel it when they enter the unfamiliar—but we need to learn to live with this anxiety when crossing cultural boundaries. It is a part of the world we live in, and as individuals as well as marketers, we have enormous opportunities to grow with what we can learn.

Why a Cultural Approach to Marketing?

Marketers need to know how to ask the right questions. This book justifies the need for a cultural approach to Hispanic marketing as key to this capability.

- Instead of asking "How can we translate our ad so it reaches Hispanics?" the marketer should learn to ask "What will be the right motivational appeal to emotionally reach Hispanics?"

- Instead of asking "Can our general market campaign be effective with Hispanics?" the marketer should ask "Is there one positioning that can work with Hispanics and non-Hispanics?"

- Instead of asking "Do we have to put a Hispanic in our ad to reach Hispanics?" the marketer ought to start asking "What are the elements of cultural identification that I need to have in my ad?"

These are just some examples of ways of asking that illustrate the benefits of a cultural approach to Hispanic marketing. Although overall marketing knowledge will always be important and relevant to everyday marketing practice, asking culturally appropriate questions can be more important.

Many marketers find themselves intimidated by the black box of Hispanic culture and desperately look for any answer that will alleviate their fear of failure. They are frequently under pressure to put together ad campaigns, often with tight budgets. It is precisely a knowledge base about the culture, accompanied by a critical perspective, that will prevent failures. No one has all the answers about how to market anything. However, that lack of certainty is even more pronounced when crossing cultural boundaries.

When marketing across cultures, the marketer needs to:

- Suspend judgment
- Live with uncertainty
- Question any quick answers and remedies
- Be a first-hand analyst of cultural information
- Learn about what questions are more likely to lead to usable answers

A Psycho-Socio-Cultural Approach

Marketing is the science of making others fall in love with your products, services, and ideas. Love is the fundamental center of marketing. Historically it was more of a persuasion endeavor but it has gradually become the art of establishing relationships with consumers. This evolution is due to the increased skepticism elicited by the manipulative image that the industry had created for itself. Another factor contributing to the evolution of marketing as a relationship-oriented discipline has been the increased use of research to inform marketing decisions. The more marketers know customers the more they identify with them and the more they attempt to meet their needs and expectations. Further, the advent of new interactive technologies is increasingly making it possible for consumers and marketers to literally interact virtually.

When marketing to consumers from other cultures, making them fall in love with our products and ideas becomes challenging. If establishing interpersonal human relationships is difficult with members of our own culture, establishing those relationships with members from other cultures is many times more difficult. And that is because we lack sufficient information to make sense of who they are and how to relate to them.

Accurate Predictions of Behavior

Having enough information is the key to marketing in general, but when marketing across cultures the amount of required information is just so much greater. Charles Berger and Michael Burgoon, in their edited 1995 book, *Communication and Social Influence Processes*, explain how uncertainty reduction is part of relationship building.[2] Marketing and communication are effective when they make accurate predictions. When the marketer accurately predicts how consumers will receive a product they succeed at product design. When they accurately predict how consumers will react to their commercial message about a product they succeed in their communication.

To be effective marketers need to behave like dedicated lovers or good friends. They need to gather information about the other person so that they achieve their objective of establishing a relationship. By accumulating evidence they can position themselves better to be liked and accepted. In the cross-cultural case, there is much more evidence that needs to be collected to achieve these ends.

There are different types of information that individuals may need to collect in order to reduce uncertainty:[3] psychological, societal, and cultural. These domains overlap, as can be seen in Figure 1.5.

The overlap suggests that there is a correlation between psychological, sociological, and cultural domains. As discussed earlier, the modal personality is what characterizes a culture, thus it is not surprising that these domains overlap and mutually influence each other. The overlap becomes more obvious when we think of human characteristics as ascending in order of abstraction as they go from psychological to

Figure 1.5

The overlap between psychological, sociological, and cultural domains

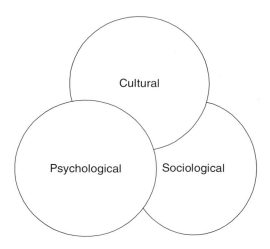

sociological and to cultural. The unit of analysis in the psychological domain is the individual, the unit of analysis at the sociological level is the group, and at the cultural level the unit of analysis is the aggregate of social groups that have a common view of the world.

Within the same culture the amount of information that needs to be collected is relatively small because it is almost a constant for most members of the culture, who are socialized from childhood or for a large portion of their lives within it. In any culture there are different social classes, social structures, and norms, and most marketers and communicators will have to collect some sociological information, for marketing both within and across cultures. This type of sociological information is largely demographic, and also includes social norms regarding specific situations.

When working within one culture the psychological information will probably be the most challenging. Understanding the idiosyncratic aspects of individuals, as marketers know, can be demanding. This psychological information usually is referred to as *psychographics*. The marketer working within a one culture situation aggregates some sociological data and much psychological data in order to make accurate predictions. For example, the target for a particular product could be women heads-of-household, 28 to 40, with at least one child under 18 living at home, who enjoy arts and crafts and tend to be heavily home and family oriented. They tend to be "other oriented," and enjoy being there for others.

In the cross-cultural case, the arrangement of these dimensions changes. The marketer in this case is more likely to have some psychological and perhaps sociological information, but very little cultural information. Thus the ability to make predictions decreases dramatically. Not only does the marketer require an understanding of demographics and psychographics, but also needs *culturegraphics*.

The problem with culturegraphics is that they are less accessible to the marketer via direct data collection. The marketer can always do a survey to find out who uses the product, how, when, for what reasons, and can even explore the appeal of a line extension. The marketer can ask lifestyle and psychological questions. But asking questions about culture is difficult, as we discussed earlier, because people have a hard time talking about the intricacies of their own culture. The marketer with total initial ignorance about the culture of the audience of interest tends to ask poor questions that lead to relatively useless information. Since the culture of a group of people is an aggregate set of experiences, the marketer needs to have some sense of what these consumers are about given their heritage.

Continuing with the case of the marketer who is unfamiliar with another culture, he or she may want to sell his or her product to female heads-of-household, ages 21 to 45, preferably with children at home, who are dedicated homemakers, enjoy catering to their family, and are highly collectivistic Hispanic consumers. For example, if the products to be marketed are refrigerated dough products, the marketer is likely to make many mistakes. The first one is approaching Hispanic women without understanding that their culture has a bias toward perceived freshness. Further, Hispanics have a negative bias toward frozen and refrigerated products because they believe that food that comes directly from nature is better for them and their family. In addition, most of these consumers have not seen, used, or purchased these types of products, so they have a vacuum of information regarding the category. Thus, if the marketer decides to pursue these consumers, he or she would need to study the target with questions informed by cultural knowledge. Then, he or she would need to approach the marketing problem with knowledge of the stamina needed to succeed in this market.

Many marketers not used to marketing to members of other cultures balk at the notion of having to educate a new customer base. That may be a warranted attitude but the situation is not much different than when their brand has had to educate non-Hispanics in the past. But when marketing to their own culture marketers seem to have a false sense of confidence that allows them to take more risks. Cross-cultural knowledge and understanding has the purpose of reducing uncertainty and anxiety in the marketer. With less uncertainty and anxiety, the marketer, similar to the lover, is more likely to take risks in courting a new market.

What Happens without Cultural Knowledge?

Simply, predictions are in error. Let us illustrate the need for cultural understanding with a relatively simple anecdote. A beer manufacturer needed to understand who among Hispanics were their customers, and what media they used. Knowledge about media preferences was to be used to inform a media plan. The questionnaire originally was formulated in English and omitted the genre of Ranchera music. The questionnaire was translated into Spanish using the term Country Music as Ranchera music. When the marketers viewed the percentages along the margins of the original English language questionnaire, they wrongly concluded that Hispanics were listening to American Country Music in large amounts.

For those reading this example, the misunderstanding may not be obvious. Ranchera music is a typical type of Mexican and Latin American music very different from Country music, even though it is literally "country music." It is very different in its sound, language, lyrics, artists, and so on. The confusion between Country and Ranchera could be obvious only to someone who has a basic understanding of the culture. And this example is just a very simple instance of the large complexity that marketers have to work with when navigating at the interface of two cultures.

The Paradox of Social Class across Cultures

A typical question marketers ask is: Can I bring our ads from Caracas, Bogota, Buenos Aires, or Mexico City to the United States and use them to communicate successfully with U.S. Hispanics? The question has much apparent merit. Just think, if one could use the same advertisements from Latin American countries in the United States, this would constitute great savings. The assumption that these markets are equivalent may come from the following logic: Mexicans in the United States make up over 67 percent of all U.S. Hispanics. If Mexicans are the majority and they come from Mexico, then they come from the same culture as those in their home country, thus they should react similarly in Mexico and in the United States.

What is missing from this logic is an understanding of the dynamics of social class across cultures. Imagine a gathering of physicians from India, Mexico, Denmark, the United States, and Japan. Will they be able to communicate among themselves? Most likely they will be able to communicate very well. That is because most have Western education, and most likely they all have lived or spent time in the United States. Further, they are affluent and cosmopolite. They value similar aspects of life. They likely aspire to be examples of Western success.

The lower middle classes and working classes of these countries are more likely to be much more different among themselves in their own country than the physicians. Further, the physicians are most likely to have more difficulties communicating with the lower middle and working classes of their own countries than with physicians from other countries. The social distance of the upper and lower classes of most countries is larger, in many cases, than the social distance of the upper classes of diverse countries among themselves.

Further, migration patterns are not independent from socio-economic class. Migrants from Mexico and Central America to the United States tend to be generally from the working class. These are people that come to the United States to get a major break in their financial situations and lifestyle. Many of these migrants to the United States were subsistence farmers and factory workers in their countries of origin. They did not have the economic capacity in their own countries to access packaged consumer goods to any large extent. Fundamentally these are people that become consumers when they come to the United States.

Their more affluent counterparts in their countries of origin are not as likely to migrate to the United States because they can enjoy a relatively comfortable life at home. The migration pressure is so much stronger on the poor. These less affluent individuals have not had as much access to manufactured goods before coming to the United States. The commercial messages designed in Mexico City target those who have the resources to purchase manufactured products. They do not target the poor and the disadvantaged.

Messages in Mexico can be high on image and low on information because they are communicating with a commercially experienced audience. Here in the United States, however, the masses of consumers need communications that are high on information and low on image. This is because they are inexperienced as consumers and eager to learn the basics about products. This is why ads from Mexico City are not likely to be as effective here as they were there.

Consider that less than 30 percent of Mexico's households make US$10,000 or more per year. The 70 percent below this income level, in the bottom of the distribution, are the ones more likely to migrate to the United States. They have very different perspectives on life, and that is what marketers need to work with. The marketer is not just dealing with a national culture but with a set of experiences heavily characterized by poverty. These are people who are willing to risk everything to improve the standard of life for themselves and their children. They generally do not come to the United States with middle class perspectives and experiences. The majority of migrants to the United States from Mexico and different parts of Central America tend to have little formal education, and many times their first language is not Spanish but a language native to the continent such as Maya, Quiche, Zapoteca, Nahuatl, and so forth.

When coming to the United States, these consumers go through a transformation in their ability to deal with the world economically. This transition, many times, is very difficult and frustrating. A large number of these migrants are young men who have left behind their parents, siblings, spouses, children, and everything that is dear to them. When they arrive in the United States, their main need is to learn the ways of the new culture. Ads from the big cities advocating the use of products with ethereal images emanating from cosmopolite advertising agencies in Mexico City or Buenos Aires have little to do with the lives of these people.

The Challenge Facing Hispanic Ad Agencies

Advertising and communications geared to this population need to take into consideration the information and lifestyle needs of these large numbers of migrants. U.S. advertising agencies face interesting challenges since, of course, there is ample variability among Hispanics in the United States. Indeed, there are those who have been described in the largest waves of immigration. Nevertheless, among those who move to the United States there are different levels of education, experience, and consumer sophistication. Further, once migrants become established, their perspective on the world changes. They become more sophisticated consumers than they were a few years before.

So, how is the marketer supposed to establish a target when it can be quite heterogeneous in experience? Clearly, a common denominator has to be established to make sense of the complexities of the U.S. Hispanic population. Overall, the U.S. Hispanic consumer will be relatively unlikely to relate to advertisements from metropolitan areas in Latin America. Socioeconomic class will generally be a complicating factor when deciding on communication strategies directed to U.S. Hispanics. The topic will be touched upon frequently in this book.

A Targetable Market?

Although it is true that the U.S. Hispanic market is complex, there are specific variables that make it quite desirable to marketers. It is true that some marketers unrealistically have attempted to reach the Hispanic market as a homogeneous whole and have failed. It is also true that many smart marketers specifically have targeted segments of the Hispanic market with much success.

Size

The speed of growth of the Hispanic market has exceeded the expectations of most observers and analysts. The Bureau of the Census estimates that there are now about 40,000 Hispanics in the United States. That is four times the size of the official size of the market in 1980.

And, of course, those figures do not say much about those who have entered and continued to live in the United States without official documentation. For the 2000 Census the Bureau of the Census exerted an unprecedented effort in trying to appeal to undocumented immigrants to be counted. Officials of the Census deserve great credit for that effort. Nevertheless, it would be illogical to think that people who live in this country without documentation would complete official Census forms. Thus, there are many more Hispanics in the United States than the official figures suggest. The problem is that no one knows exactly how many.

The Office of Immigration Statistics of the Department of Homeland Security states that in 2002 alone, 1.1 million deportable aliens were located in the United States. Further, between 1981 and 2000 there were almost 27 million deportable aliens located, and over 90 percent of them were Mexican. Conservative estimates by the same office and institutions such as the Pew Hispanic Center and the Selig Center for Economic Growth roughly estimate that there are about 11 million undocumented individuals in the United States, of which at least eight and a half million are Hispanic.

If the eight and a half million figure were accurate that would put the Hispanic population of the United States at a minimum of about 48.5 million in 2004. But that figure is likely to be understated as well. Just think that if the number of deportable aliens from Mexico between 1980 and 2000 was about 24 million, the number of unidentified individuals must have been at least as large as another 24 million. This makes sense since the former Immigration and Naturalization Service would have had a seemingly insurmountable task of identifying most deportable individuals.

No one really knows what the total number of U.S. Hispanics is, but a very conservative estimate is that in 2005 there were at least 48.5 million of them. That makes the U.S. Hispanic market the second largest in the world, after Mexico. In 2004, Spain had only an estimated 41 million inhabitants, placing it as the third largest Hispanic country in the world.

Now, a population of 48.5 million Hispanics, affluent in comparison with the rest of Latin America and Spain, becomes a very desirable aggregate of consumers. Clearly, not all Hispanics are the same, and the entire 48.5 million are not necessarily the target of almost any one product or service. Still, the specific segments within it can be substantive and very lucrative. According to an H&AMCR (Hispanic & Asian Marketing Communication Research) survey of 900 Hispanics conducted in 1997 in Los Angeles, New York, and Miami, it was found that almost half the households interviewed had children in diapers. That is an outstanding opportunity for marketers of diapers, formula, baby food, wipes, and many other products for children. The numbers justify marketing efforts directed to Hispanics. Clearly, there are other aspects that need to be considered.

Purchasing Power

The Selig Center for Economic Growth placed the purchasing power of U.S. Hispanics in 2004 at approximately 700 billion dollars. A conservative estimate according to the same source is that by 2008 the purchasing power of U.S. Hispanics will be over one trillion dollars.

For proportionality, consider that Mexico had the tenth largest GDP in the world in 2002 with 642 billion dollars.[4] The spending power of the U.S. Hispanic market in 2004 is larger than that.

The spending power of U.S. Hispanics compared with Latin Americans is outstandingly high. It is disproportionate and it is not surprising that immigration to the United States continues to be vigorous. Most Hispanic immigrants greatly improve their standards of living by moving here. As stated earlier, many of these Latin American immigrants become consumers of manufactured goods here in the United States. That is something that many of them could not afford in their countries of origin. And here is also where they become the dream of marketers, precisely because of their spending power.

Shared Perceptions, Motivations, Beliefs, and Values

It Is Not a Race

What makes Hispanics Hispanic is not their race. Most U.S. marketers do not yet understand that Hispanics are not a race. Hispanics can be of any race. They are African blacks, they are Asian from almost all Asian countries, they are Semites, they are Caucasian, they are Native Americans,[5] they are mestizos,[6] mulatos, and many other races.

Most of the Atlantic coast of Latin America contains people from African backgrounds that were brought to this continent as slaves. In contrast to the United States, in many Latin American countries African blacks melded with the rest of the population, which contains many shades of brown, black, yellow, and white. In Mexico, for example, individuals of African background are simply Mexican. In the United States racial differentiation is still quite prevalent, but in Mexico and the rest of Latin America the differentiation between people tends to be made on the basis of socio-economic class rather than race.

In most of Latin America there are people from China, Japan, and Korea in relatively large numbers. A well-known piece of evidence of their integration in the societies of Latin America is that an individual like Alberto Fujimori, of Japanese background, became President of Peru. Lebanese, Syrian, Jewish, Iranian, and many other Semite groups are found in most of Latin America. Well-known individuals of Semite backgrounds include Shakira, a singer from Colombia, and Salma Hayek, an actor from Mexico. Caucasians have occupied prominent places in Latin America for a long time. A prominent case is President Fox of Mexico. The O'Farrill family of Mexico has been prominent in the Media industry of that country.

These examples make the point that being Hispanic is not a race but a common heritage and culture. This common background is what makes Hispanics homogeneous in many interesting respects: beliefs, values, perceptions, and orientations derived from a common experience that goes back to the common roots of the colonization of most of Latin America by Spain. The largest country in Latin America is Brazil with approximately 180 million people in 2004. They are not Hispanic, but their Portuguese heritage shares many cultural similarities with Spain.

A Common Heritage

The cultural domination of Spanish-speaking America by Spain is one of the most important sources of influence on the way in which Hispanics perceive the world. The complexities of the Spanish cultural heritage and the process of colonization include the following.

- The Catholic religion has dramatically influenced the way of thinking and feeling of the continent. The notions of original sin and guilt permeate the culture and dramatically differentiate Hispanics from other cultural groups. Related to Catholicism is a value for hierarchical relationships, and also a stoic view of life as a suffering experience, *un valle de lágrimas*.[7] Popular television shows like the *telenovelas* clearly reflect orientations that reflect the notions of sin, destiny, suffering, and anomie.

- Linguistic elements and values derived from 800 years of Arab domination over Spain. Many aspects of Spanish language vocabulary can be traced back to the Arabic language. Examples include *zapato, pantalón, camisa, bodega, algebra, café, cero, azúcar, aceite, adobe, ajedrez, mascara, mazapán, momia, talco, toronja, zanahoria,*[8] and many more. Among the many other Arabic influences on Hispanic culture is the notion of Ah-Riba. This concept refers to the prohibition to collect interest on debt, and scholars debate whether different types of insurance are included in the prohibition of Riba as well.

  Hispanic heritage combines these and many other aspects of Arabic culture that have important implications for marketing. If the concepts of "interest" and "insurance" are problematic in the heritage of the culture then it is reasonable to assume that selling on credit and selling insurance to Hispanics would be more difficult than selling the same to non-Hispanics. Then, as will be seen later in the book, the words and language that people use have important implications for the way in which people think.

- Shared values and ways of looking at the world, including:
  - Collectivism as opposed to individualism: The family and the group are more important than the individual. Reference groups are more motivational than appeals to the individual. This orientation has implications for the purchases of large ticket items as well as the way in which consumers can be persuaded to appreciate the benefits of a product.
  - Polychronism as opposed to monochronism: The nonlinear use of time or doing multiple activities simultaneously as opposed to doing one thing at a time.[9] Customer service is expected to be polychronic. That is, a customer service representative should be able and willing to address different topics simultaneously and handle requests from different people at the same time. The consumer is likely to use products intended for one specific time during the day, on many occasions throughout the day instead. The idea of insisting that orange juice consumption be studied as a breakfast beverage exclusively may not make sense for Hispanic consumers.

○ Polymorphic opinion leadership as opposed to monomorphic opinion leadership: Opinion leadership on many topics and areas of expertise tends to be concentrated in a few individuals as opposed to having many specialized leaders on individual areas of knowledge.[10] The realtor becomes family counselor, economic advisor, immigration expert, instead of just being seen as a specialist in his or her own area of expertise. Thus, training of agents in the real estate, insurance, and other industries requires knowledge of these expectations.

○ A sense of fatalism or lack of control over the environment: Human beings seen as subordinate to nature as opposed to being the masters of it.[11] For example, emphasizing product benefits having to do with the control of events and life may not be as convincing as using arguments that talk about family benefits and potential for spiritual growth.

○ Reverence for tradition, older relatives, and ancestors: In contrast to other cultures, Hispanics generally have positive feelings and respect for tradition, age, and life experience. Denigrating tradition in favor of the "new generation" may backfire in marketing communications because Hispanic youth does not perceive itself to be divorced from its ancestry and history. An example of a snafu in this category of values is an ad for a cereal that showed a grandmother hoarding the cereal because it was so good that she did not want to share it with her family. This ad failed quite dramatically. Consumers stated that a Hispanic grandmother would never hide food from her children and grandchildren. They were offended because they felt the dignity of the grandmother had been offended.

○ Value for introspection and spirituality, and strong faith in the supernatural. The relevance of products and services to enhance human experience as opposed to sheer materialism can be very appealing to Hispanics. Being aware of the spirituality of the Hispanic market can make a strong difference in creative efforts. Lack of sensitivity about these issues can result in very negative consequences.

This discussion emphasizes how culture and its constituent values, beliefs, perceptions, and orientations make the overall Hispanic market targetable. Clearly, specific subgroups must be delineated for effective segmentation. Still, there is a significant core of homogeneity within the heterogeneity of the Hispanic market. Knowledge of this is a clear asset to marketers as they think through their approach to this culture.

A Common Language

The Spanish language, as part of the heritage from Spain, is one of the most unifying aspects of the U.S. Hispanic market. The Spanish language is the glue that keeps Hispanics relatively homogeneous. An Argentinean and a Mexican can communicate with each other with relatively little difficulty. A Cuban and a Peruvian can understand each other quite well.

There are regional dialectical language variations in Latin America. These variations tend to concentrate in specific areas. One of the areas of most variability is the nomenclature for food items. Still, most Spanish speakers in the world can communicate quite efficiently with each other. They may ask for clarification of a couple of terms when interacting but they get the overall gist of almost any message regardless of specific Hispanic origin.

There are some who argue that the Spanish spoken in each country is idiosyncratic. That is not more accurate than stating that the Spanish spoken in different regions within any Latin American country has its own idiosyncrasies. In a country like Mexico, the reader will find differences in the Spanish dialect spoken in the Atlantic coast as compared with the Pacific, Mexico City, the northern border states and the states of the south like Yucatan and Quintana Roo. Still, Mexicans can communicate with each other relatively well. Their communication is as good as the communication between people from New York and those of Georgia, each with their dialectical differences.

The notion that there is a "Walter Cronkite" Spanish is somewhat misleading; there is not unaccented Spanish because there is no dialect that does not have some specific peculiarities. Since Mexico with Televisa has been the dominant source of television exports to the rest of Latin America, it is true that formal Mexican broadcast Spanish has become a sort of standard by default. Some people argue that Colombian Spanish is "pure" and most understandable. The disappointing news is that there is no such thing as pure Spanish. Nevertheless, people from Latin America and Spain do understand each other.

The commonality of the Spanish language has been one of the most salient common denominators that make the Hispanic market highly targetable. Things are evolving, nevertheless, and the Hispanic market is becoming increasingly more complicated in this respect. There are Hispanics that are more targetable in English and others who are targetable in Spanish but in English media. In many cases a culturally relevant message strategy is more important than the actual language.

Still, the Spanish language is an important part of the culture and constitutes an axle around which the Hispanic culture revolves. Spanish is still the language that is likely to reach the majority of the market, depending on the specific target and media.

Media Facilitate Specific Targeting

Spanish language media has been the most important facilitator of specific Hispanic consumer targeting over the past 25 years. It is not only that sizable portions of the market can be reached in Spanish, but that there have been communication channels to do so. Univision, Telemundo, several radio networks, newspapers, and magazines have been dedicated to reach the Hispanic market for a long time. The spectrum of media outlets has been dramatically expanded over the last few years, and consolidation has also played a role. Now there are specialized Internet channels like AOL Latino, Terra Networks, Yahoo en Español, that also facilitate targeting in the virtual interactive world. Notable new broadcast media channels include Mun2, Telefutura, Azteca America, and in print there are noteworthy developments that will be discussed in more detail later in this book.

The SRDS Hispanic Media & Markets periodical is a fundamental media resource for buyers of Spanish language media that lists hundreds of outlets locally and nationally. Spanish language media is abundant and has become increasingly specialized. It is a great resource that further makes the Hispanic market highly targetable and reachable.

Geographic Concentration

Geographic concentration is one more of the elements that has made Hispanics a very identifiable and reachable market. California and Texas contain more than 50 percent of all U.S. Hispanics. Other remarkable areas of great Hispanic concentration are the metropolitan areas such as New York, Miami, and Chicago.

This concentration makes it relatively inexpensive to reach large numbers of Hispanic consumers. This tendency toward concentration traditionally has been associated with the pull of family and friends. Friends and family attract others and that becomes a multiplying and effervescent growth effect.

It should be carefully noted, however, that in the past ten years there has been an important geographic dispersion movement toward the center of the country and away from the coasts and the southern border. Markets like Minneapolis, Charlotte, Chapel Hill, Atlanta,

Las Vegas, and Denver have experienced disproportionate Hispanic growth in comparison with the rest of the country. This trend should be monitored carefully by marketers even though it is not yet a dominant tendency.

A Cultural Perspective Makes the Difference

The intent of this first chapter was to orient you to the philosophy and intent that motivates this book. It is important to understand the statistics and parameters that describe the U.S. Hispanic market. It is more important, however, to understand where Hispanics come from so that the marketer can establish strong links with them.

Clearly, the seasoned marketer will need to know the demographic and psychographic characteristics of the segment he or she wants to reach. As indicated earlier, overlaying culturegraphics makes the connection so much more meaningful when the marketer and the target are from different cultures.

When marketers can look at the Hispanic market from a culture-graphic perspective they add communication intimacy to their strategy. Knowing how members of the culture feel about life, the future, love, death, children, career, art, sex, and so on empowers the marketer to formulate the right questions. Further, the marketer is also in the position to interpret the results of research and tests in light of the culture. This helps make sense of the consumer's perspective. It is looking at consumers in a more holistic approach.

As an example, the marketer of an orange fruit drink may know that demographically his audience is composed of kids 5 to 14 and their mothers. The marketer may know that psychographically these families are active, engaged, and that the mothers are heavily involved in the food and drink choices of their children. If this marketer also understands that culturegraphically these mothers are likely to experience a guilt syndrome derived from their heritage they can add an important dimension to their marketing effort. The marketer can then position the product as a beverage that helps the mother manage guilt in some interesting ways. If the kids drink too much soda the mother may feel that she has not done enough for the nutrition of the children. If, however, she is able to substitute an orange fruit drink for sodas she reduces guilt feelings because she is doing something positive for her kids. This motivational force can be made sense of only with cultural sensitivity; that is, if the marketer understands at least some of the cultural aspects that are related to the marketing problem at hand.

In making sense of the Hispanic market, Chapter 2 looks at critical dimensions of the Hispanic market.

References

1 Hall, Edward Twitchell. *Beyond culture*. New York: Anchor Books/Doubleday, 1989.
2 *Communication and social influence processes*. Edited by Charles R. Berger and Michael Burgoon. East Lansing, Mich.: Michigan State University Press, 1998.
3 According to the article by Michael Roloff entitled "Interpersonal Influence: The View from Between People" in *Communication and social influence processes*. Edited by Charles R. Berger and Michael Burgoon. East Lansing, Mich.: Michigan State University Press, 1998.
4 http://www.studentsoftheworld.info/infopays/rank/PIB2.html
5 Native Americans in this book are any of the peoples considered to be indigenous to the American continent. Many times they are incorrectly called Indians because Christopher Columbus thought he had arrived in India when he discovered the American continent.
6 This is the resulting mix of Spaniards and Native Americans.
7 Life is a valley of tears.
8 Shoe, pants, shirt, warehouse, algebra, café, zero, sugar, oil, adobe, chess, mask, marzipan, mummy, powder, grapefruit, carrot.
9 Hall, Edward Twitchell. *Beyond culture*. New York: Anchor Books/Doubleday, 1989.
10 Rogers, Everett M. *Diffusion of innovations*, 5th ed. New York: Free Press, 2003.
11 Kluckhohn, Florence (Rockwood) and Fred L. Strodtbeck, with the assistance of John M. Roberts [and others]. *Variations in value orientations*. Westport, Conn.: Greenwood Press, 1975.

Characteristics of the Hispanic Market

2

Cultural and Historical Origins of Hispanics

The essence of being Hispanic is the sharing of a common heritage. That cultural heritage is traced back to the rich history of the Iberian Peninsula, where Iberians, Celts, Phoenicians, Visigoths, Greeks, Carthaginians, Romans, and Arabs created the ethnic and cultural base of the peninsula. The Romans left the indelible seal of Christianity. The Arabs made scientific, architectural, literary, and philosophical contributions. All of these peoples influenced the character and the language of the inhabitants of Iberia. These people eventually influenced deeply the cultures of Latin America.

Iberian Diversity and Commonality

Lusitania, the area of Iberia that is currently occupied by Portugal, was part of a larger conglomerate dominated by Visigoths. Portugal became a separate entity and later on a country, given the mountainous barriers that separate it from the rest of the peninsula. The war against the Arabs, who dominated the Iberian Peninsula for almost eight centuries, further consolidated the identity and relative independence of Portugal. That separation was emphasized as strife against the Arabs continued. Still, the modern countries of Spain and Portugal share much in common in terms of cultural heritage and history despite linguistic differences.

The fact that Portuguese is a different language does not detract from the great similarities that the Portuguese share with the rest of the peninsula. In fact, many regions of Spain have other languages as their main communication tools. Those in Galicia speak Galician, Asturians speak Asturian, Basques speak Basque, Catalonians speak Catalan, Valencianos speak Valenciano, and those in the center of Spain have what is commonly known as Spanish as their language. The inhabitants of Iberia have in common a cultural heritage that goes beyond language. That is why Brazilians and most other countries of Latin America share vast amounts of a common heritage.

What Constitutes the Hispanic Market

The Romans named the Iberian Peninsula Hispania, and from there the name of the modern nation of Spain derived. Hispanics in the United States, therefore, are all those who are descendents from countries conquered or dominated by Spain. These are people who trace their origins to any of the following countries:

Argentina
Bolivia
Chile
Colombia
Costa Rica
Cuba
Dominican Republic
Ecuador
El Salvador
Guatemala
Honduras
Mexico
Nicaragua
Panama
Paraguay
Peru
Uruguay
Venezuela

Of course this includes the people of Puerto Rico and Spain as well. Brazil usually is not included because of its linguistic identity, that is, the Portuguese language. Nevertheless, Brazilians share a large amount of the background that characterizes Hispanic countries.

At this point you may be wondering why Hispanics are sometimes called Latinos, or conversely why Latinos are sometimes called Hispanics. The origin and complexity of labels will be addressed later in this book. For now, the term Hispanic is used for simplicity. The

Bureau of the Census decided to use the term Hispanic to denote all people who share the background of tracing their roots to a Spanish-speaking country.

This book will argue and provide evidence that U.S. Hispanics share among themselves a cultural background that makes them relatively homogeneous. In the area of implicit culture, the belief and value systems, thought patterns, psychological and sociological make-up of the different Hispanic nationalities are surprisingly uniform. Even more evident, the material culture of Spanish-speaking countries exhibits great similarities in architecture, music, poetry, literature, and some aspects of food and dress.

Hispanic Immigration and How the Border Was Left Behind

The history of Hispanization of the United States is long and full of important benchmarks that have characterized the relationships between the United States and the rest of Latin America and Spain. The relationship between the United States and Mexico has been the closest and most influential.

A famous statement by the prominent Mexican writer Miguel Leon Portilla characterizes the relationship between Mexico and the United States: "Poor Mexico, so far from God and so close to the United States." The relationship with Mexico and the rest of Latin America has been colored by power differences. Although there is a profound interest and admiration for some aspects of life in the United States, there is also an underlying resentment of the influence the United States wields in their countries and lives.

Mexico as the Largest Contributor

After the discovery of the New World by Christopher Columbus in 1492 the influence of Spain was felt in most of the North American continent, including the current territory of the United States. Mexico held vast territories of the continent. However, it lost more than half of that territory to the United States in 1848, including Texas, California, Arizona, New Mexico, Nevada, Utah, and Colorado. The treaty of Guadalupe Hidalgo[1] consummated this loss of territory, marked an end to hostilities between the two countries, and guaranteed the rights of the inhabitants of these states that were previously part of Mexico. The degree to which those rights have been honored by the United States has been debated intensively over the years.

Still, those left behind when the border crossed them constituted the first massive contingent of Mexican nationals to live in U.S. territory. Since then Mexico has been the largest exporter of Hispanics to the United States. Because of dramatic changes in economic conditions in Mexico around 1980, the official growth of Hispanics in the United States has been dramatic and surprising. The official number of U.S. Hispanics in 1980 was approximately 10 million. By 1990 the figure was about 22 million, and by 2004 the official figure was almost 40 million. Understandably, official figures are likely to be greatly understated because of the huge influx of undocumented workers that cross the border between the United States and Mexico every day.

Mexicans now constitute at least 67 percent of all U.S. Hispanics. Mexico is likely to continue being the major contributor to the growth of the Hispanic market in the United States for the foreseeable future. There are politicians and segments of the American public that condemn Mexican immigration as a danger to the economic stability of the United States. Labor unions fear the impact of people that are willing to work for lower wages. Ideological pundits espouse the idea that immigrants who have different values will erode the protestant ethic that has characterized the United States. The constituencies politicians serve divide them. Some support the legalization and recognition of immigration as part of the engine of U.S. society. Others oppose it on the grounds of national integrity.

Despite this controversy, if all Mexicans left the United States, a major crisis would ensue. A 2004 movie produced by Televisa[2] for the U.S. market addresses this specific issue. The movie, "A Day without a Mexican," addresses the hypothetical situation in which all Mexicans disappear for one day with disastrous and distressing consequences. The immigration controversy contains paradoxes that are not being directly addressed. Both sides of the border depend on each other.

The United States depends on Hispanics, particularly Mexicans, for the labor that different sectors of the economy demand: agriculture, building, landscaping and gardening, hospitality, janitorial, and many other trades and services. In addition, there are relatively small but important groups of professionals and entrepreneurs that energize the American economy. Mexico depends on U.S. Hispanics for many reasons. The most important contributions U.S. Hispanics make to Mexico are money remittances to relatives and friends. In 2003 the value of these remittances was estimated to be about 13.3 billion dollars[3] but industry speculation is that these remittances were over 20 billion in 2004. This constitutes the second largest source of income for Mexico, second only to the oil industry.

The majority of Mexican immigrants to the United States trace their origins to agriculture, manufacturing, and other relatively low earning occupations in Mexico. They had few funds available to purchase other than staples in their home country. Therefore, many of these immigrants learn to become full fledged consumers once they are in the United States. This background of inexperience in buying products and services for themselves and their families strongly characterizes patterns of purchase and consumption behaviors in the United States. Since these consumers tend to be relatively new to the economy of the United States they require information and education to incorporate themselves into the mainstream of U.S. consumption.

Many companies have recognized that the large Mexican population in the United States provides an excellent target market for their products. Marbo, a small firm in 1997, recognized the potential business opportunity for their juice-based drink in the U.S. Mexican market. They launched the Tampico brand in the face of competition from the largest beverage companies in the United States, and through culturally astute marketing have become a leader in the fruit drink category (see The Marbo Tampico Case Study at the end of the chapter).

Puerto Rico

Puerto Ricans are American citizens whose culture is more similar to Latin American countries than to the United States. The Spanish American War of 1898, when the United States took Puerto Rico, Cuba, and the Philippines from Spain,[4] marked the beginning of U.S. control over the Island of Borinquen, as Puerto Rico is known. In 1917 the United States granted U.S. citizenship to Puerto Ricans, and in 1952, Puerto Rico was granted Commonwealth status. Important controversies over the political status of the island have marked the United States–Puerto Rico relationship into the present. Since World War II, the influx of Puerto Ricans to the United States has been important. At the time of this writing, there are almost as many people of Puerto Rican origin in the U.S. mainland as there are in Puerto Rico. According to estimates by the Bureau of the Census, there are about 3.9 million residents in Puerto Rico and about 3.8 million people of Puerto Rican origin living in the United States. Puerto Ricans in the United States constituted almost 9 percent of the U.S. Hispanic population in 2002 according to the Current Population Survey of the Bureau of the Census.[5]

Puerto Ricans are unique in many ways. For one they can travel freely between their homeland and the United States. They are also unique in that most Puerto Ricans have access to consumer products from the United States. Thus, they are familiar with the U.S. consumer culture. Ethnically, they represent a variety and an amalgamation of Spanish, Native Americans, and Africans.

Cuba

The population of Cuba was a mixture of Spaniard, African Blacks, and Indians early in Cuba's history, scarcely 100 years after the discovery of the Island.[6] The Indians were decimated by the treatment they received from the Spanish conquerors and by the diseases these intruders brought. It was a very similar case to what happened to Indians[7] in most of Latin America. Cuba declared its independence from Spain in 1868 but it was never consummated. It was not until 1898, when the United Stated defeated the Spanish in the Spanish American war that the United Stated occupied Cuba. Americans intermittently occupied and maneuvered the politics of Cuba up to the point when they influenced the system to place Fulgencio Batista as president.

During the era of American Prohibition (1919 to 1933), Cuba developed an important tourism industry, which included prostitution. Batista presided over Cuba and further contributed to the development of casinos, hotels, and bordellos for the enjoyment of Americans. Fidel Castro and his communist revolution obtained strong support from those that were left behind by the tourism prosperity. Fidel Castro became the communist leader of Cuba in 1959.

From 1960 to 1991 Cuba partnered with the Soviet Union and Soviets had a strong presence in the island for those 31 years. Many Cuban children were given Russian names, and the way of thinking of the population at large was strongly influenced by Soviet thinking.

A large number of elite and well-educated Cubans left the island in 1960. A vast majority of them came to the United States as refugees from the Castro regime. This sophisticated group of immigrants has been part of the progress and "Latinization" of South Florida. Many other legal and illegal refuges from Cuba have arrived in South Florida since Castro took over. Of particular interest was the Mariel boatlift that consisted of about 125,000 Cubans that were allowed to leave Cuba for the United States. Castro played rough because among the emigrants he mixed undesirable individuals he released from prisons and insane asylums. The Cuban emigration to the United States had consisted of elites at first and then of much less affluent individuals.

The consumer experience of the first immigration of Cubans was characterized by sophistication and affluence. Working class people, who have known very little about consumer products, have characterized later migrations. Most of these individuals had been touched by Soviet ways of thinking. Because of this social class dichotomy, Cubans in the United States do not represent a group of consumers with homogeneous experiences. Some are highly demanding and very knowledgeable. Others indicate they want more consumer education and information. According to the Current Population Survey of the U.S. Bureau of the Census in 2002,[8] the estimated population of individuals of Cuban origin in the United States was almost 4 percent.

Central America

It is difficult to speak of Central America as if it were a unit even though the U.S. Bureau of the Census and other organizations speak of it as such. It is a conglomeration of countries in a relatively small geographic area. These countries, however, are quite diverse. The Spanish-speaking countries of Central America are Guatemala, El Salvador, Honduras, Nicaragua, Costa Rica, and Panama. Belize is English-speaking.

The population of Native American Indians in Guatemala is the largest of any country in Latin America. About 40 percent of the people of Guatemala are Maya Indians.[9] El Salvador, Nicaragua, and Honduras are largely mestizo, like Mexico. Costa Rica is mostly European with a heritage of Spanish, German, and Italian among the most prevalent origins. Costa Rica also has a strong component of citizens of African origin. Panama has the largest population of African heritage among the countries of Central America.

Migration from Central America to the United States has been characterized by economic and political need. Many migrants from Central America pass through Mexico. Mexico has had its own illegal immigration problems due to this influx. The largest population of Central Americans in the United States is of Salvadorans, most of whom came as official or unofficial political refugees during the unrest of the 1980s. It is estimated that about half a million Salvadorans came to the United States during that time. They have settled mostly in Los Angeles, San Francisco, Washington, D.C., and South Florida. Guatemalans constitute the second largest contingent of Central Americans in the United States, Nicaraguans are the third largest group. Other Central American country contingents in the United States are relatively small. In the aggregate, all people of Central American background accounted for roughly 9 percent among U.S. Hispanics.[10]

South America

If clumping all countries in Central America as a unit is arbitrary, it is even more arbitrary to do so with all of South America. Despite its large magnitude, according to Synovate, in 2004 only 5 percent[11] of U.S. Hispanics traced their origin to South America. This is a small but influential contingent because of their important contributions to Hispanic culture in the United States. South Americans are dispersed throughout the United States but tend to concentrate in South Florida and in the areas surrounding and including New York State. Some groups have concentrated in specific areas that have become magnets for others from the same country in Latin America. For example, there is concentration of Peruvians in the Bay Area of San Francisco.

Brazil is not heavily represented in the United States and it is not considered to be a Hispanic country because of its Portuguese background. Still, Brazil was the largest Latin American country in 2004 with over 184 million people.[12]

The richness of Spanish-speaking South America is beyond the scope of this book. Immigrants from Argentina, Chile, Venezuela, Colombia, Ecuador, Peru, Bolivia, Uruguay, and Paraguay enrich Hispanic life in the United States. Because of the distance from the United States, immigrants from these countries tend to be somewhat more affluent and educated than those from countries that are closer to the United States. More affluent individuals are much more likely to afford travel to the United States. And due to education and exposure to international marketing efforts, these consumers tend to be somewhat more sophisticated about consumption than some of their less cosmopolite counterparts.

Dominicans

The Dominican Republic has been a strong contributor of immigrants to the United States in recent years. The New York/New Jersey area used to be predominantly Puerto Rican, but Dominicans have increasingly challenged that prevalence. In 2004 Dominicans constituted 3 percent of all U.S. Hispanics.[13] Dominicans share with Puerto Ricans a heritage of Spanish and African backgrounds and many common cultural patterns. Still, Dominicans have the unique idiosyncrasies of their history. Dominicans share their island with Haiti and were dominated by them for a period of time. Dominicans are not U.S. citizens as Puerto Ricans are and immigration is a struggle they share with the majority of other Hispanic immigrants to the United States. Dominicans do have a history of exposure to American and global brands, and many come to the United States with some knowledge of those brands.

Implications of Homogeneity and Diversity

As indicated in the preceding overview, there are specific tendencies that make the Hispanic market targetable. You also should have become cognizant of the variability that exists in the aggregate of people covered under the label Hispanic.

The homogeneity of the market is due to historical and cultural roots. Hispanics do share a rich history marked by the Spanish conquest of the continent and a struggle for independence. Political turmoil and instability has been omnipresent in many Spanish speaking countries. That background colors the experience of Latin Americans and their relative distrust in institutions including governments, banks, and hospitals, and phone companies.

Religion, language, and many other aspects of Hispanic culture serve as the glue that ties Hispanics together. It is the commonality that makes them an ideal marketing target. It is difficult to find many other niche markets in the United States that share so much in common.

Clearly, there are dominant tendencies in the market. Mexicans are the vast majority of all Hispanics. They represent the single most relatively homogeneous group within the overall Hispanic market. Many product categories benefit from attracting the interest of Mexicans first. That is one way of acquiring momentum. Still, the marketer needs to remember that even consumers of Mexican origin are not all similar to each other.

There are some whose ancestors were in current U.S. territory before modern Mexico existed. There are affluent Mexicans that live in Coronado, La Jolla, Houston, and Miami. They do not have a lot in common with the large number of Mexicans that come from more humble backgrounds to start a new and better life from scratch in the United States. There are those who depend on the Spanish language for their understanding of basic aspects of shopping and using products; those who can handle English and Spanish almost interchangeably; and those who are English dominant.

Still, a common Mexican origin provides a very strong point of origin and cultural commonality.

Testing the Assumption of Homogeneity

When a marketer decides to have a national campaign he or she may want to test the assumption that Hispanics are quite homogeneous. In practice it has been found that an acid test is to "talk" with Mexican consumers in Los Angeles and also with consumers of Cuban background in Miami. If the brand, product, commercial, stimulus, and so on has similar reactions with groups in both locations, then the marketer can confidently conclude that the object of the research will probably behave similarly across most groups of Hispanics.

Mexicans and Cubans are as different as Hispanics can be among themselves given their history. If an idea is interpreted and appreciated equally in both markets, the marketer can trust it is a general Hispanic concept. If Cubans and Mexicans disagree, then there is a need for much more investigating. The marketer then would need to learn how several of the other subgroups think and feel about the idea under consideration.

Food products and other iconic items that are very specific to a country may not be for widespread dissemination. For example, there is a frying condiment that Cubans, Puerto Ricans, and Dominicans use, called *sofrito*. It would be unlikely that Mexicans would relate to it without some education and persuasion effort.

There was the case of an advertising campaign that used the Aztec calendar as part of the symbolism of the ad. East coast Hispanics generally rejected the message as being "too Mexican." Clearly, Cubans or Puerto Ricans have very little to do with the Aztecs. This basic cultural sensitivity can be part of the challenge in attempting to reach across Hispanic groups.

Nevertheless, there are striking similarities in very complicated cultural beliefs. Through qualitative research the authors have found that beliefs about stomach upset are widely shared among Hispanics. For example, there is the belief that if a food is spoiled or does not agree with the person eating it, it gets stuck in the gut. This is called *empacho*. Consumers from Mexico, Cuba, Puerto Rico, Venezuela, and other countries know about this phenomenon and even agree about the basic treatment for it. Some rub and stretch the skin of the back of the patient and others rub the legs. Still the basic premise is that by stretching and rubbing they release the food that is stuck in the stomach. There are many cultural beliefs like this, that transcend country of origin. The marketer that connects with the consumer at the level of cultural beliefs is likely to reap windfall profits.

An example of a common cultural tendency across various Hispanic countries of origin, discovered by Procter & Gamble and Bromley Communications, their advertising agency for Charmin toilet paper, is the preference for scented products. P&G revitalized the Charmin brand and grew Hispanic sales with a national Spanish language "Scents" line campaign in 2003 (refer to the Bromley Charmin Case Study at the end of the chapter).

This exploration will continue, particularly when addressing the notion of cultural archetypes.

Geographic Trends

The geography distribution of Hispanics in the United States is a function of physical nearness to different parts of Mexico and the Caribbean. The map in Figure 2.1 shows the distribution of Hispanics in 2000.[14]

This distribution and the relative densities have been fairly constant but the actual numbers have increased dramatically. This dramatic increase from 10 million Hispanics in 1980 to almost 40 million in 2004, documented by the U.S. Census, has awakened the interest of marketers, politicians, educators, and most other sectors of U.S. society.

The geographic concentration of Hispanics in the west, the southwest, and select areas of the east of the United States has traditionally singled out the Hispanic population as a highly targetable aggregate of consumers. Typically, media purchases have tended to be focused on those areas of high Hispanic density.

But with the growth of the Hispanic population there has also been dispersion as well. Internally, in the United States, Hispanics have been exploring new geographies—areas that had not had a strong presence

Figure 2.1

Distribution of Hispanics in the United States

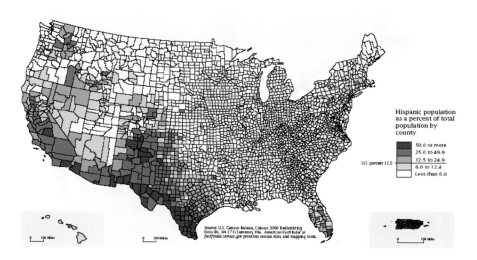

Hispanic population as a percent of total population by county

50.0 or more
25.0 to 49.9
12.5 to 24.9
6.0 to 12.4
Less than 6.0

U.S. percent 12.5

Source: U.S. Census Bureau, Census 2000 Redistricting Data (RL. 94-171) Summary File. American FactFinder at factfinder.census.gov provides census data and mapping tools.

of Hispanics in the recent past. Some of these areas have experienced surprising changes in their Hispanic population. An interesting example of this migration trend, according to self-reports, is that from 1995 to 2000, 160,374 Hispanics reported moving to the state of California, and 505,947 indicated they moved out.[15] This means that more than three times as many Hispanics already residing in the United States moved out of California as moved in.

Among the states that have gained Hispanic population is Colorado, which experienced in-migration of 503,409 and out-migration of 388,356. Other states that experienced pronounced gains in Hispanic population include Florida, Georgia, Indiana, Iowa, Kansas, Kentucky, Michigan, Minnesota, Nebraska, Nevada, North Carolina, South Carolina, and Tennessee.

Some of these states have made dramatic gains. For example, from 1995 to 2000, Nevada gained 87,917 and lost only 26,267. North Carolina gained 71,268 and lost only 30,197. Regardless of cold winter weather, Minnesota gained 26,137 Hispanics and lost only 11,405. Texas, however, a highly Hispanic state, like California, did not change much according to Census-measured internal migration. New York, on the other hand, gained 67,273 and lost 225,429 Hispanics. These dramatic migratory changes are just for those who moved within the United States, not for those that came from abroad during those years. Still, what this internal migration dynamic indicates is that there appears to be an increasing trend toward dispersion of the U.S. Hispanic population.

The map[16] in Figure 2.2 from the U.S. census shows the U.S. counties that experienced gains in Hispanic population from 1990 to 2000. Comparing the map in Figure 2.1 with this one shows that the areas of more pronounced growth are those that were not typically where Hispanics have lived until recently.

This trend is likely to be due to several factors:

1. Migration out of states with a high cost of living, like California and New York.
2. Migration toward states with increasing labor needs. Due to the tourism industry, for example, Nevada and Florida have been magnets of Hispanic migration. Other states that have experienced population growth have become magnets in the construction, landscaping, janitorial, and other service industries.
3. The pressure of increasing Hispanic population growth in the United States has also made migration out of centers of high concentration attractive. Areas of lesser Hispanic density present less competition and more opportunities.

Figure 2.2

Changes in Hispanic population by county

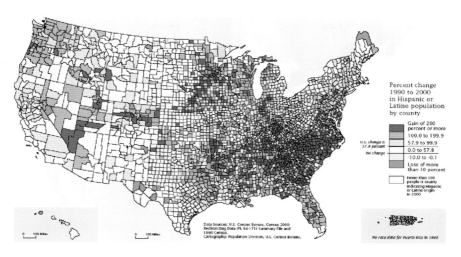

Not only have Hispanics discovered the benefits of dispersing geographically but towns in states like Indiana have been keen in welcoming Hispanics. In order to make Hispanics feel welcomed, Indiana's Governor Frank O'Bannon decided to allow the *matricula consular* as a form of identification for undocumented immigrants from Mexico.

The *matricula consular* is an identification card that Mexico has used for many years to identify its own undocumented nationals who venture into the United States. Mexican Consulates grant these IDs to those bearing a Mexican birth certificate and other forms of Mexican legal identification. In some cases, when immigrants have no IDs, consular officers quiz the petitioners. If they can verify they are from Mexico they grant them a *matricula*.

"More than 80 cities and 900 police departments in 13 states accept the matricula as a legitimate form of identification."[17] These entities are realistically addressing the issue of illegal immigration. They know that by allowing the *matricular consular* as a form of identification they can track those who use them as opposed to having no record of illegal immigrants in their midst. Also, many of these entities recognize the contributions of Hispanics to their economy and communities and attempt to facilitate their lives by recognizing these documents.

Geographic dispersion of Hispanics is likely to have strong implications for Hispanic marketing in the future:

1. As Hispanics increasingly distribute themselves among the non-Hispanic population, they will have more influence on the culture of the United States furthering the Hispanization of America. More non-Hispanics likely will have friends, acquaintances, workers, neighbors, mates, relatives, and professional relationships with Hispanics. These associations and relationships will further enhance the mutual influence of both Hispanic and U.S. cultures.

2. Hispanics likely will have to speed up the acquisition of English as a second language in these new environments. It cannot be denied that as it happens in most human contexts, Hispanics will seek the companionship of other Hispanics. Still, the opportunity for non-Hispanic contact will increase. Becoming bilingual and bicultural will be a more pressing priority for Hispanics.

3. Having Hispanics less concentrated will force marketers to reach them via media that is not considered to be typically Hispanic. Campaigns on television, radio, print, and other outlets will have to be customized to reach Hispanics in Spanish and/or English in places where Spanish language media is not as accessible as it is in major metropolitan areas.

4. Hispanics likely will preserve their cultural roots due to the pride and desirability of the Spanish language and Hispanic culture in the United States. Thus, instead of assimilation, bicultural acculturation is more likely to take place. This will further contribute to the interest of the larger U.S. culture in the Spanish language and Hispanic culture.

These trends will challenge the assumptions that marketers have made thus far about marketing to United States Hispanics. The Hispanic market will continue to be profitable as a cultural entity because of its attachment to its origins, values, and way of life. There are fundamental differences in the vision of the world held by Hispanics as contrasted with their largely Protestant Anglo counterparts.

Socioeconomic Trends

Perhaps one of the most important predictors of culturally based behaviors is the social and economic standing of U.S. Hispanics. Those that trace their origins to the elites of Latin America are very different from those who were the working classes in those countries. And these two extremes are also different from the middle class Hispanics who immigrate to the United States.

The Elite

The elites that immigrate to the United States constitute relatively small numbers of people. These are those who had made it so big in their country of origin that they found it more comfortable and convenient to have their base in the United States. Some of them are actually afraid to live in their own countries because of the danger of kidnappings and prevalent crime. Others are simply rich retirees that fondly remember their shopping trips to the United States, and eventually make a life of spending their money in the United States.

They go back and forth to their countries of origin and live a very affluent cosmopolite existence. They live in places like La Jolla, Coronado, San Francisco, Aspen, Dallas, Houston, Miami, Atlanta, and New York. They are likely to have servants that come from their own country of origin. This is not the subgroup that best defines the Hispanic market in the United States, however they are great targets for large investment companies, luxury cars, expensive real estate concerns, and other goods and services that define the affluent elite.

The Middle Class

Those from the middle classes who immigrated are also a relatively small group. The middle classes in Latin America are small in each country and tend to be strongly attached to their societies. They do not easily emigrate to the United States because they leave behind status, prestige, credentials, titles, licenses, and so on.

For example, Mexican physicians do not make as much money, in general, as their U.S. counterparts. Nevertheless they enjoy great prestige and a comfortable lifestyle. If they emigrate to the United States they need to obtain their license to practice again, which is a very cumbersome and time-consuming process. The middle class businessman or businesswoman knows that to get started in the United States they need to confront very difficult obstacles. They have much to lose.

Basically, having much to lose is what keeps the middle classes anchored to their countries. They do not make the sacrifice to come to the United States until economic pressure is so strong in their country of origin that they feel they have no further recourse. Middle class emigrations to the United States from Latin America tend to be defined by economic crises in specific countries. For example, after the economic disaster in Mexico in 1994, there were physicians, attorneys, and others who came illegally to the United States to work in the fields or as construction workers. The economic pressure was too much at that time. When that pressure subsided, however, many of these professionals returned precisely because of the difficulties of obtaining their credentials back in the United States.

Some of those middle class members that emigrate to the United States do extremely well. They perform well because they had a head start in their country. They were provided with entrepreneurial tools and they brought them here. An interesting success story that illustrates the potential of this middle class is that of Lulu's Dessert Corporation.

In 1982 there was a major economic crisis in Mexico. As previously stated these are the occasions when the middle class is willing to take a risk in the United States. A cultural custom in Mexico is to consume ready-to-eat gelatins—beautiful and colorful cup-size gelatins that children and adults buy as snacks in bakeries, supermarkets, small specialized stores, and street vendors. Of course, moms also make these gelatins for children's parties and just for healthy snacks.

Maria de Lourdes "Lulu" Sobrino worked for a travel and conventions company in Mexico that failed due to the economic downturn that year. She noticed that ready-to-eat gelatins were not available in the United States. She also thought about the fact that the U.S. Hispanic market was growing fast, particularly in Los Angeles. She decided to open a gelatin factory and store in Los Angeles. That was an entrepreneurial innovation. Maria de Lourdes took an opportunity that no one else had seen. She started from nothing, making 300 gelatins per day and having a hard time selling them in her small store in Los Angeles, and grew to 15 million dollars per year in sales today. She represents the quintessential case of the middle class immigrant to the United States that becomes a success story. Her photo, along with her large line of products is shown in Figure 2.3.

The Working Class Mass

The working class mass is the bulk of the U.S. Hispanic consumer in the United States. This is a large contingent characterized by those who have come to the United States, many illegally, to find a better standard of life. These are individuals who in their country of origin had very little, or nothing to lose by coming to the United States.

Many of these immigrants come from subsistence farming backgrounds—people who produce what they consume, and have little extra to sell for money. They come to the United States for survival, not for luxury. Many of these are people who could have starved if they had not had the courage to take a risk for a better life. Their

Figure 2.3

Maria de Lourdes "Lulu" Sobrino

attachments to their country of origin are not titles, money, professions, licenses, or material goods, but just their friends and family. Those friends and family keep them loyal to the land where they had very little.

These are people that might have been factory workers in cities, but who had very little disposable income to enjoy the material life of their environments. Some of them had been domestic servants. Some of them had been occupied in a mixture of agricultural and industrial low level jobs that barely allowed them to enjoy any of the benefits of a materialistic society.

They come to the United States with nothing. Many cross illegally. Others come as tourists and stay. The many that are here already claim others as relatives and obtain immigration permits for them. They arrive with very little background and experience regarding consumer products. The little they learn at first is taught to them by those who preceded them. Those brands that had done a good job in penetrating the market are perpetuated in the minds of new arrivals.

These new arrivals tend to be courageous young men who have left their mothers, fathers, wives, family, and friends behind in search of fortune. That is a fortune that eludes them in the highly stratified society of Mexico and most Latin American countries. They come to the land of opportunity and take the risk of perishing for it, often being abused and discriminated against once they arrive. Communities find it offensive that these men hang around on street corners waiting for temporary jobs. Most of these young people suffer loneliness and despair. Their hoped-for reward is to make money to go back to their country and share it with their families. They dream of a house and perhaps building a business. The reason so many are willing to take the risk is because they know of many relatives and acquaintances who have made it.

These recent immigrants send money to their country routinely. They live a hellish life for a while with the reward of knowing that their loved ones are enjoying the fruit of their labor. Eventually, the young men start saving money, moving to better occupations, and deciding either to marry[18] or bring the women and wives they have left behind.

These couples start having children. These children are American citizens by law, but not recognized as such until they are 18 years of age. Some of these kids are denied public education because of the illegality of their parents even if they themselves are U.S. citizens. However, generally the children grow up and learn English in school. The Spanish they learn at home tends to be modest because many of their parents did not have the privilege of extended formal education. They bring the English language home and teach their parents about the world of consumerism in the United States.

The parents nurture the dream of going back "home." They continue sending money to Mexico and other countries. They may buy a piece of land, a home, and perhaps a small business in Mexico to be there for them upon their return. The children grow up, and despite their parents' dreams, they prefer to stay in the United States. Thus the dream of going back home remains just a dream for many of them. The parents tend to be heavily dedicated to the success and well-being of their children in the United States. They sacrifice and pay for their education. Many children of parents who did not finish elementary school become professionals and prosper in the United States.

Many of these immigrants just decide to stay in the United States because of tougher immigration measures along the borders. The so-called "war against terrorism" inadvertently keeps many illegal immigrants in the United States. Many of them give up their homeland just to avoid having to cross back and forth. These are dangerous and dreaded crossings. Things could be very different if the United States had a migrant worker program that would make the process legal and easier for everyone.

Reality in 2005 is that the ranks of U.S. Hispanics who come from humble backgrounds are rapidly growing. These consumers start with little consumer knowledge and evolve into the U.S. consumer society as many forces, including their children, lead them to learn to function in the United States. Here is where many marketers have missed an opportunity.

The Hispanic market has a complexity that makes it different from the U.S. general market. Marketers typically have assumed that, like the mainstream market, the decision-making unit is the individual. However, in reality, it is the family. Further, these families are likely to have members with different levels of acculturation. Children may be English dominant, the father may be bilingual, the mother may be Spanish dominant. And, the grandmother that lives with them is definitely Spanish dominant.

Let us think about the instance in which the family decides it is time to buy a new car. The input is going to come from everyone. The kids will have seen ads on English-language television and may have friends whose father has a car brand X. The father has seen ads in English and Spanish for brand X but he is confused because the ads in English and Spanish emphasize contradictory attributes. The mother's friends have told her that brand X is OK but that the family should consider brand Y. The grandmother definitely goes for brand Y.

If the integrated marketing communication campaign for brand X had made use of a uniform message that took into consideration the different decision making inputs, the decision would have been X. But since the brand X message was equivocal, the family goes for tradition and purchases Y. This is a brand X missed opportunity due to the marketer's lack of consumer understanding.

Income Levels

According to the U.S. Census Bureau,[19] Hispanic household income declined from a median of $34,099 in 2001 to $33,103 in 2002. The overall population was about $9,000 above the Hispanic median, and also had a declining tendency. That was not surprising because of the tragic events of September 11, 2001 and the overall decline of the U.S. economy. In 2004, with an improving economy most projections are that income levels will show an increase across the board. Still, the central point is that Hispanics lag economically and that their lag is substantive. What has not been systematically quantified and analyzed is the relative difference in standard of living, for those who are first generation immigrants, between their country of origin and the United States.

The distribution of household income in 2002 is symptomatic of current levels of disparity between the overall U.S. population and those of Hispanic origin. Table 2.1 illustrates the pattern.[20]

In 2002 Hispanic income lagged substantially with respect to the overall population. The percentage of those households with incomes over $100,000 in the overall population was double that of Hispanics. For those over $50,000 Hispanics lagged by over 25%. Further, in the overall population there are many fewer households in the lower levels of income. These differences are expected to decline over time. Still, these disparities overlook the fact that the meaning of "getting by" is different when you have had a background of deprivation. Even though everyone suffered economically from 2001 to at least 2003, Hispanics in general appear to have retained their optimism and be thankful for what they have. Starting out with very little makes every step forward seem larger.

The 2003 Yankelovich Multicultural Study in Collaboration with Cheskin and Images USA may serve as an illustration.[21] One of the tables from that study shows how different cultural groups describe their financial situation (see Table 2.2).

At face value we can observe that Hispanics and African Americans perceive their situation as being less well off than non-Hispanic whites and that is very likely to be accurate. Nevertheless, understanding the history and development of the market, it seems logical that the subjective interpretation of "Just have enough to get by" would have higher value to Hispanics than to African Americans and non-Hispanic whites. That is because for many Hispanics, particularly those who are recent immigrants, "Just have enough to get by" is better than not having enough to get by, as is the case for many who come from less affluent strata in Latin America.

Family Size and Economic Behavior

Even though Hispanics lag economically, they consume large amounts of products for the home and family. According to the U.S. Census Bureau,[22] in 2002, Hispanic households with five or more people were 26.5 percent of all Hispanic households, and Mexican origin households with five or more people were 30.8 percent of the total. Comparatively, only 10.8 percent of non-Hispanic whites had households with five or more members. This is a clear opportunity for mar-

Table 2.1

	Under $5,000	$5,000 to $9,999	$10,000 to $14,999	$15,000 to $24,999	$25,000 to $34,999	$35,000 to $49,999	$50,000 to $74,999	$75,000 to $99,999	$100,000 and over	$50,000 and over
All Households	3.2	5.9	7	13.2	12.3	15.1	18.3	11	14.1	43.4
Hispanic Households	4.3	6.7	8.1	17.2	15.7	16.4	16.9	7.5	7.2	31.6

Percentage of Households for Different Brackets of Total Income in 2002

Table 2.2

How Different Cultural Groups Describe Their Financial Situation			
	African-Americans	Hispanics	Non-Hispanic Whites
Comfortable financially	31%	32%	53%
Just have enough to get by	46	48	37
Have financial difficulties	23	20	10

keters of products for home and children including food, beverages, diapers and other paper products, home improvement, and clothing.

A large family size is a function of two factors. One is the presence of more children due to a pro-natal attitude in the culture. The second factor is that Hispanic families are likely to host friends and relatives for extended periods of time. New immigrants tend to establish their residence in the home of someone that preceded them. Sometimes a parent, a sibling, or someone else comes to visit and stays for very extended periods of time. These friends and relatives can sometimes live with a family for years before finding their own way in American society. Some take care of elderly relatives until they pass on. Many Hispanic families still serve as "social security" for elderly, sick, or poor relatives. The concept of family among Hispanics is more inclusive than among Anglos. It encompasses members of the extended family, and many times, others.

An additional complication is that many Hispanic families that are in the process of escalating the economic ladder in the United States simply join households. It is common to find two families sharing a rented home for some time. It is also common for families who own a home to rent part of the house to another family.

These patterns make for complications in understanding some of the consumer behavior of Hispanics. The income of the household may actually be more than what the nuclear family makes. Relatives that live in the home are likely to contribute in many ways. A tangential issue is that many Hispanics work in jobs that pay cash and thus operate in the underground and unreported economy. Their income may be significantly higher than what they report.

Education

One of the most important issues facing the U.S. Hispanic market is education. According to 2002 U.S. Census Bureau Statistics,[23] only 46 percent of U.S. Hispanics 25 years of age and older had completed high school. That is compared to almost 60 percent of non-Hispanic whites. The educational gap is a challenge that the United States needs to address in the near future with determination. As the non-Hispanic white population decreases proportionally, and as it gets older with the bulk of the baby boomers at the forefront, Hispanics and African Americans will be the supporting pillars of the U.S. economy in the future. These two groups will largely bear the burden of supporting the aging non-Hispanic white population. But, with limited education, their ability to generate income and advance the causes of the U.S. economy will be precarious. To avoid that potential disaster, U.S. politicians and their constituencies need to come to terms with a potential disastrous future featuring a very large underclass.

For marketers, it is important to understand that the future of the Hispanic market will indeed be brighter if higher levels of education are attained. Even if Hispanics need to face limited educational opportunities, marketers will continue to have profitable Hispanic ventures. Still, it is in the best interest of marketers and their clients to contribute to the education of the market. The higher the education that Hispanics achieve, the better the opportunities they will have to increase their income and consume more extensively.

It is paradoxical and interesting that the market's economy seems to be doing more for Hispanics these days than are established social institutions. It was not until the market became worthy of the attention of marketers that other institutions started attributing importance to Hispanics in the United States. This economic power is likely to continue to grow and attract further respect and interest in U.S. Hispanics.

The Selig Center for Economic Growth at the University of Georgia estimates that Hispanic buying power in 2003 was $653 billion, and that by the year 2008 it will be over a trillion dollars.[24] Interestingly, that will put the U.S. Hispanic market among the top economies in the world, close to the GDP of Mexico (Mexico is the tenth largest economy in the world in 2003). The tenor of the discourse about U.S. Hispanics will evolve into the Hispanization of America and the Americanization of Hispanics, in a mutual flow of influence and benefit.

Conclusions and Implications for Marketers

This chapter has provided a demographic and geographic perspective on the U.S. Hispanic market. The overwhelming message is that this is a substantial population segment that marketers will either ignore at the peril of their competitiveness, or take notice of for potentially great benefits to their companies. This chapter has shown that this market is dynamic, changing rapidly in overall numbers and geographic configurations. These facts compel the attention of marketers to provide informed guidance for their businesses.

Implications for Marketers

- Avoid jumping to conclusions based on the broad demographic picture of this market. Understand how your products, services, and business objectives match specific needs and characteristics of the Hispanic market. Investigate Hispanic consumer tendencies through secondary research to develop hypotheses. Then, test these assumptions by gathering primary consumer data.

  For example, it is relatively simple to understand where the largest bulges in the Hispanic population are (i.e., Mexicans in California, Texas, and Illinois). However, if your product is a luxury item, it may be more appropriate for higher income Hispanics, who are better educated, U.S. born, and predominantly English-speaking. These Hispanics may come from various Hispanic countries of origin and live on both U.S. coasts.

- Consider both short- and long-term strategy in planning for the U.S. Hispanic market. Given the demographic overview in this chapter, you can get the current picture of where the market is. In addition, you can also develop a vision of where it may be in only three to five years.

  Good strategic planning for your business could include such burgeoning Hispanic markets as Las Vegas and Denver. Getting into rapidly expanding markets for relevant products and services could prove advantageous. For example, money transfers or mortgage lending could provide valuable services for Hispanics who are growing their incomes. Many will surely send money back to relatives in their home countries, and plan on building homes for their growing families.

- Consider what speaking to the hearts and minds of Hispanic consumers means for your business, from a cultural perspective. This chapter has presented the common aspects of Hispanic culture derived from the language, religion, and heritage of Spain. Certain products, services, and communication campaigns are likely to fit with these shared Hispanic traditional values and beliefs. This knowledge allows the marketer to make initial considerations about the Hispanic market.

  For example, Procter & Gamble has been enormously successful with their Pampers brand by using culturally compatible images. Their advertising depicts the loving Hispanic mother smiling over her baby and indicating her confidence that she is providing the best start in life for her baby by using Pampers. P&G has indeed been so successful with their Pampers' campaigns that Hispanics use the name Pampers as a generic name for diapers.

Although these ads seem intuitive, P&G continuously conducts research to make sure that they are close to the heartstrings and concerns of the Hispanic consumer prior to launching any new advertising campaign. Through research, P&G discovered the cultural insight regarding Hispanic mothers' deeply felt need to provide their babies with the best start.

- Don't forget to take into account educational levels. There are large numbers of Hispanic consumers who read only in Spanish, or who are functionally illiterate because of their low levels of education and lack of practice. For those who read only in Spanish it is obviously important to provide them with materials in their own language. For those who do not read well or at all, it is not feasible to provide them solely with written materials.

  Therefore, symbols like the famous Pillsbury doughboy make a brand easily recognizable without words. In addition, directions with figurative drawings or photos, and TV or radio advertising that explains the wide array of new brands in Spanish can all be effective ways to promote them. Think, if you suddenly move to Greece or Japan and are exposed to an array of new products and services, how disorienting this could be without guidance in ways that go beyond the written word!

All in all, this chapter clarifies that the characteristics of the U.S. Hispanic market make it an enticing avenue for companies and their marketers. The basic understanding of the historical and demographic materials presented in this chapter provides the framework for considering and approaching the Hispanic market for many U.S. companies. Here, the marketer has learned an overview of commonalities that can generate enthusiasm and guide initial consideration of whether a campaign seems like a good idea. The marketer has also learned that this market is complex, and that careful research is required prior to moving ahead. Capturing the hearts and minds of these consumers with an informed strategy can indeed result in enormous benefits for both the companies that market to them and the consumers themselves.

Case Study: *Marbo – Tampico*

Company/Organization: Marbo Inc.
Advertising Agency: Casanova Pendrill
Campaign: Development and launch of the new Tampico brand
Intended customers/clients: Hispanic market in high density Hispanic cities

Background:

Owners of Marbo wanted to leverage their previous beverage experience and to develop a new brand of juice-based drinks that did not require refrigeration, did not need to be shipped long distances, and could appeal to a large-volume consumer. They wanted to do this without going up against the major juice brand producers, who had budgets that could blow away a private company just entering the market.

Discovery Process/Research:

Marbo had a hypothesis that the Hispanic market could make an ideal target based on their criteria. They researched this niche to understand: what were the consumption patterns of U.S. Hispanics for juice drink products (they had some understanding of this already from the prior work experience), what locations would be ideal for initial targeting, and what production and delivery channels would be optimal.

Cultural Insights:

They reconfirmed through primary and secondary research that indeed Hispanics had larger than average family size and that they over-indexed in sweet juice drink consumption. They learned that not only do all family members drink juice drinks, not just children, but they consume juice drinks all day long, not just at meals or for special occasions. They also determined that Hispanics' shopping habits and patterns differ from those of the general market, i.e., they shop frequently at *bodegas* or independent grocery stores, where they can find familiar products from their countries of origin, not available in the big supermarket chains.

They also delved into the culture to understand the nature of colors and design which appeal to Hispanic shoppers. Through primary research they determined that brightly colored packaging clearly depicting the product inside is preferred. They also learned the importance of face-to-face and personal-style marketing with in-store and community promotions, which they geared to the more modest level lifestyle of these consumers. They understood that these Hispanic consumers want both quality in taste and product, but also value in costs for the large volume of beverages consumed in their households.

Expression of Insights in the Campaign:

Marbo named their brand Tampico after a city in Mexico, realizing this would resonate positively and directly with the largest Hispanic consumer group, the U.S. Mexican population, and would be favorable to and easy to pronounce for the remainder of the Hispanic community. Their initial packaging was in gallon sizes to respond to the needs of the larger than average Hispanic family size. They created a sweet juice drink product to appeal to the sweet palate of Hispanics. They branded it to underscore that this was an established product, something important to create trust with Hispanic consumers. They priced the product affordably so Hispanic families could afford it for a family drink. In order to control costs and build distribution quickly, they decided to go to market via a bottling network. Through these arrangements Marbo was able to have a promotion, production, and distribution model that made them strongly competitive.

Marbo created a brightly colored package design for Tampico which incorporated photographs of the fruits represented in each drink's flavor. With a small marketing budget they took advantage of the buzz which can be engendered by a community with high face-to-face communication networks. They used Spanish language advertising in Spanish language media, which was less expensive than mainstream media.

In all of their campaigns, they relied most heavily on their face-to-face "personal" promotions. They created in-store, in-community, and in-culture promotions that brought their sales staff and products close to these Hispanic consumers. In their in-store promotions they featured mini-sweepstakes with prizes like bikes and coolers, in contrast to the cars and other more pricey products of large affluent beverage companies. These modest sweepstakes helped them stay within their budget, yet created interest and relevant prizes for these Hispanic consumers.

They had bilingual signage in stores to cater to the language realities of these consumers who were at various levels of speaking and reading Spanish and/or English. Later in their marketing, as their product took off, they also used Spanish-language billboards and even more in-language radio and TV.

Marbo also launched Tampico in Mexico, the Caribbean, Central and South America. Their intent was to increase the volume of their business with a product they felt certain would have strong appeal. However, this effort also positively affected their U.S. Hispanic market sales since those who emigrated from these Latin American countries arrived in the U.S. already familiar with the brand.

Figure 2.4

Tampico in-community promotion

Effect of the Campaign:

Based on its overall integrated campaign and with a limited budget compared to major juice drink brands, Tampico became a leading brand in the fruit drink category. Its strong growth trajectory included these achievements: From launch through 1999 Tampico had double-digit growth; it is the #1 refrigerated juice drink brand in U.S. groceries; and its Tampico Citrus Punch 128 ounce size is the #1 branded sku in the U.S. grocery juice drink category. Additionally, Tampico has become a leader in the juice drink category throughout the Caribbean, Central and South America, and around the world.

Case Study: *Bromley – Charmin*

Company/Organization: Procter & Gamble, Charmin
Advertising Agency: Bromley Communications
Campaign: "Scent"
Intended Customers: Spanish-speaking Hispanic women 25–49, with children under age 18 living at home, who are "Scent-seekers"

Background:

Decommoditizing the category

Toilet paper is toilet paper, right? Judging by consumers' purchasing behaviors in the category, one might think so. There is almost constant switching; with competitive pricing strategies and promotions continuously giving consumers reasons to alternate among different brands. Although consumers claim that softness and strength are desired attributes in the category, they believe that most brands satisfy these requirements. In other words, just about any toilet paper brand is "good enough." This prevailing consumer attitude threatens to erode Charmin's historical dominance of the category. In an effort to halt dollar share declines and counter competitive merchandising, the brand decided it had to get Charmin "back on a roll" by giving consumers something new to talk about at the shelf.

For U.S. Hispanic consumers, many of whom are immigrants, the toilet paper category is even more complex. The overall quality of the category in the U.S. is far superior to the toilet paper found abroad. For them, the category is even more commoditized, as almost all brands initially exceed their expectations. Despite this variety of superior products at the shelf, few brands are communicating directly with Spanish-speaking consumers. Historically, Charmin has been the only toilet paper brand advertising in Spanish to this segment. However, in an increasingly price-sensitive and merchandising-driven category, Charmin faces intense competition from players like Scott, Cottonelle, and Quilted Northern.

In an attempt to de-commoditize the category and set itself apart from the "pack," Charmin launched its Scents line in April 2003 with the Wildflower Fresh product. Scents was given the challenge of getting Charmin "back on a roll" by 1) driving trial at the shelf, 2) increasing Charmin's overall share in the U.S. Hispanic market, and 3) bringing excitement and energy back to the brand.

Discovery Process/Research:

Procter and Gamble conducted a series of quantitative and qualitative concept and use tests to assess the viability of the Charmin Scents line within the Hispanic market. During early 2003, qualitative exploratory research was conducted by Procter and Gamble and their Hispanic advertising agency, Bromley Communications, in order to assess desired consumer product end benefits as well as the most effective and impactful ways to communicate the new Scent product to the Hispanic market. Following the development and production of television executions, quantitative copy-testing was conducted to assess the potential convincingness, engagingness, recall, and likeability ratings of the execution.

Cultural Insights:

Quantitative analysis of the category told Bromley that an overwhelming majority of Hispanic women are "scent seekers" or acceptors. They buy all sorts of scented products for the home including detergent, dish liquid, candles, air fresheners, shampoo and lotions. While Hispanic moms proactively seek out scented products and are willing to pay more for these little "extras," their general market counterparts are more selective in their acceptance of these products. In the general market, scented toilet paper proves to be a fairly polarizing product offering.

Qualitative research indicated that Hispanic consumers desire aesthetic as well as functional benefits in the toilet paper category (*Qualitative Research April 2003, Procter & Gamble Concept & Use Testing*). Conversely, qualitative research on Scents with general market consumers demonstrated that this market has fundamental hygiene concerns with a scented toilet paper. As such, initial emphasis in general market advertising was placed on thwarting hygiene concerns by calling out the "scent on the tube, not on the paper" message.

As avid "scent seekers," Hispanic women use these products as a little way to make their homes feel special and inviting to the constant flow of visiting friends and family. It's the little things, like toilet paper, that allow her to pamper her family. She takes great pride in keeping the home smelling clean and fresh; especially the bathroom.

Hispanic female consumers did not demonstrate a significant hygiene aversion to scented toilet paper, and in fact, they easily recognized that the scent was on the tube, not the paper. Therefore, our communications were able to go beyond the expected functional message, to capture the sensorial benefit of "leaves your bathroom smelling fresh and clean." In this way, we positioned Charmin Scents to offer a benefit that was unique and tailored to our Hispanic scent-seeking consumer. Research indicated that a scented toilet paper helped to "enhance" the bathroom experience for our consumers on several different levels: 1) scent makes her feel as if the bathroom is cleaner, 2) scent makes her bathroom more presentable and enjoyable for guests, 3) scented toilet paper works longer and more consistently than an air freshener and 4) positive comments from family and friends about the scent make her feel as if she's a "scent-sational mother."

Although the end benefit went beyond the paper, consumers were reassured about the fact that Charmin Scents features "scent on the tube, not on the paper." This piece of important functional information was called out clearly in all pieces of advertising to address any potential hygiene issues.

Copy-testing results in the general market later demonstrated that general market consumers were also looking for a bigger end benefit than a purely functional call-out, and messaging was adjusted to mirror the Hispanic communications strategy.

Expression of Insights in Campaign:

Charmin's global animated "Call of Nature" campaign, featuring a bear family, has been on air for over three years. Bromley's challenge was to launch Scents within the existing campaign—reinforcing established brand equities and getting across the new product message. It was also important to maintain synergy with general market and international efforts.

Media support of this campaign included television and print executions. Both Bromley's television and print executions clearly called out the fact that the scent was on the tube, not on the paper; thereby eliminating any potential hygiene concerns with consumers. In order to demonstrate the enhanced bathroom experience that Charmin Scents provides, the print execution featured a very happy bear smelling the flowers that emanated from the tube of the Charmin toilet paper. In the television execution, baby bear cubs were featured rolling around in a flower bed, enjoying the "wildflower fresh" scent; similar to that of Charmin Scents Wildflower Fresh. The father bear looked on happily in the background as the cubs enjoyed the experience.

The Agency's tagline in the Hispanic market, *Mimalos con Charmin* (Pamper them with Charmin) helps to highlight the little "extra" that the consumer is providing for her family with the purchase of Charmin Scents.

Figure 2.5

Charmin scent campaign

Effect of the Campaign:

According to Bromley, the results of the Hispanic Campaign indicate that Scents is off to a "scent-sational" start for the brand.

Drive Trial:

By June/July 2003, all key Hispanic customers (retailers) were carrying Scents and as a result, the Scents line already accounted for 4% of total Hispanic Charmin sales. To date, Scents accounts for 6% of the total Hispanic brand sales vs. 3% of the general market brand sales, making Scents over-developed in the Hispanic market. Retailers are selling the Scents line and are receiving positive consumer feedback on the product.

Among consumers, Charmin Scents achieved trial of 8% and awareness of 32% behind television and print support through March 2004. Importantly, Scents drove strong repeat purchase (84%), highlighting its ability to drive loyalty for the brand.

(Source: P&G internal tracking, AC Nielsen)

Increase Share:

In June/July of 2003, just three months after its launch, Charmin Scents dollar share in the U.S. Hispanic market exceeded goals by an index of 115. During FY 2003/2004, Charmin Scents delivered much stronger share results in the Hispanic market than in the general market, delivering a 125 index vs. general market. Additionally, strong Hispanic shares of Scents have spurred the potential development of other scented products designed specifically for this market.

(Source: P&G internal tracking)

Create Excitement:

Consumer qualitative research, with in-home use of the Wildflower Fresh product, indicated that for both Charmin Loyals* and Switchers,** Scents not only met their expectations of a Charmin product, but actually seemed to have a positive halo effect on the Charmin brand.

Consumer advertising, which clearly called out the "keeps your bathroom smelling fresh and clean" benefit, created consumer excitement in a relatively low-interest category, and generated the

---

*Loyal Charmin consumers buy Charmin most of the time
**Switcher consumers buy Charmin and another brand

desire to "try for myself" among key consumer segments—especially switchers. In addition, consumers indicated another use for Charmin Scents that we had not considered—they indicated that they would use the product instead of air fresheners, not only in the bathroom, but also in linen closets and bedrooms. In this way, Charmin Scents saves our price-sensitive consumer money and offers something that no other product in the category can provide.
(Source: Consumer Qualitative Research, TNS, April 2003)

References

1 "Treaty of Guadalupe Hidalgo." *Encyclopædia Britannica Online*, 25 June 2004, <http://search.eb.com.proxy.lib.fsu.edu/eb/article?eu=39059>.

2 The largest Mexican television network.

3 Orozco, Manuel. *The Remittance Marketplace: Prices, Policy and Financial Institutions.* A Pew Hispanic Center Report, Washington, D.C., June 2004.

4 "Puerto Rico." *Encyclopædia Britannica Online*, 25 June 2004, <http://search.eb.com.proxy.lib.fsu.edu/eb/article?eu=127868>.

5 US Census Bureau. *US Hispanic Population: 2002.* Ethnicity and Ancestry Branch, US Census Bureau. June 29, 2004. <http://www.census.gov/population/socdemo/hispanic/ppl-165/slideshow/286,1,U.S. Hispanic Population: 2002>.

6 "Cuba." *Encyclopædia Britannica Online*, 28 June 2004, <http://search.eb.com/eb/article?eu=127845>.

7 In today's vocabulary these would be considered Native Americans, as all the indigenous people of the continent.

8 *US Hispanic Population: 2002.* Ethnicity and Ancestry Branch, US Census Bureau. June 29, 2004. <http://www.census.gov/population/socdemo/hispanic/ppl-165/slideshow/286,1,U.S. Hispanic Population: 2002>.

9 "Central America." *Encyclopædia Britannica Online*, 28 June 2004, <http://search.eb.com/eb/article?eu=118689>.

10 *2004 Hispanic Market Report.* Synovate, Miami, Florida, 2004.

11 Ibidem.

12 *Brazil.* The World Factbook 2004. Central Intelligence Agency. Washington, D.C. June 29, 2004. <http://www.odci.gov/cia/publications/factbook/print/br.html>.

13 *2004 Hispanic Market Report.* Synovate, Miami, Florida, 2004.

14 U.S. Census. *Census Brief 2000: The Hispanic Population 2000.* Document C2KBR/01-3. U.S. Department of Commerce, Economics and Statistics Administration, U.S. Census Bureau, Washington, D.C., May 2001.

15 Census 2000 PHC-T-25. Migration by Race and Hispanic Origin for the Population 5 Years and Over for the United States, Regions, States, and Puerto Rico, 2000.
Table 1. Gross and Net Migration by Race and Hispanic Origin for the Population 5 Years and Over for the United States, Regions, and States: 2000. June 30, 2004. http://www.census.gov/population/cen2000/phc-t25/tab01.pdf.

16 Data Sources: U.S. Census Bureau, Census 2000 Redistricting Data (PL 94–171) Summary File and 1990 Census. Cartography: Population Division, U.S. Census Bureau.

17 Aguilera calls for acceptance of the matricula. July 2, 2004. http://www.state.in.us/legislative/hdpr/R12_07162003.html.

18 Many of these individuals do not necessarily legally marry but they cohabitate and form a family that could last a lifetime. When asked, many of them state they are married just to avoid a longer and less desirable explanation.

19 U.S. Census Bureau. *Income in the United States: 2002. Consumer Income.* Current Population Report. Washington, D.C., September 2003. July 7, 2004. http://www.census.gov/prod/2003pubs/p60-221.pdf.

20 Adapted from Ibidem.

21 2003 Yankelovich Multicultural Marketing Study in Collaboration with Cheskin and Images USA. Chapel Hill, North Carolina, 2003.

22 U.S. Census Bureau. The Hispanic Population in the United States: March 2002. U.S. Department of Commerce, Economics and Statistics Administration, U.S. Census Bureau, June, 2003.

23 Ibidem.

24 Jeffrey M. Humphreys. *The multicultural economy 2003: America's minority buying power.* Selig Center for Economic Growth. Georgia Business and Economic Conditions. The University of Georgia. Vol. 63, No. 2. Athens, Georgia, Second quarter, 2003.

What Makes Hispanics "Hispanic"

The Role of Cultural Identity in Marketing

Reference Groups as the Basis of Cultural Identity

Humans, as social beings, generally identify with groups they belong to, and sometimes with groups they do not belong to. These can be referred to as belongingness groups and reference groups. They overlap many times, but not always. People may not belong to a social group and still use that group as a reference group to derive the criteria and standards they need in making decisions about courses of action or judgments.[1] Usually these are aspirational groups. Individuals may identify with these groups without necessarily being part of them.

Marketers need to understand the reference groups that Hispanic consumers use for their consumer decision making. Also, a key point is to understand which reference groups Hispanics may use under varying circumstances. This is particularly interesting in the case of U.S. Hispanics who maintain cultural ties, but also live within the context of the U.S. mainstream culture.

Individuals do not necessarily hold only one cultural identity. Cultural identity refers to the cultural group that individuals use in specific circumstances for selecting courses of action or evaluating ideas or objects. If a Hispanic consumer uses the cultural reference group of the non-Hispanic U.S. middle class when purchasing a car, then there would be little difference in the way in which this individual and a non-Hispanic make decisions. In addition, it is possible that an individual may use different cultural reference groups in different situations.

For example, a Hispanic may use the reference group of coworkers when making a decision about insurance, regardless of his or her Hispanic heritage. He or she may make decisions about reading materials using the reference group of his or her schoolmates despite his or her cultural heritage. This person may choose to behave like an African American in a dance club. He or she could also order food in a restaurant using non-Hispanic neighbors as reference. This is because reference groups may have different saliency in different circumstances. The extent to which different reference groups become salient in different circumstances has to do with the emotionally perceived links between the situation and the reference group.

Social Learning Theory and Reference Groups

Non-Hispanic role models can guide Hispanic consumer behavior. The key to social influence is identification. Albert Bandura's Social Learning Theory[2] establishes the conditions under which humans learn behavior from others through observation and modeling. Models that are similar to the observer and those models who have aspirational status are more likely to be emulated.

Similarity and Homophily

The principle of similarity or homophily strengthens the notion that Hispanics are more likely to identify with other Hispanics. Homophily is the degree to which individuals who engage in communication share common attitudes, values, aspirations, and beliefs.[3] Hispanics, like most human beings, are expected to engage in communication and learn from others who are similar to themselves. The typical scene of the cocktail party in which those who already know each other interact with each other is an illustration of this principle. We tend to seek those with whom we are familiar and with whom we have certain traits in common.

Thus Hispanics are more likely to identify with other Hispanics and to use them as their reference group under many circumstances. If a consumer's cousin purchased a car from dealership A and he or she indicates having had a good experience with the car, then the consumer is more likely to go to dealership A than B. That is because the cousin possesses credibility in the eyes of the consumer. The consumer perceives his or her cousin to be very similar to him- or herself. This similarity provides confidence that the resulting experience will be similarly good.

Nissan and Acento, their Hispanic Advertising Agency, developed a campaign for California and Arizona dealerships to address a loss in their Hispanic market share. They learned that Hispanics felt unfamiliar, or out of their own "homophilic" reference group, with the whole car-purchasing process; they would not even enter a dealership without already knowing someone there or going with a friend or family member. Nissan, supported by Acento, created a multifaceted approach to develop a more personal Hispanic image at the dealership, including a fictional Spanish-speaking mechanic to invite them into the dealership and a store-readiness program to create a respectful, comprehensible, and *amable* (kind) environment. The campaign turned around Hispanic sales at these dealerships and led to strong sales results (see The Acento Nissan Case Study at the end of this chapter).

Expertise and Successful Models

Social learning is not based on similarity alone. Social learning theory also indicates that individuals will emulate behaviors of people they admire. Thus Hispanics may admire others outside their own "Hispanic" group. These role models could be people who are aspirational because they are successful in different aspects of life.

A large number of U.S. Hispanics and/or their predecessors come to the United States for economic advantage. They yearn for success. It is not unlikely that many Hispanics adopt role models and reference groups that are not Hispanic. Hispanic individuals can easily look up to their bosses, their neighbors, their schoolmates, and others for examples of behavior. Thus, Hispanics can learn consumer social behavior from both Hispanics and non-Hispanics.

This is very important because advertising models and portrayals may be more or less aspirational and credible depending on their relevance. In some cases Anglo role models could be more appealing and in others, Hispanic role models could be more persuasive. Understanding the circumstances under which each of these models can be most effective can be very important in marketing.

Even an Oppressor Can Be a Model

Clearly, a non-Hispanic reference group can be appealing in some aspects but aversive in others. Understanding this possible ambivalence can be highly instrumental in conducting advertising research. In 2003, 78 percent of U.S. Hispanics indicated that discrimination is still a part of Hispanics' day-to-day lives.[4] If Hispanics believe that they have been discriminated against in the United States, they may be cautious in modeling the behaviors of those who have shown negative behaviors against them. However, discrimination does not come from everyone nor from every group, thus there is plenty of room for Hispanics to find non-Hispanic models that they can relate to and look up to.

Even in cases of overall feelings of being discriminated, the potential for identification is still possible. The social-psychological literature has shown that there are circumstances under which victims identify with victimizers.[5] As a prototypical example of this, recall how Patty Hearst identified with her captors of the Symbionese Liberation Army and took on their values and behaviors.[6] Under certain circumstances, victims take on the values of their victimizers.

Thus there is ample opportunity for Hispanics to use non-Hispanic reference groups under certain circumstances. These processes and their surrounding circumstances are an important area of inquiry when investigating cross-cultural marketing.

Empirical Determination of Models

It seems most logical that generally, Hispanics will identify with other Hispanics. Thus, advertisements and testimonials featuring Hispanics should be more impactful than if these were non-Hispanics. Still, because of the reasons just elaborated, it is very likely that for certain types of decisions some Hispanics will use non-Hispanic reference groups and individuals. This is particularly true of the immigrant experience of these Hispanic consumers who are exposed to a constant bombardment of information regarding the accomplishments of those in the mainstream culture.

If the United States has been the land of aspirations and the realization of dreams, then Anglos can be powerful influences because of their success. Would a Hispanic that has been able to attain some degree of success in U.S. society be more likely to go to a bank like Banco Popular because of affinity, or to a bank like Bank of America because that is where successful Anglos go? This is not a simple question, and marketers need to address this question taking into consideration the salience of the role models and situations. The dimensions of success/expertise and homophily/similarity are likely to influence which reference group is used for specific consumer decision-making situations. Table 3.1 illustrates potential options.

The cells in Table 3.1 contain example "importance" scores. Thus, a Hispanic looking to purchase a new home may have a combination of reference group influences in his or her mind. For example, he or she may use an Anglo reference group and assign to it an importance score of 75 on a 100-point scale, because this consumer has seen that Anglos he or she knows have been very successful at purchasing their homes.

Table 3.1

Importance Scores by Salience, Success, and Homophily		
Situation Salience	**Hispanic Model**	**Anglo Model**
Success	50	75
Homophily	90	25

Nevertheless, this consumer also feels that other Hispanics he or she knows have been successful at getting their home, but not as much as Anglos.

Because of these considerations this consumer assigns an importance score of 75 to Anglos on the "success" criterion, and a score of 50 to Hispanics. When it comes to homophily (or similarity) this consumer feels much more comfortable listening to Hispanics and assigns them a score of 90 because they are very much like him or her. They have gone through the same issues and problems. He or she also feels some homophily with Anglos, but less, and so assigns this cell a score of 25.

In the course of a quantitative study, Hispanics could be asked to assign importance scores to the reference group by the dimensions of credibility: success and homophily. Across many individuals an advertiser would be able to determine what type of role models would be most impactful to the Hispanic consumer of interest.

The main conclusions that the marketer would be able to derive from this set of scores include:

1. A successful Anglo model is likely to be highly appealing.
2. A successful Hispanic model has appeal.
3. Hispanics are most likely to feel similar to the Hispanic model and thus believe that his or her probability of success is higher with company X if Hispanics are portrayed as succeeding in getting mortgages from this company.
4. A communication should indicate that both Anglos and Hispanics succeed when applying for a mortgage with company X, and that Hispanics, like the consumer him- or herself, recommend company X.

This conclusion provides an initial template for a communication with high probability of credibility and increased sales. Notice that this rough template does not include creative nuances of any type. It only addresses the need for both Anglo and Hispanic characterizations of success, and Hispanic characterizations of homophily in connecting with the consumer. The results of this analysis may be counterintuitive to many who have thought for many years that only Hispanic models should be used when selling to Hispanics.

The key point here is to remember that the "importance" scores are the ones that determine the inclusion of characterizations in ads. What this perspective emphasizes is that reference groups may vary by their degree of relevance in specific situations in which consumers are expected to make decisions.

Macy's West with Enlace Communications, their Hispanic marketing partner, conducted research to assess Hispanic females' image of their California and Arizona department stores vs. competitors. They learned that Macy's strong brand equity in the Anglo market did not carry over to Hispanic consumers, and that they needed to work to improve store impressions of being Hispanic-friendly. In this case, Macy's needed to maintain their success orientation as an upscale store of quality, yet build on their connection with their Hispanic customers' homophily. As a result of this finding, Macy's West and Enlace developed an in-store program called *Vida, Estilo y Sabor Latino* (VESL) (Life, Style, and Latino Flavor or Joie de Vive). This program reached out to prominent Hispanic performers, included events of interest to Hispanic shoppers and their families, and even gave access to Hispanic-oriented nonprofit organizations (see Enlace Macy's West Case Study at the end of the chapter).

Identity and Socialization

Our sense of identity is defined socially.[7] It is in the course of social interaction that we acquire a sense of self. This is somewhat paradoxical because in common parlance many individuals argue that they want to be themselves, as if being like the group detracts from who they are.

But there is no way of *not* being part of some group, at least in one's mind. Humans, to be "human," must be socialized in at least one social group. That group or groups become the standard against which the individual compares the rest of the world. In contemporary Western society it is difficult to think of individuals who are socialized in only one social or cultural group. Still, as it happens in parts of Latin America, there are individuals for whom their original socialization group continues to be the most important and a unique source of influence for a long time.

Individuals who become socialized in rural, isolated, or socially segregated societies are more likely than others to have an almost exclusive cultural reference group. But the media may also present reference groups to which people may relate. Thus, even if an individual was raised in a remote community, he or she may have built a mental and emotional image of another group that the media portrayed. Thus soap-opera characters or actors from western films can become relevant reference groups.

The key issue emphasized in this section is that the identity of Hispanics is likely to be influenced by multiple sources. Although the main source of influence is generally the one in which the individual was socialized from childhood, there are other sources that need to be known. Understanding the reference groups that form the identity of specific Hispanic segments is crucial for effective Hispanic segmentation and targeting.

Marketers' Need for Predictability

Marketers, advertisers, and the media need stability and predictability in looking at consumer behavior. The assumption of behavioral consistency over time is necessary for any marketing planning to make sense. In this vein, it is assumed that the cultural identity of Hispanics is relatively stable and that Hispanics use the people of their own culture as their reference group in most situations. This is justifiable in the sense that one's culture of origin should have primacy or dominance in many situations.

Still, the empirical question of cultural reference groups is crucial as is the case with most consumer behavior. Even within the realm of Hispanic reference groups the consumer may have different subsets as reference groups. Recent immigrants from Mexico may have reference groups that are more specific than just Hispanic. For example, the new immigrant may be thinking about how his peers and siblings would approach a purchase situation, even though those peers and siblings may still be in Mexico.

Many marketers ask the question about what kind of models they should put in their commercials; that is, models that Hispanic consumers can identify with. The answer can vary from very specific to very general. The accuracy of a communication effort is likely to increase with a more accurate understanding of the reference groups Hispanic consumers have in mind when making decisions. An example of a specific reference group ladder in ascending order of abstraction is presented in Figure 3.1.

The marketer can derive more accurate predictions and create more precisely targeted communications at the lower level of abstraction.[8] Nevertheless, it can get very expensive to target consumers at the lowest level of abstraction in terms of their reference groups. Thus a com-

Figure 3.1

Reference group ladder example

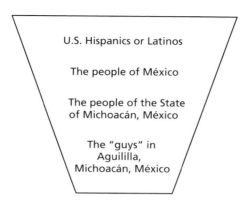

U.S. Hispanics or Latinos

The people of México

The people of the State
of Michoacán, México

The "guys" in
Aguililla,
Michoacán, México

promise level needs to be arrived at. This compromise will always be troublesome. It is almost like the dilemma between globalization and localization. What is important is that the market researchers need to consider and include in their studies the notion of reference groups. This is so the marketing decision maker can make an informed decision as to how specific or general the reference group ought to be to reach a specific target.

Hispanic Identities and Labels

The Question Influences the Answer

Many marketers have endorsed the idea that the label that people use to describe themselves represents their cultural identity. If you ponder this assertion, you may realize that this is a necessary but not sufficient condition. If Hispanics don't consider themselves Hispanics in some way, then they just don't belong to the classification at all. On the other hand, people may indicate being Hispanics for many different reasons depending on who asks the question, where the question is being asked, and the purpose of the question.

Other things being equal, if an Anglo asks a person of Mexican background what "he is," the person is likely to respond Hispanic or Latino because that is the category that more Anglos are likely to understand and relate to. The reason for using the general label, however, may be related to a desire to avoid negative stereotypes. These authors have heard multiple consumers of Mexican origin state that they answer Hispanic or Latino instead of Mexican because "they don't like Mexicans." Assumed prejudice is a reason for using one label instead of another, and again, that depends on who asks the question.

If the question is being asked in the context of a group of Hispanics of different national backgrounds, then the salient identity would be Mexican or Colombian, as opposed to the more general Hispanic. The context has inherent demand characteristics that make it relevant to use one label as opposed to another.

Further, the purpose of the question can have a strong impact in the response. If the question is for the Census then there is no choice. Hispanic or Latino is the overarching label available. If the question is asked in an application for a grant, scholarship, license, loan, and so on, then marking Hispanic or Latino is very likely because it is common knowledge that preference quotas and Federal mandates provide certain benefits to members of specific classes of persons, in this case, Hispanics.

Essentially Hispanic?

The essentialist question whether one is really Hispanic or not is not likely to be productive. The marketing question should be, "What is the most prevalent identification of the group of Hispanics under consideration?" Finding out the prevalent identification can be very useful. It provides specific tactical and strategic guidance for generating marketing communication pieces.

Labels

Hispanics have variedly described themselves in many ways, including:

- The label of the country of origin such as Cuban, Puerto Rican, Mexican, Salvadoran, Argentinean, and so on
- Chicanos
- Raza
- Mexican-Americans
- Latin-Americans
- Hispanics
- Latinos

- New Yoricans
- Boricuas
- American

There are more varied labels for Mexicans because they have constituted the majority group of Hispanics in the United States. It should be stated again that in this book the label Hispanic is used to include all people who trace their origins to a Spanish-speaking country. That does not mean that those included necessarily accept the label or that they identify with any Hispanic background at all.

If someone describes him- or herself as Mexican-American, the assumption is that the individual identifies and uses as his or her most salient reference group that which is composed of Mexicans who also feel American. When someone describes him- or herself as Chicano, we expect that the person using that label will be someone whose most salient reference group is that of people of Mexican origin who feel they are not Mexican or Americans, but who have a new identity born from those two. A Boricua is usually a person who thinks of the people of the island of Puerto Rico as their main reference group.

Different labels have different origins. Some of these labels have been born out of convenience and others out of pride. Some have emerged out of political impetus. Sometimes Hispanics describe themselves with the label of their nationality or that of their ancestors. These nationality self-descriptors seem to indicate that the individual using them feels the people of that country are his or her closest cultural reference group.

The use of labels, however, is complicated. Hispanics have been shown to use a different label depending on who asks.[9] So, for example, when an Anglo in Orange County, California asks a Mexican something along the lines of "What are you?" or "How do you describe yourself?" the person may respond Hispanic or Latino. When the person inquiring is also Mexican, however, the respondent may be more likely to describe him- or herself as Mexican.

For marketing purposes, it does not really matter what is the absolute label the person uses; what is important is the meaning of the label to that person. If in the preceding case, the term Hispanic and Mexican refer to the same cultural reference group, then the label is not necessarily denoting a substantive difference. If the person, on the other hand, takes great pride in being Mexican, then using the term Hispanic in marketing communications may not be emotionally effective.

Hispanic or Latino?

The label Hispanic traces its roots to the U.S. Census Bureau attempt to collectively label all those people in the United States who traced their origins to Spanish-speaking countries. This label was instituted in the 1970s, and was first used in the 1980 Census as a general denominator for Hispanics.

Different Hispanic constituencies felt differently about this label. The more politically active segment of the Hispanic community argued and still continues to argue that this label was imposed from the outside and that it represents the roots of oppression from Spain. That is because Hispania was the name of one of the Roman provinces that now constitutes Spain.

These same politically oriented individuals, after much debate, came up with the label "Latino" as better representing the community. Still, the label is controversial because it encompasses almost anyone from a culture with Latin roots. That could be Italians, Roumanians, Portuguese, French, and so on.

Despite the controversy, the term "Hispanic" is the more widely accepted as a general denominator. The 2002 National Survey of Latinos by the Pew Hispanic Center and the Kaiser Family Foundation[10] found that 34 percent of Hispanics prefer Hispanic, 13 percent prefer Latino, and the rest do not have a preference for one or the other.

The Measurement Challenge

Label Choice as Equivalent of Identity

For years the Hispanic marketing industry alleged the way of identifying Hispanics was to ask them to "self-identify." If individuals identified themselves as Hispanics or Latinos then they were classified as such. This procedure has intuitive merit. The argument is that if someone identifies him- or herself as Hispanic that is all that matters.

But from what we have seen earlier, Hispanics may identify themselves as "Hispanics" because of the person asking, the context, or the purpose of the question. Thus, this type of self identification may not necessarily reflect either the subjective or the objective meaning of the term.

Classification Based on Country of Origin/Ancestry

An alternative used in multiple research studies has been to ask people to indicate what country or countries they trace their ancestry to. If they mention any Spanish-speaking country in Latin America or Spain, then they are classified as Hispanics. This is a viable option from an objective perspective. It is a relatively simple alternative that has shown itself to reliably classify individuals who have roots in Spanish-speaking countries. Still, this approach renders a necessary but not sufficient condition for subjective identification with Hispanic culture.

This measure can be used in combination with a follow up question like: "Which of the following labels best represents how you feel about yourself?" This usually is followed by a series of alternatives including the labels listed earlier. This combines an objective and a subjective measure having some Hispanic reference group. Most efforts to classify Hispanic identity revolve around the ones described here.

Further Identity/Reference Group Measures

This book suggests that further reference group measures be used to more finely target specific groups of Hispanics. Clearly, this may pay off only when the reference group can be practically refined to achieve a more specific marketing objective. For example, when thinking about money remittances, the marketer may benefit from knowing that the communication is likely to be more effective if the reference group used is specifically Mexican from "small rural towns." This would allow careful targeting and effective message design.

The following is a list of ideas for measures that can be used to better define Hispanics according to their identity. Some of the measures are behavioral or "objective" in that they ask for actual actions. The other measures are subjective and deal with identification with aspects of culture.

Behavioral/Objective Measures

- How many times in a normal month[11] do you call friends or relatives in your hometown in _____?
- How many times in a normal month do you send e-mails to friends or relatives in your hometown in _____?
- How many of your friends and relatives from your hometown are now with you in the US? _____

- How many times during a normal month do you read a paper from your hometown either via the Internet or on paper? _____

- Whom do you usually go to for advice when you are in the process of purchasing a _____ (product category)? Please specify who these person or persons are, where they are from, and why you go to them.

These sample measures exemplify the degree to which the hometown is behaviorally salient to the individual. Other measures could include items like "snail mail" correspondence as indicators of contact with the hometown.

The battery of items should also include more general measures referring to the country as opposed to the hometown, like:

- How often do you watch television programs from _____ _____ (country of origin)?

- How often do you listen to music from _____ (country of origin)?

- What proportion of your circle of friends in the United States is from _____ (country of origin)?

These broader measures assist in understanding the degree to which the country of origin is present in the person's daily life.

Subjective Cultural Identification

- When we make purchases, we often remember advice and the ways of thinking of people we respect. Please indicate with a number from 0 to 10, 10 being the most important, the importance of each of the following types of people that are in your mind when making decisions about purchasing _____ (specific type of purchase)?
  - ○ _____ Family and friends from your hometown in _____ (country of origin).
  - ○ _____ Family and friends from _____ (country of origin) in general.
  - ○ _____ American friends and acquaintances in the United States.
  - ○ _____ Hispanics/Latinos in the United States, in general.
  - ○ _____ Family and friends who are here with you in the United States.

- How often do you find yourself thinking about the people in your hometown in _____ (country of origin)?

- How often do you find yourself missing your hometown in _____ (country of origin)?
- How important is it for you to celebrate the customs of your hometown in _____ (country of origin)?
- When thinking about your own identity, do you identify more strongly with your hometown or with your country of origin? _____ Hometown _____ Country of Origin _____ Both equally
- Now in the United States, how well does each one of the following labels describe how you think about yourself? Please rate on a scale of 0 to 10 with 10 being the most descriptive.
  - Hispanic _____
  - Latino _____
  - Mexican-American _____
  - And so on, depending on the nature of the study and sample

These questions constitute examples of items that have been used in different studies in trying to measure cultural identification. There are no standardized batteries with established validity and reliability. In marketing practice the measures used tend to depend largely on the specific needs and objectives of the particular study. Nevertheless, it will be important for the field to develop more standardization than what is now available in the measurement of important concepts such as the ones handled in this chapter.

Conclusions

What makes Hispanics "Hispanic" involves a complicated set of considerations. By now you should have an appreciation of the issues to consider when attempting to address the cultural identity of Hispanic consumers. Identity is a complex construct that is socially determined, thus Hispanic identity varies with the social context in which the individual interacts.

This chapter has provided guidance for marketers on what constitutes the social identity of U.S. Hispanic consumers and how to peer through that veil of self-definition to deepen understanding of consumer motivation. We learned the importance of clarifying the reference groups that influence Hispanics in making a decision on products or services. Hispanics may look toward "belongingness" groups from their countries of origin, or from other "reference" groups from their U.S. exposure, to guide their purchase behavior.

We also developed awareness of other key elements in this complex construct under girding Hispanic identity. We considered Hispanic social group identification as a function of homophily (feeling close to others like oneself from the home country) and success (looking up to others who achieve in the United States), and how identity on these dimensions varied according to the marketing objective. We also looked at the potential impact of a hierarchy of group influences across the socialization process, ranging from hometown, to particular area in the home country, to entire country of origin, to new country of residence. Further, we considered the adjustment of self-identification, that is, whether a person defines the self as Hispanic, Latino, Mexican, or Puerto Rican, as a function of who is asking the question and what the respondent feels will be the best response in that situation.

As marketers seek predictability about their Hispanic target consumers, they should keep Hispanic identity constructs in mind. Who people think they are strongly impacts their emotions. To address Hispanics as they see themselves can create powerful allies for a company and its products; to address them inappropriately can sink marketing aspirations. It is essential to develop an understanding of Hispanic identity related to a marketing objective, and to use this consumer knowledge subsequently for guidance on marketing decisions.

Implications for Marketers

- Resist the temptation to assume that all Hispanics primarily use their country of origin belongingness group as the reference for making purchase or adoption decisions. This leads to stereotyping that could dampen consumer interest. Although closeness to one's own people may be the main influence for certain products or services, it's important to check this out with research for your particular marketing objective.

- Clarify the levels of identity that relate to your marketing objective. This means consider whether Hispanic consumers identify with their town or area of origin, their country of origin, their community in the United States or their U.S. affiliations when they make decisions regarding your product or service.

- Don't get blind-sided by labels. Thinking about Hispanic, Latino, Chicano, Mexican-American, or Colombian labels may rattle your comfort level, and that could be appropriately so. The key is to find how people themselves consider their identity; how they would prefer to be addressed either directly or strategically.

Understanding this self-identification may be the key to their motivation, and the foundation for building a powerful campaign.

- Check out the combination of influences from both homophily groups and success groups in order to build a subtle campaign clearly adapted to your brand. This will aid in discovering your Hispanic target's comfort level regarding a product or service, as well as their aspirations. Reliance on homophily groups may be stronger for those who have immigrated to the United States more recently, whereas a tendency toward success groups may increase as Hispanics become more acculturated over time.

- Use both behavioral and subjective research questions to understand how Hispanic consumers identify themselves related to your marketing objective. It is important to listen not only to who people say they are, but how they tend to behave in staying close to particular reference groups. This takes into account that Hispanics tend to gear their identity answers to who they think is asking the question and why it's being asked and provides a behavioral basis for assessing identity.

- Keep in mind the influence of the mainstream U.S. culture on Hispanic identity. Hispanics have constant exposure to non-Hispanic success models in the media, in the business world, at work, and in various day-to-day settings. Although Hispanics may clearly see themselves as identified with other Hispanics, they also may pick out aspects of mainstream U.S. identity that directly relate to your business.

  For example, Hispanics may identify with American heads of household when thinking through the importance of life insurance products, since these products are not common in their countries of origin. Although they may need the comfort level of speaking with a Hispanic agent about insurance, they may indeed emulate the aspirational level of Americans who protect their families in this way.

Case Study: *Acento – Nissan*

Company/Organization: Nissan Southwestern Dealers (California & Arizona)
Advertising Agency: Acento
Campaign: The caring automobile dealer committed to Hispanics
Intended customers/clients: Hispanic potential automobile purchasers for Nissan dealerships in California and Arizona

Background:

While automobile sales were growing, Nissan sales were declining. Nissan dealers wanted an advertising strategy specifically targeted to Hispanic consumers. Their purpose was to motivate Hispanics to purchase Nissan automobiles, not just come in and look. Their goal was to turn around the company's current loss of market share in these California and Arizona dealerships.

Research:

Through research both qualitative and quantitative, Nissan and Acento, its Hispanic Advertising Agency, developed an understanding of the Hispanic purchase decision-making cycle. They conducted positioning research to develop insight into the key benefits Hispanic buyers look for in a car and how they perceive Nissan. They visited Nissan dealerships to understand the thinking and sales strategies directed to Hispanic potential buyers. They conducted quantitative research with Hispanics already thinking about buying an automobile to assess their attitudes and purchase behaviors. They conducted mystery shopping in dealerships to develop insight into the Nissan buying experience for Hispanics.

Cultural Insights:

Hispanics need a personal experience in purchasing an automobile. They will not even enter a dealership without knowing someone there already, or without coming in with a friend or relative who has a contact. They have little understanding of the purchase process typical in a U.S. dealership, and they mainly focus on price and service when they select a car.

Hispanics tend to collaborate with others in the decision-making process. They look for approval from friends and family, and while males may be principal decision-makers, wives have a strong influence and can veto their decision. Potential Hispanic car purchasers for these dealerships look for a *personal* connection with the sales person and prefer that their interaction is in Spanish. They want to feel at home in the dealership and comfortable with an environment that is compatible with their culture.

Hispanics in the research did not perceive Nissan as a brand with a style that demonstrated their success, and they found the Nissan less appealing than Toyota and Honda, the brand's main Japanese competitors. When they chose the brand they did so because of cost benefits through cash-backs, rebates, and other offers, not because they preferred the brand itself. In addition, these Hispanic in the research could not differentiate the brand's current advertising strategy; they found that all the automobiles in the automotive ads looked basically the same.

Expression of Insights in the Campaign:

Nissan, supported by Acento, their marketing communications agency, responded to the insights gleaned from their research by developing a two-prong strategy. They created a new advertising campaign and targeted the dealerships with a "store readiness" initiative. They developed an integrated model for all of the components of the overall campaign to speak to the personalization theme for the brand.

In their advertising campaign Acento humanized the face of the dealers so that Hispanics felt invited into their dealerships, and could differentiate Nissan from the competition. Acento created advertising with a fictional Nissan mechanic, who spoke Spanish and talked about cars in the same manner as his Hispanic customers. To create a welcoming attitude, the Nissan mechanic in the advertising invited Hispanics to the dealerships. They titled the campaign: Concesionarios Nissan: Pensamos en ti (Nissan dealerships: we're thinking of/caring about you). They created ads to convey the feeling that only Southern California Nissan dealerships make you feel at home.

To address store readiness, the Agency prepared a how-to Hispanic Alert Kit to educate the sales persons in the dealership about Hispanic car buyers. The Kit contained important psychographic and demographic information. Most importantly it included information on how to attract these consumers in a culturally appropriate way. Acento emphasized the imperative to hire more bilingual personnel. They also provided assistance on how to create an environment that looked and felt homelike to

Hispanics including relevant and appealing point of purchase materials.

To round out their personal focus for the dealerships, Spanish speakers from Nissan were placed at community events, concerts, and in locations frequented by Hispanics. Nissan showcased their vehicles so Hispanics could both see and touch them, and learn about them from Hispanic experts. They made a continuous effort to be present at Hispanic cultural events.

Figure 3.2

Nissan campaign

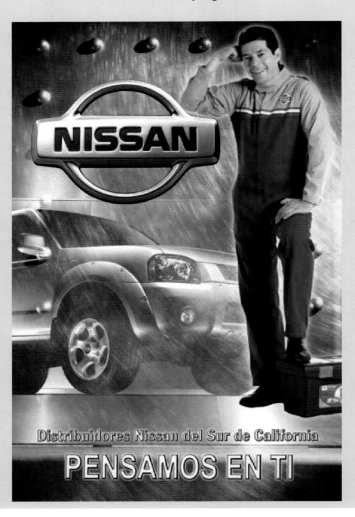

Distribuidores Nissan del Sur de California

PENSAMOS EN TI

Effect of the Campaign:

This campaign achieved strong sales results: First year 31% sales increase, second year sales increase 87% higher than any other brand, third year .4% increase compared to 10% decrease in the General Market, fourth year sales to Hispanics reached 35.9% penetration, the highest among all brands in Los Angeles. This campaign was consistent for over three years and created a character that Hispanics could trust. It was in synergy with the General Market campaign, but focused on the cultural themes that were specific to this market. The campaign won an Effie Award for one of the best automotive campaigns in any language.

Case Study: *Enlace – Macy's West*

Company/Organization: Macy's West
Advertising Agency: Enlace Communications
Campaign: Vida, Estilo y Sabor Latino (Life, Style, and Latino Flavor or Joie de Vive)
Intended customers/clients: Hispanic female department store shoppers in Macy's West California and Texas Stores

Background:

In 1998, following the acquisition of Broadway department stores by Macy's West, Enlace Communications, Inc. was selected by Macy's West as the department store's U.S. Hispanic marketing partner. Enlace had the hypothesis that the equity Macy's had with Anglo-Americans (as a result of its New York presence and its icon status reinforced annually by the Macy's Thanksgiving Day Parade and by the Christmas classic movie Miracle on 34th Street), did not exist with U.S. Hispanics. They needed to test this supposition, and to assess the relative attraction for Hispanic female shoppers of Macy's key competitors in their areas.

Discovery Process/Research:

Enlace's first step was to utilize research to determine the existing attitudes of Latino consumers (most specifically Latinas 18–45 with individual incomes of no less than 30K) toward the Macy's brand. Research, conducted by a specialist research firm H&AMCR, confirmed Enlace's existing hypothesis that the equity that Macy's had with Anglo Americans did not exist with U.S. Hispanics. The research not only confirmed this, but revealed that Macys had work to do in relation to its image as "Hispanic-friendly" vis-à-vis competitors like Robinson-May, JC Penney's, Sears, and others.

Cultural Insights:

The research revealed that what Hispanic female shoppers looked for in a department store was both quality and value. While price was a concern to these shoppers, who tended to have the expenses related to large families, they did not want to sacrifice the quality of purchases for obtaining competitive pricing. These Hispanic females also wanted a department store that demonstrated care for Hispanic consumers and their families. They wanted service personnel available who spoke in Spanish, and signs in the store in Spanish.

Expression of Insights in the Campaign:

In order to build a dynamic image that stood for quality and value, and care for the needs of Hispanic shoppers and their families, Enlace and Macy's West embarked on an integrated Hispanic marketing program. This campaign included tailored advertising messages, carefully designed media plans utilizing Spanish-language media, English-language programs with Latino appeal, merchandising work, credit card efforts, select bilingual signage and collateral efforts, HR involvement, and a series of off- and on-site event marketing programs.

One of the signature programs of the Macy's West Hispanic marketing initiative, was an in-store program called Vida, Estilo y Sabor Latino [VESL] (Life, Style, and Latino Flavor or Joie de Vive.) This bilingual, bicultural event program was designed to resonate with Hispanic consumers in particular, while being accessible to non-Latino shoppers. VESL, implemented in six Macy's stores, included a program of events, which focused on relevant lifestyle, fashion and "flavor" areas of interest. VESL utilized Latino celebrities, spokespeople, and other Latino authorities and community representatives of interest to the target shopper.

Hispanic female shoppers and their families had the opportunity to see Latina fashion shows focusing on the small business owners' needs of going from day to evening quickly, listen to storytelling for children by Latina PBS storyteller Marabina Jaimes, hear panel discussions from the cast of Selena, enjoy an Edward James Olmos talk on empowerment, learn from cooking demonstrations by

Latino chefs and cookbook authors, and take salsa lessons. In addition, non-profits were allowed to participate in-store with information about their efforts and in some cases to benefit from sales or to do fundraising efforts in-store.

Enlace promoted VESL via direct to home calendar of events, newspaper advertising, radio tags, flyers, and posters. Additionally, VESL generated a great deal of positive public relations in print and on broadcast in both English and Spanish. The community focus of the events and the inclusion of community leaders from relevant non-profits created strong word-of-mouth buzz about Macy's West and its dedicated efforts for Hispanic shoppers and the community.

Figure 3.3

Macy's West in-store program

Effect of the Campaign:

On-going research of a qualitative nature confirmed the Hispanic consumer's interest in this type of initiative. Research also reported positive trends in image transformation as a result of the integrated marketing program as a whole, and with indications that VESL was a contributing factor.

Specific outcomes of the campaign were: increased store sales, exceeding sales goals by 60% in some cases; a tangible relationship between community organizations and Macy's; involvement of Latino and non-Latino store management and staff which facilitated improved customer and employee relations; vendor participation resulting in budget contributions; press coverage; a "template" turn-key event structure that later became Latina Live (in partnership with Latina magazine).

References

1 Kemper, Theodore D. "Reference groups, socialization and achievement." *American sociological review*, Vol. 33, No. 1. Feb., 1968, pp. 31–45. *http://links.jstor.org/sici?sici=0003-1224%28196802%2933%3A1%3C 31%3ARGSAA%3E2.0.CO%3B2-W*.

2 Bandura, Albert. *Social learning theory*. Englewood Cliffs, NJ: Prentice Hall, 1977.

3 Rogers, Everett M. *Diffusion of innovations*, 5th ed. New York: Free Press, 2003.

4 2003 Yankelovich Monitor Multicultural Marketing Study in Collaboration with Cheskin and Images USA. Yankelovich, Chapel Hill, NC, 2003.

5 Davies, Jody Messler and Mary Gail Frawley. *Treating the adult survivor of childhood sexual abuse: a psychoanalytic perspective*. New York, NY: BasicBooks, 1994.

6 Zimbardo, Philip G., Ebbe B. Ebbesen, and Christina Maslach. *Influencing attitudes and changing behavior: an introduction to method, theory, and applications of social control and personal power*, 2nd ed. Topics in social psychology. New York: Random House, 1977.

7 Berger, Peter L. and Thomas Luckmann. *The social construction of reality: a treatise in the sociology of knowledge*. New York: Anchor Books, 1990.

8 Terry, Deborah J. and Michael A. Hogg, eds. *Attitudes, behavior, and social context: The role of norms and group membership*. Mahwah, NJ: Lawrence Erlbaum Associates, 2000.

9 Generalization based on multiple qualitative observations by the authors.

10 *http://www.pewhispanic.org/site/docs/pdf/LatinoSurveyReportFinal.pdf*.

11 Clearly, respondents need to be qualified by an initial screening question like: "Do you ever call friends or relatives in your home town of _____?"

The Role of Language in Hispanic Marketing

4

The Relationship between Language and Culture

It is interesting to hear marketers and advertising managers talk about language and culture as if they were two separate entities. In the educational process our institutions teach language as if it were an empty code—as if by learning words and syntax rules one would be able to put together any possible thought into the empty vessel that language is supposed to represent.

But language is not an empty vessel. For example, Esperanto, the supposedly ideal universal language, has not become popular among peoples of different countries because this language is disconnected from its social context. As humans evolved into what we are now, we use sounds along with pointers and objects to share experience. Experience and language are not separate from each other. They are fundamentally connected.

The connection between language and culture is similar to the way in which memory and emotion are linked. People are more likely to recall experiences that have some emotional value to them. In a parallel way, language gets shaped and acquires rich meaning as humans associate experiences with words, sentences, poems, books, and so on.

Humans appear to have an innate capacity for language. Sociolinguist Noam Chomsky[1] coherently argues that humans can distinguish acceptable word sequences from nonacceptable ones with little or no formal learning. Humans may have a universal capacity for language, but the specific words and content of the language are not universal.

Languages are made of words and syntax. The syntax is the set of rules for assembling words in a language. Words are the product of experience. Words have roots that can be traced to other languages. Still, words are tied to the experience of a group of people. If the referent for a word has positive connotations it is because the experience of a people with that word had been generally positive.

Let's look at an example of a word that has roots in a different language but that has a specific emotional connotation for the culture that adapted it. The word *mariachi*, which refers to a musician, a band of musicians, and to a genre of Mexican music, comes from the French word for marriage or *mariage*. Allegedly, these were the musicians who played at weddings in the Mexican state of Jalisco. The French had a strong influence on Jalisco. The root of the term *mariachi*, however, has relatively little to do with the term the way it is now used by Mexicans and others who refer to that type of music or musicians. The word Mariachi evokes strong Mexican nationalism and pride. The emotion associated with the word *mariachi* has more to do with the experience of Mexicans while listening to mariachis and mariachi music than with any reminiscence of the French influence over Mexico in the 19th century. Mariachi music evokes colorful events, great food, and music that speak loudly of the pain of love, love of the fatherland, the joy of living, and the pain of dying. The typical Mexican scream that accompanies mariachi music is a sound associated with both pain and joy simultaneously. And this is just one word. Talk about mariachis with Mexicans and the term alone is likely to evoke an emotional response.

Although there are some words in any language that are similarly enunciated and that have a similar meaning across cultures, the majority do not. An example of such similar words are the archetypical mother, mamá, ima, mutter, and so on, which all stand for the same referent "mother" and sound similar when spoken. Also, these words generally have an emotionally charged connotation that is positive. These are basic words that speak of our common human heritage. Many of these almost universal words are onomatopoeias in that they resemble the sound of what they represent. In this case it is the sound of a baby drinking milk from the mother's breast.

Onomatopoeias are a useful example of the connection between language and human experience. Intuitively, we understand that these words are linked to human life. More abstract words that are not connected to their referent by similarities are also linked to experience, but the connection is less obvious and they are more culture bound. For example, certain types of worms have been a source of food and nutrition to a cultural group. *Gusanos de maguey* (or cactus worms) hold a positive connotation contained in the social experience of many Mexicans. For members of another culture the thought of eating cactus worms can be revolting. Words are not neutral universal equivalents but conveyors of experience. In a very powerful way words carry the meaning of the experience of a culture. A culture represents the sets of tools that a human group assembled over time in order to preserve the physical, intellectual, and spiritual integrity of its members. One of these tools is the language that this group managed to use in order to maintain cohesion, share experience, allow for coordination, and enable self defense.

There are further complexities in the conceptualization of language and culture. Words are not the only carriers of cultural experience. Sentences, phrases, sayings, proverbs, poems, books, and other linguistic manifestations are associated with cultural experiences. Proverbs like *al que madruga Dios lo ayuda*[2] are difficult if not impossible to translate. This difficulty is due to the cultural experience accumulated behind the phrase. In addition, the way in which we emphasize and enunciate words can carry cultural meaning as well.

Language conveys the richness and texture of human experience in a synthetic way. A people whose culture shares a sense of fatalism use words and expressions that help suggest the experience of fatalism. In such cultures one typically hears expressions like "If God wills," because the members of that culture doubt their self-efficacy and ability to alter the course of events. But fatalism is not an arbitrary construct. Groups of people who have been subjected to much uncertainty and oppression in their history are fatalistic for a reason. Their experience taught them that they could not overcome the forces of the supernatural, and their language and expressions reflect that. Language in its diverse forms is like the container that holds or reflects the experience of people.

Language is an adaptive mechanism that serves us, but in some ways also enslaves us. Our language expands horizons or limits them. Some languages are said to be better for the communication of affection and love than others. Language, then, is not the simple tool we learn in school for when we have to talk to others who use the language. Language encompasses the accumulated and collective evolution of human groups. Learning a language is more than pairing a term of a known language with a term of a new language. That is why it can be argued that marketing to Hispanics in Spanish and with an understanding of their culture is fundamental to secure a minimum degree of success. This does not mean, however, that all Hispanics would prefer to receive and process communications in Spanish. In some cases an understanding of the culture may be more relevant and powerful than simply communicating in Spanish.

The Art of Translation

A popular dictum is that translation inevitably betrays the original. Marketers who market to Hispanics in the United States have for many years asked the same question over and over again: "Can I just translate my English ad into Spanish?" This question is justifiable because if the answer is affirmative, the economies of scale that could be realized through translation would be substantive.

Given this discussion of the relationship between language and culture, the immediate intuitive response is that translation is not likely to work. Even if it were to work it would not work as well as if the original communication were designed to reach the intended recipient in the first place. It is very difficult for a translation to do justice to the original for the reason that the cultural elements in the original communication were not designed with the second culture in mind.

Perhaps a better response would be that Hispanic culture is not as likely to be well portrayed in a translated communication as it would be in an original version. This does not mean that for certain segments of Hispanics communications in English would not work. It means that cultural representations that connect with the consumer are more important for effectiveness than the language code alone.

Translation is an ongoing area of debate in Hispanic marketing. Regardless of how precise a translation can or should be, the results are seldom satisfactory. Some of the issues follow.

Professional Translations

Federal and state governments in the United States certify interpreters and translators. Those who qualify for the distinction of certification are definitely meritorious individuals. Nevertheless, even with certification, translators and interpreters bring biases to the interpretation situation. One bias is the notion that one's version of the language is the "correct" version.

Thus, an intellectually oriented translator from almost any Spanish-speaking country in Latin America will utilize language that is technically correct. Undoubtedly their work is worthy of the Royal Academy of the Spanish Language. However, despite adherence to established language standards, intended meanings of a communication may not be conveyed and the intended audience may be baffled by the text. The problem with translations by certified translators is that they give a false peace of mind to the marketer, and lead him or her to believe they have done their communication job.

It is not that certified or uncertified translators are unqualified to do their job. The issue is that they cannot do the job because the job is not one of translation but of cultural adaptation. It is the original cultural message that counts, not the language code in which it is cast.

Further, there is an elitism implied in most professional translations. The notion of correctness creates noise between the marketer and the consumer. Only a consumer-oriented translator/interpreter could aspire to do justice to the marketing objective of the marketer. Most consumers, including Hispanic consumers, have relatively low levels of education. There is no doubt that educational levels do compound the communication problem.

The most crucial gap between the consumer and the message generated by the translator is that the intended meaning is not likely to be there. The marketer would need to thoroughly brief the translator as to the intention and objective of the communication. In addition, the translator would need to have a sense of how the audience will interpret the message. This is something that many times not even the marketer knows. This is particularly true when crossing cultures.

Unfortunately, there is no real solution to this paradox of translation. It is generally a losing proposition. The problem becomes more evident when thinking about communicating a message in English to Hispanics. Then, it is not the "code" per se that gets in the way. In this instance, it is the cultural insights that need to be evident in the message for the consumer to connect. Here it should become apparent why sheer translation is not likely to work properly in most cases. If a translation could magically transmit the intended cultural meaning that would be ideal. Unfortunately there is no mechanism that could achieve such a feat.

Translation, Confusion, and the Reason Why

Many marketers arrive at the conclusion that they must translate all their materials to be consistent and to serve their Hispanic constituencies. Their conclusion is very understandable. They want to serve their Hispanic customers and wish to do a good job, but there are several problems in attempting this.

An overall recommendation is that, instead of translating, documents should be prepared in Spanish from scratch, if Spanish is the language that specific customers require. Further, the level of Spanish and vocabulary to be used needs to be appropriate for the Hispanic consumer that will be served. As stated earlier, translations are rarely transparent and culturally informed to connect with the consumer at the appropriate level.

If generating messages in Spanish from scratch is not possible and translations are required, then the translations must be of high quality and adapted to the specific type of consumer. Many Hispanic consumers have indicated that many times they prefer to read materials in their "poor English" rather than reading a confusing and contrived translation. If the translator does not clearly understand the objective of the translation, he or she is not likely to communicate the message appropriately through translation. Here is where the translator may need to resort to "cultural adaptation" to make the message relevant. Cultural adaptation consists of understanding the intended message and then casting it into the second language as opposed to achieving a literal translation. To fully adapt the translation to the Hispanic consumer, the marketer should not stop at the translation stage, but take one further step to verify that the translation achieves the intended meaning. This is what we have called "translation verification."[3] It consists of submitting an original and its translation to a panel of literate bilingual individuals from different Hispanic countries of origin. The panel is convened in a central location and is provided with both the English and the Spanish language versions. Individuals are then asked to discuss and debate the translation in terms of changes that are required in order to achieve the communication objective; changes that would improve the understandability of the message; and changes that would be nice but are not necessary to achieve the intended meaning.

Translating technical materials generally is not advisable. If writing for computer scientists, IT personnel, and others who have a high level of technical expertise, translating into Spanish (and many other languages) tends to make the reading of the materials more complicated. Most of these individuals generally have been trained in English. Translations of technical terms are either very difficult or impossible. Thus the translation winds up being an interesting version of "Spanglish" that few people, if any, could understand expeditiously. This is an extreme case, because it is assumed that the document is highly technical and the reader is very sophisticated regarding the technology in question. Many times high technology companies assume that by providing the translation they are doing a service to the reader when in fact the English version is generally more likely to be read.

Translating semi-technical text is very tricky and more difficult than expected. Imagine a brochure dealing with "How to obtain a home loan," or "How to open a brokerage account," or "How to use your new VOIP[4] phone." A lot of the terminology either does not exist in Spanish or the consumers are very unlikely to know it. One solution frequently utilized is to place the original word in English next to the translated term. A preferred solution is to explain the "meaning" of the intended message with common terminology. This is very difficult, however, because the translator must know the marketing issue and have the intention to do justice to the message. Again, a cultural adaptation that starts off by encoding the message originally in Spanish, and that avoids technical terms, would be most desirable. Translating words such as equity or escrow into Spanish are likely to confuse many consumers, even many of those with higher levels of education. Thus, the translator that sits at his or her desk with a dictionary and restates the message in Spanish is likely to be creating a confusing and usually useless message.

Then there is the issue of connotation. The term "mortgage" is one of those particularly complex terms. If translated as *hipoteca*, the consumer may be turned off, even if this term is possibly the most accurate translation. This is because the marketer, the translator, or both may not have considered the emotional charge of *hipoteca*. Here is where consumer understanding impacts translations and consumer reactions. In many parts of Latin America a *hipoteca* is a course of last resort. When someone is in dire straights they may resort to taking a *hipoteca* on their home. But that is generally seen as a negative course of action because one endangers the patrimony of one's children. Also, it means that the borrower is not doing well. Almost the opposite to what happens with Anglo consumers in the United States. If they get their mortgage they are starting a prosperous life. A more positive term in Spanish would be *prestamo*, or loan. A home loan would not have the negative connotation of a mortgage. Knowledge of how language is interpreted is something that few marketers, and translators, tend to consider. It is not only that technical terms need to be cast in commonly used terms, but that emotionally charged terms need to be replaced with those that are more appropriate to achieve the goals of the communication.

Should It Be in Spanish, English, or Bilingual?

Most U.S. marketers come to the point in their careers in which they need to decide whether or not they need to communicate their message to U.S. Hispanics in Spanish, English, or both. This is usually the moment at which marketers decide it is a good idea to conduct focus groups to find out the answer. The typical approach is to conduct groups with consumers that prefer Spanish with those that can go either way, and with those who prefer communicating in English.

The answer may seem obvious—those who prefer Spanish would want materials in Spanish, those who can go either way would have no preference, and those who prefer English would express a preference for English. However, things are more complicated because these consumers live in a unique social world.

The typical response in these situations is for respondents to state they would prefer bilingual materials. And this is across all language preference groups. Hispanic consumers argue that bilingual materials are important to them for several reasons, including:

- Their household tends to contain individuals who are Spanish dominant, bilingual, and English dominant. Thus, a bilingual piece would serve the different levels of language proficiency and preferences in the household. This is a very important and symptomatic aspect of U.S. Hispanic households. The marketer is seldom selling to an individual but rather to a household with different levels of language skills and preferences. Further, these consumers have large extended families with whom they share communications of interest. Thus, if they want to share with others, a bilingual piece is also useful.

- The ones who prefer Spanish express an interest in the English translation in order to learn the vocabulary in English, and the ones who prefer English tend to be interested in refreshing or learning Spanish, and those who are bilingual like the idea of comparing. A bilingual item, then, provides a learning experience.

- And, there is an overall distrust of translations. Thus having a bilingual communication helps the consumer make sure they have a way to verify that the translation they are reading is adequate.

The use of language by Hispanics is complicated because their socio-cultural environment is complex. Consumer insights are crucial for effective outreach and communication design. Language is not just an issue of moving a message from one code to another.

Language and Thought

At this point, let's try an experiment. Close your eyes and try to think without words. Close your eyes and try to articulate thoughts and ideas and see if you can do it without words. When doing this exercise some people claim they can think without words, and others say they cannot. In general, most humans would agree that language plays a part in their thinking even if not exclusively.

Thinking is similar to language. Thoughts are formed of words and other symbols, or representations, and these are linked by rules. That is what logic is about. That is why we can distinguish between sound thoughts and conclusions and faulty thoughts and conclusions. This is similar to the way in which we can judge if a sentence is correct or incorrect. People talk to themselves and call that process thinking. The more abstract the thinking process the more likely it is to be verbal. Words are symbols or abstractions that represent generalizations and concepts. Higher order thinking involves concepts that are difficult to cast in any other way but in language.

Edward Sapir and Benjamin Whorf, early in the 20th century, advanced the notions of linguistic determinism and relativism.[5] They argued that language determines the way people think, and that because of this determinism, members of different cultural groups would think and perceive the world relative to their language. Thus, the experience of members of different linguistic groups or cultures would be different enough so that their thinking would not necessarily converge.

Sapir and Whorf's theory has been highly controversial and widely debated. There have been tests and revisions of this theoretical approach. Still, one of the main conclusions is that even if the language we speak does not determine the way we think, the language we use does have an influence on the way in which we organize information. This would be a softer interpretation of the main tenets of the theory.

A key problem with linguistic determinism in an absolute sense is that there is no way to test the proposition that language determines thinking. That is because there is no way to observe thinking without language. The "strong" statement of the theory is considered to be a tautology of the "egg and chicken" form.

Why Market in Spanish?

If the Spanish language, with its multiple influences, actually shapes the way Hispanics think, then communicating with Hispanics in Spanish has a different effect from communicating with them in English. This is true even if the Hispanic consumer can understand both languages. The emotional impact of messages is different. It is not the same thing to say to someone "you are very kind" as it is to say "*usted es muy amable.*" The two expressions are equivalent in terms of translation, but not in terms of emotional value.

Further, the images and connotations that are evoked by one language are likely to be different from those evoked by another language.[6] Many of these images are the concepts that cultures use to perpetuate themselves. The concept of fatalism, for example, can be found in the colloquial Mexican expression *valemadrismo*. This expression is not really translatable, and it is generally understood only by those who were raised in the context of a specific way of thinking. *Me vale madres*, is a vulgar expression that connotes the frustration of repeated failure and the inability to shape one's life. It is like Aesop's fable of the fox and the unripe sour grapes. The expression reflects an attitude and view of the world that is unique to a set of cultural circumstances.

Speaking Spanish or a variety of Spanish specifically touches emotional cords. The common wisdom in the Hispanic marketing industry is that communicating in Spanish even with those Hispanics who are fluent, but not monolingual, in English, can be more productive than doing so in English. The explanation for this is that language is related to our perception of ourself and the world.

In a study conducted by e-mail in 1999 on the subject of acculturation, it was found that the Spanish language provided Hispanic consumers with specific perceptions of self. The study quotes a 24-year-old Hispanic born in the United States:

> "Spanish is my mother tongue, and it is the tongue of my mother. Spanish is still the tongue which I feel most clearly speaks from my heart. It calls out from my childhood. What I mean is that it encompasses my sense of identity by its sound and rhythm, and the fact that it is the language which I speak to my family with. It speaks not of the identity which I project in public now, but rather of my personality and sense of self since birth. When I speak in Spanish, I feel I speak from my soul."[7]

This testimonial emphasizes the emotional quality of the Spanish language for the individual. It describes how the language relates to a sense of self. Perhaps most importantly it refers to the duality of identities that this bilingual speaker identifies with. Each language and hence each identity has a different domain. Language differentiates the public and the private selves. Spanish best characterizes, according to him, his private or more personal sense of self.

For Corona Extra and their agency, Español Marketing and Communications, their successful campaign in Spanish on Spanish Language media focused on Mexican pride in the beauty of their home country. The target for this campaign, *orgullosamente mexicana* (proudly Mexican), were Mexican male beer drinkers. There was no doubt that the overall constellation of product, target, and Mexican heritage required the use of the Spanish language to convey the message. The Corona Extra communication campaign with its combination of Spanish with beautiful images of Mexico resulted in increased consumption occasions for Corona over domestic beers, as well as solid increases for the brand overall (see the Español Corona Extra Case Study at the end of this chapter).

Reach Out and Touch Someone

Advertisements for long distance personal telephone services, like the one quoted previously, will be more effective with Hispanic consumers if they are in Spanish. Even if the target consumers speak English, communicating with them in Spanish about establishing contact with home will establish a better emotional connection. This is not just because these consumers feel closer to the Spanish language, but because the Spanish language touches them in places where an English message could not. And this is due to context as well. If long distance conversations take place totally or mostly in Spanish, then the emotion of the experience in marketing communications is best conveyed in Spanish. This is true even if one or both of the interlocutors are fluent in English.

The symbols imbedded in the language conjure images, thoughts, and emotions that are different from those evoked by the English language. A large part of the difference can be accounted for by culturally accumulated experience. Karl Jung spoke of the collective unconscious, conceptualized as a repository of human experience.[8] That common experience is composed of the experiences of many groups of people over time. If the experience of humanity is accumulated in our biological heritage, then these are parts of different cultures that become salient when in a similar cultural context. A different part of oneself is awakened when interacting in a different culture.

It is common to hear travelers talk about how they discover new parts of themselves when experiencing another culture and/or speaking another language. This line of reasoning explains why one language would be more or less effective in conveying images and experiences than another. That is because the aggregated part of human experience in the collective unconscious can be better evoked or made relevant within a specific language. That is the language in which the experience was learned. Perhaps that is why popular wisdom has characterized different languages as reflecting different approaches to life. Italian, French, and Spanish are said to be languages of love, whereas German and English tend be characterized as languages of work and efficiency.

Language then becomes not just a filter or an influencer of thinking and experience but part of being and behaving differently in different cultures. Advertising and marketing in Spanish, when dealing with those who prefer the Spanish language, touch realms of experience that could not be touched in English. The phrase *caminante no hay camino, se hace camino al andar*[9] evokes images of nostalgia and fatalism that can hardly be conveyed in English. Using this well-known phrase to communicate the virtues of an automobile could be highly effective. The effectiveness would come from the familiarity with the phrase. Most of the impact of the phrase, however, has to do with the cultural imagery associated with the meaning; that is, lack of clear destiny because destiny is made as one lives. This way of talking and thinking finds affinity among Hispanics. The Anglo Saxon view of control over the environment is in sharp contrast with fatalism. Living life as we evolve with it conveys a sense of harmony with the universe, not of dominance.

In simple (but transcendental) phrases like *caminante, no hay camino, se hace camino al andar*, cultures encode their archetypes and communicate them to other members of the culture. This is an important way in which language influences the way in which the marketer and the communicator can establish relationships that go beyond the surface.

These pieces of cultural thought reflected in sentences are like memes.[10] Memes are ideas or pieces of knowledge that for different reasons spread through societies and become part of them. They are basic units of cultural continuation and reproduction.[11] Some ideas find better receptivity in certain cultures because they are compatible with existing beliefs and they evoke emotional reactions that favor their diffusion.

Advertising, marketing, and communication across cultures largely depend on their ability to reach out and conjure in the minds of recipients the images intended. To do this, the symbols must find resonance among customers. These symbols that replicate themselves are memes.[12] And they are heavily dependent on language, much like poetry depends on the language in which it is cast for its appeal.

For example, when Ameritech wanted to introduce their caller ID device to the Hispanic market in Chicago, they needed to "personalize" it in Spanish as *El Aparato Para Sonreir* (The Smiling Device). This positioning and its imagery brought the Hispanic consumer closer to callers rather than creating the screening barrier desired by non-Hispanic U.S. customers. The campaign was successful in interesting Hispanic consumers in Caller ID, and outsold the English language campaign by three to four multiples (see the San Jose Group Ameritech Caller ID Case Study at the end of this chapter).

Studies have been conducted to test the degree to which the Spanish language is more or less effective than English in reaching Hispanics. Peter Roslow of Roslow Research found in a study he published in August 2000 that among Hispanics the recall of commercials in Spanish was 61 percent higher than that of commercials in English. He also found an increase in message communication effectiveness of 57 percent over commercials in English, and also reported that Spanish commercials were four and one half times more persuasive than ads in English.[13] The study contained both Spanish dominant and bilingual individuals and used an ample number of commercials across several categories of products.

Other research on the impact of Spanish vs. English language content was a 1996 study of Hispanic, Spanish preferred, women heads of household in the Bay Area of San Francisco. The research revealed that although these Hispanic women watch both Spanish and English television, their perception of being influenced by Spanish language television was substantially stronger. Respondents were asked: "Think about the products you have purchased in the past month. Did any advertisement you saw on Spanish language television influence any of these purchases?" Forty-six percent of the sample indicated they had been influenced in this manner, but only 23 percent of the sample answered yes to a parallel question about English language television.[14] In this case the respondents were predisposed in favor of the Spanish language, thus the results are not as striking as those in the Roslow Study. Still, marketers routinely ask if Spanish speakers could be influenced by English-language commercials. The answer appears to be yes, but to a much lesser degree than if the communication is in Spanish.

These findings serve as partial substantiation of the claims made here. According to these accounts, the Spanish language is able to better connect even with those who are able to comprehend the message in English. The marketer who takes the trouble to understand the Hispanic consumer and to identify the memes and archetypes that best connect with him/her will be most effective. Language plays an integral part in this effectiveness. In many cases the Spanish language will be most effective, particularly those cases in which language and cultural experience are strongly linked.

"Spanglish," Code-Switching, and the Future

The term "Spanglish" has been popularized in the U.S. marketing industry. The term has been used by Hispanics for a long time to refer to the common practice of mixing the lexicon of both Spanish and English in the same sentence, or to adapt English terminology to the Spanish language. Mixing words or sentences of both languages generally is known in academic circles as code switching. Spanglish is a special case of mixing languages in individual words themselves as opposed to mixing elements of language within sentences, paragraphs, or complete statements. Thus, for example, technically, code switching can be exemplified with:

> "Oye Juan, traeme la calabaza (Hey Juan, bring me the pumpkin), because my Mom wants to cook it." Here languages are mixed in one sentence, and it is grammatically correct in both languages.

Examples of Spanglish would be:

> "Voy a vacunar la carpeta" (I am going to vacuum the carpet)
> "Soy un picador" (I am a cotton picker)
> "Necesito filiar la aplicacion" (I need to fill out the application)
> These examples are adaptations of English vocabulary into Spanish despite the fact that the expressions can be considered illogical and even offensive by more educated Spanish speakers. The meaning of code switching can be stretched to include Spanglish because, in a sense, the switching is inside the words themselves. The English words are Spanisized.

The practice of code switching or Spanglish among US Hispanics is widespread for different reasons:

- Language users acquire vocabularies relevant to specific situations or contexts. So, for example, the language of the family includes vocabulary about food, cooking, family love, role relationships, home, garden, pets, and so on, and this vocabulary is very likely to have been acquired in Spanish. On the other hand the language of work and school, including technical terminology and vocabulary about peer relationships, and other relevant language clusters are likely to be learned in English. Then, when the Hispanic consumer gets together with Hispanic coworkers, he or she speaks in English but introduces Spanish language terms when referring to family and other home and emotional issues. When at home, with family, this consumer is likely to speak

Spanish but mix some English when referring to work or friends outside the home.

- Many Hispanics who come to the United States for economic opportunity have had relatively little formal education. Many are not fully fluent in Spanish and are functionally illiterate. For some the Spanish language can be a second language, since their first language could have been Otomi, Zapotec, Mayan, or any of the many native languages of Mexico and Central America. For these individuals communicating in Spanish can be as difficult as communicating in English. In these cases mixing Spanish and English has more to do with not having enough vocabulary in any one language and mixing English and Spanish to make do in different situations. Terms are Spanisized and words like "application" becomes *aplicación*, "truck" becomes *troca*, "pitching" becomes *pichear*, a "quarter" becomes a *cora*, and so on.

- In many circumstances, after years of living in the United States, even those Hispanics who have had more formal education mix terms of the "other" language when speaking in one of them for the sake of saving energy, as Zipf's law would predict.[15] It becomes just too difficult to build complete sentences in one language as one retrieves terms from different repositories in the neural mass.

- Young Hispanics experience a mix of these conditions. They find themselves learning the Spanish of their grandmother and generally have no formal education in Spanish. Most of their verbal life is in English, but they do get together with other Hispanics and bring in terms from Spanish as they become relevant and emotionally satisfying.

None of these scenarios are pure cases because they can combine and juxtapose depending on the circumstances. Also, some form of Spanglish has been used in Latin America and Spain for many years as the result of the adoption of cultural and consumer products from the United States.

Marketers have most recently expressed a common concern regarding Spanglish. They have been told that to reach young Hispanics they should communicate with them in Spanglish. That creates anguish and uncertainty on the part of Anglo marketers who generally do not understand this phenomenon. They hypothesize that if young Hispanics mix English and Spanish, advertising directed to them should emulate their communication style. This makes sense. The only problem is that there is no Spanglish per se as distinctive language. It is a way of speaking, not a formal language with a defined vocabulary and syntax.

A Language or a Style of Communication?

Ilan Stavans recently published a book entitled *Spanglish: The Making of a New American Language*. For him, Spanglish is the result of the meeting of the Hispanic and Anglo worlds.[16] Stavans espouses the reasonable perspective that languages evolve and change as other living organisms. He defines a large number of terms that are used as Spanish terms but are based on English roots. The English and the Spanish languages will continue to evolve to recognize the existence of each other as a result of the interaction of the cultures. Still, Spanglish is not a language, at least not yet, because it includes only a series of words but no syntax that rules how and when the terms are to be mixed.

Thus, communicating with Hispanic youth in Spanglish is not something that is possible. What is possible is to communicate with these consumers in a style that is relevant to them. That is, a communication style in which they can see their own image and values.

Although it has been observed that code-switching does have certain regularities in its performance, there is no way to predict what term will be used when or where. Marketing managers need to understand their audience in this case, as in any. If their audience mixes Spanish and English, their communication with the customer should mirror this pattern for the purposes of promoting identification and homophily.[17]

Purism vs. Pragmatism

There already have been several examples of television advertisements that use some type of mixture of Spanish and English. There are many relatively more educated Spanish speakers that object to the mixture of languages. For them the dictionary or the Royal Academy of the Spanish Language still rules how Spanish should be spoken. Many do not realize that the modern Spanish has many Arabic, English, Germanic, and other words with origins from many other cultures. Still there is a tendency toward the preservation of languages in some kind of pure state.

There are reasons for speakers of a language to resist the invasion by other languages. It is very confusing to have languages change rapidly in different regions because speakers of the language do not catch up with each other and eventually they experience a phenomenon similar to that of the Tower of Babel. Keeping constancy and predictability in the language has practical implications. Eventually, despite all efforts to the contrary, neologisms born from the encounter of the two cultures will emerge and will become indistinguishable parts of the language.

The extent to which the marketer allows its communication partners to use Spanglish ought to be to reflect the lifestyle and values of their current and prospective customers. There is no dogma and no absolute Spanglish, just an understanding of the customers in their cultural context.

The Emerging Bilingual Hispanic Market

The Spanish language will continue to be important to U.S. Hispanics for a long time to come. The only reasons why the Spanish language may lose ground in the United States include:

- A potential major turn to conservatism in the United States that would punish Hispanics, as happened before the 1980s, for speaking Spanish and ostracize them for preserving their culture. In the past 25 years Hispanics have become salient in U.S. society because a philosophy of multiculturalism has fertilized the seed of emergent differences in the United States. If conservative nationalistic tendencies re-emerge, then the Spanish language will likely go back in the closet. In the 1960s you could find Hispanics in Los Angeles who would not speak Spanish for fear of being marginalized, even though they were marginalized anyway. Richard Rodriguez, a well-known Hispanic writer, is an example of that fear of marginalization.[18] In his autobiography he speaks of the way in which his youth was punctuated by discrimination.

- The emergence of a set of circumstances such that the border with Mexico gets reinforced with a concrete barrier so that nothing or no one can enter the United States without official documentation. The obstruction of border flow, added to increased xenophobia, would make the Spanish language fall in disrepute.

Other than these unlikely scenarios, the Spanish language will continue to thrive in the United States for many reasons, including:

- A continuing drive toward cultural preservation that has been observed on the part of Hispanics over the past quarter of a century.

- An interest on the part of non-Hispanics to have an insider's view of Hispanic culture and an interest in communicating with Hispanics in Spanish.
- A perceived economic advantage on the part of both Hispanics and non-Hispanics because bilingualism pays better when it comes to jobs and other opportunities.
- A trend toward retro-acculturation by which Hispanics who are established in the United States two, three generations and beyond, feel a drive to re-engage with their Hispanic culture because of its revitalization in the United States. These are also the individuals who would encourage their children to go back to their roots.

These scenarios are the most plausible ones for the U.S. Hispanic future. Nevertheless, Hispanics will continue to master the English language. And bilingualism is likely to become more prevalent than it has been for Hispanics. Ignoring this tendency would be unrealistic. The English language is part of the fabric of the United States and it is the key to success for many Hispanics. We already see tendencies that point toward a bilingual future.

The Growing Importance of Marketing to Hispanics in English

Because of pragmatic and emotional reasons, the U.S. Hispanic marketing industry has generally endorsed the idea that communicating with Hispanics in Spanish would be the most effective approach. That perspective is still valid, particularly when dealing with Hispanics who depend on or strongly prefer the Spanish language for comprehension, or the large number who are emotionally attached to the language. However, it is important to consider whether communicating in Spanish is in tune with marketing objectives, or whether English could be a more effective option.

Spanish-Speaking Hispanics Are Easy to Target

One of the key reasons for reaching out to those Hispanics who either depend on or prefer the Spanish language is that they tend to be geographically concentrated in neighborhoods. The notion of the *barrio* or neighborhood where Hispanics concentrate is prevalent among those who are relatively newer to the United States. They tend to concentrate in specific areas where the language and consumer environment is favorable to their needs and meets their expectations. They have traditionally concentrated in urban areas and in a few States including California, Texas, Arizona, New Mexico, Colorado, Florida, Illinois, and New York. It is in these states that the largest majority of those who speak a language other than English at home concentrate, and clearly that other language is Spanish in the vast majority of cases.[19]

These consumers tend to have highly homogeneous perspectives on life and the products they need. They are easy to target in Spanish because they are exposed to Spanish-language media more than to English-language media. Spanish media outlets generally have been less complex and less expensive to purchase than English-language media. Thus geographic concentration and highly targeted and relatively inexpensive media channels make for a very good marketing "deal." SABMiller signed a three-year contract for $100 million with Univision in October 2004 for advertising in its radio and television properties, which provide broadcast and cable programming exclusively in Spanish.[20] This unprecedented contract highlights the confidence that SABMiller places in targeting Hispanics that depend on or prefer to communicate in Spanish. They have obviously concluded that their investment constitutes a good business proposition instead of going with other, less targeted media.

Also, it has been argued consistently that the Spanish dependent or preferred consumer is the majority. Several studies have provided evidence that a large majority (60% or more) of adult Hispanic consumers prefer to communicate in Spanish when given a choice.[21] One of the key reasons for targeting separately, and in Spanish, those who prefer the Spanish language is that these consumers ought to be the ones that logically preserve the customs of their countries of origin and thus are more specifically targetable. Those who do not prefer the Spanish language any more should be less likely to relate to communications targeted to them culturally.

Why Not Target English-Speaking Hispanics?

Typical arguments against targeting English-speaking Hispanics have included the notion that these consumers are too dispersed in the population and they do not form a cohesive entity like those who prefer the Spanish language. The idea is that including these consumers in some other segmentation or grouping that is more relevant for them would work better than to continue to think of them as Hispanic. The assumption has been that these individuals are separate from those who prefer to communicate in Spanish, that their values have changed, and, that from a geographic standpoint, they are not identifiable.

An Overlooked Language Opportunity

Although the importance of targeting Hispanics in Spanish cannot be denied, depending on the specifics of the marketing problem, it seems that marketers may have overlooked interesting English language opportunities. Consider the following archetypical narrative that pertains to recent Hispanic immigrants to the United States.

Maria Hernandez arrived in the United States 15 years ago when she was 20 years old. She came illegally from Mexico to join her boyfriend, Juan, who had come two years earlier, and already learned a lot about how to live in the United States. Juan taught Maria much about what products to purchase, and where, and introduced her to new customs he developed in those two years. Juan and Maria soon had a baby girl, Martha.

When Martha was three years old she got twin brothers, Mario and Miguel. At seven years of age Martha and her younger brothers spoke the Spanish their parents taught them. Martha also learned English at school and when playing with kids in the neighborhood. The kids watched Spanish-language TV with their parents in the evening, but during the day they watched English-language shows. They learned a lot from those shows, including a lot of their English. Juan and Maria both worked and earned a good enough income to qualify for a home loan. They purchased their first home. That was one of their dreams.

Juan and Maria thought they would like to have some of the abuelitos (their own parents and the grandparents of Martha) join them so they could enjoy their company, but also they could help by being at home with Martha and her two brothers while they were at work. Soon the household was composed of two parents, two grandparents, and three children. Each of them had a different level of proficiency in English and in Spanish.

The decisions about what to eat, what to drink, what movie to see, what car to buy, and many others were made by means of family discussions. Since they all shared the consequences of most purchases, all had an interest in the decisions. The kids became very important in product decision making because they were the best informed about what is available in the market place. When Martha turned 12 and her brothers 9, they had an important influence in at least 60 percent of the purchases relevant to the family. Their parents and grandparents listened to them with respect because these kids just "knew more."

> *Maria and Juan also tended to indulge their kids quite a bit because they wanted the children to enjoy what they did not have when they were young. In many ways these kids grew up prematurely by U.S. standards, but they grew up happy and loved. When the kids were teens they wanted what all teens want except that they felt proud when Hispanic stars became popular and the Americans would look up to Hispanics.*
>
> *These kids grew up in a cultural conundrum but with pride. In their early adulthood they became good citizens and in many ways reclaimed a lot of their Hispanic heritage that had been diluted during their teen years. Some enlightened marketers that understood the trajectory of this archetypal family did well with the millions of families like them.*

This narrative illustrates that even new immigrants soon find themselves in a household where both the Spanish and English languages are forced to live together. Different generations and different language abilities coexist. Therefore, this scenario of the Hispanic household presents yet another cue to marketers that language decisions, Spanish, English, or both, should be taken only after informed consideration.

The Language Numbers Game

Consider that in 2000, when the Census reported that there were 35.3 million Hispanics, 28 million (of those 5 years of age and older) were reported to speak Spanish at home. That is, more than 80 percent of Hispanics spoke Spanish at home. But, according to that same data, over 20 million of the 28 million that spoke Spanish at home in 2000 also spoke English well or very well; that is, over 70 percent of those who spoke Spanish. Since these data include young people, those that typical marketing studies do not include, the findings are surprising. The US Census data includes kids 5–18, who are not usually interviewed in consumer studies, and these are more likely to be proficient in English than their older counterparts.

In July 2003, the U.S. Census Bureau estimated that there are 39,898,889[22] Hispanics in the United States. The number of Hispanics who speak Spanish at home, and those who speak English well or very well, should be proportionally higher than they were in the Census of 2000. But this figure is also likely to be an underestimate.

The Office of Immigration Statistics of the Department of Homeland Security states that in 2002 alone 1.1 million deportable

Figure 4.1

Estimates of the unauthorized resident population in the top 15 countries of origin and states of residence: January 1990 and 2000 (thousands)

Country of origin	Population		State of residence	Population	
	2000	1990		2000	1990
All countries	7,000	3,500	All states	7,000	3,500
Mexico	4,808	2,040	California	2,209	1,476
El Salvador	189	298	Texas	1,041	438
Guatemala	144	118	New York	489	357
Colombia	141	51	Illinois	432	194
Honduras'	138	42	Florida	337	239
China	115	70	Arizona	283	88
Ecuador	108	37	Georgia	228	34
Dominican Republic	91	46	New Jersey	221	95
Philippines	85	70	North Carolina	206	26
Brazil	77	20	Colorado	144	31
Haiti	76	67	Washington	136	39
India	70	28	Virginia	103	48
Peru	61	27	Nevada	101	27
Korea	55	24	Oregon	90	26
Canada	47	25	Massachusetts	87	53
Other	795	537	Other	892	328

[1] The estimate for 2000 includes 105,000 Hondurans who were granted temporary protected stants in December 1998.

aliens were located in the United States.[23] According to the same source, between 1981 and 2000 there were almost 27 million deportable aliens located, and over 90 percent of them were Mexican. This official source also offers estimates of undocumented Hispanics in the United States; the table in Figure 4.1 is reproduced from their report.[24]

As Figure 4.1 shows, the largest proportion of estimated illegal or unauthorized U.S. residents in 2000 were from Latin America, and the largest majority were from Mexico. According to a 2005 Pew Hispanic Center Report, there are approximately 8.5 million illegal Hispanics in the United States. Most likely these are underestimates, but since there is no other reliable source of information about this phenomenon let us take these figures as indicators. Undocumented individuals are very unlikely to have participated in the 2000 Census. It is well known that the US Census Bureau went out of its way in 2000 to encourage everyone to complete census forms, including illegal residents. Still, it is a stretch of the imagination to think that any substantive number of illegal residents would fill out official Census forms. Most likely these illegal immigrants are in addition to the approximately 40 million

Hispanics accounted for by the Census. Conservatively then, in 2005, at the time of this writing, it could be safely estimated that there are about 48.5 million Hispanics in the United States.

If approximately 80 percent of the conservative estimate of 48.5 million speak Spanish at home, and 70 percent of those speak English well or very well, then over 27 million are proficient in English. If one adds up the 20 percent of those who do not speak Spanish, the total of U.S. Hispanics proficient in English can be up to 76 percent.

The 2003 Yankelovich Multicultural Monitor

These calculations lead us to the conclusion that when using official data and estimates, the majority of Hispanics can communicate in English. Further substantiation of these trends was found in the data for the 2003 Yankelovich Multicultural Monitor conducted in collaboration with Cheskin and Images USA. A small portion of that data was analyzed by these authors to explore Hispanic language use trends.

The 2003 Yankelovich Multicultural Monitor study design included a two-step data collection method. The first step consisted of a 20-minute phone interview about general attitudes, demographics, and ethnic-specific questions in the language of the respondent's choice. This was followed up by a 30- to 45-minute self-administered survey via mail or Internet about industry-specific behavior and attitudes on a variety of topics, in the language of the respondent's choice.

Participants for the study were selected using random sampling and placed into specified racial/ethnic allocation quotas. Quotas that remained unfilled were completed using enhanced RDD based on Hispanic surname within areas of high Hispanic population density. Participation was dependent on agreement to complete both steps. The final distribution of completed interviews by individuals aged 16+ included 900 Hispanics, 1,081 African-Americans, and 1,218 non-Hispanic whites. These samples were weighted to be nationally representative. The data presented in Tables 4.2 through 4.6 corresponds to the Hispanic sample only.

English Language Understanding

Table 4.1 shows data resulting from the cross-tabulation of "How well do you understand English" by "What was the first language you learned to speak as a child." The results show that of those who first learned Spanish, 44 percent indicate they understand English "very well" and another 18 percent indicate "somewhat." Thus, over 60

Table 4.1

English Language Understanding by First Language Learned						
First Language Learned to Speak as a Child		**How Well Understand English**				**Total**
		1 Not at All	**2 A Little**	**3 Somewhat**	**4 Very Well**	
SPANISH	Count	29	215	116	286	646
	%	4	33	18	44	100
ENGLISH	Count	0	4	4	230	238
	%	0	2	2	97	100
BOTH AT THE SAME TIME	Count	0	0	0	3	3
	%	0	0	0	100	100
OTHER (SPECIFY)	Count	0	0	0	9	9
	%	0	0	0	100	100
Total	Count	29	219	120	528	896
	%	3	24	13	59	100

percent of Hispanics whose first language was Spanish claim to be very or somewhat proficient in English.

Table 4.2, shows the cross-tabulation of language spoken at home by "How well do you understand English." This table shows that almost half of those who speak Spanish more than English at home are likely to understand English "somewhat" or "very well." And of those who speak Spanish and English about equally at home are highly likely to understand English very well. Overall, almost 60 percent of Hispanics indicate they understand English very well. This is not at all an argument against the use of the Spanish language in marketing but a realization that the English language has been underutilized in Hispanic marketing.

Those Who First Learned Spanish Watch Half Their TV in English

Table 4.3 shows that those Hispanics who were raised with the Spanish language watch about half their television fare in English and half in Spanish. This is informative in that it speaks of the overall media environment in which Hispanics are submerged. In any U.S. market there may be zero to perhaps three Spanish-language television outlets, but there may be five to 500 English-language options. English-language television is not likely to be avoided because it contains content that Hispanics wish to watch and also because it is a way

Table 4.2

English Language Understanding by Language Spoken at Home						
Language Speak at Home		How Well Understand English				Total
		1 Not at All	2 A Little	3 Somewhat	4 Very Well	
SPANISH ALL THE TIME	Count	29	109	28	23	189
	%	15	58	15	12	100
SPANISH MORE THAN ENGLISH	Count	0	82	49	39	170
	%	0	48	29	23	100
SPANISH AND ENGLISH EQUALLY	Count	1	25	34	152	212
	%	0	12	16	72	100
ENGLISH MORE THAN SPANISH	Count	0	0	7	160	167
	%	0	0	4	96	100
ENGLISH ALL THE TIME	Count	0	3	3	156	162
	%	0	2	2	96	100
Total	Count	30	219	121	530	900
	%	3	24	13	59	100

Table 4.3

English and Spanish TV Exposure by First Language			
First Language Learned to Speak as a Child		Weekly Hours English TV	Weekly Hours Spanish TV
SPANISH	Mean	13.64	13.48
	N	640	641
ENGLISH	Mean	28.15	5.21
	N	229	233
Total	Mean	17.47	11.28
	N	869	874

of learning the English language and further acculturating to the United States. If half of the television exposure of those who were born with Spanish is in English, then English-language television should hold implications for marketing to many U.S. Hispanics.

What this picture seems to be saying is that the language world of U.S. Hispanics is more complex than previously thought.

Language Ambivalence

We can observe linguistic ambivalence in the meaning of the following statements endorsed by the majority of Hispanics according to the 2003 Yankelovich Multicultural Monitor:

- 84 percent agree that "all immigrants should learn English if they plan to stay in this country"
- 70 percent indicate that Spanish is one of "the aspects of your culture and traditions that you feel are most important to preserve"
- 62 percent agree that "the Spanish language is more important to me than it was five years ago"

Thus, the English language is understood as a necessity and reality of U.S. life. On the other hand, consumers exalt the value of the Spanish language. It is part of Hispanic heritage and culture, and it keeps growing in importance. This precise duality of Hispanic life in the United States seems to have been absent from past discourse on Hispanic marketing. The reality of Hispanic life needs to be understood in its bicultural nature. This complexity is illustrated by responses to the question, "What language would you prefer to use if you could only use one?" The distribution of responses to this question can be seen in Table 4.4.

A slight majority of these respondents would choose the English language, and 15 percent do not have a strong preference. There is a significant, and relatively stable, segment of the Hispanic population of about 35 percent that shows a strong loyalty to the Spanish language. Still, the argument that communication with Hispanics should be in Spanish for effectiveness receives a strong qualification when confronted with this data.

Trust in Brands and Ad Persuasiveness

Table 4.5 presents the distribution of agreement/disagreement with a statement regarding trust in brands that advertise in Spanish as opposed to those who do not.

Table 4.4

Language Preference If Could Only Use One	
Language	**Percent**
SPANISH	34
ENGLISH	51
BOTH EQUALLY/NO PREFERENCE	15
Total	100

Table 4.5

Brand Trust Depending on Language of Ad	
"I trust a brand that is advertised in Spanish more than those that are not."	**Percent**
Strongly Agree	9%
Agree	24%
Disagree	53%
Strongly Disagree	12%

Sixty-five percent of the respondents in the study disagree or strongly disagree that their trust in brands is related to their being communicated in Spanish. They are not saying that the Spanish language is not important to them. They are saying that trust is not necessarily associated with the language used to build brand equity. Those who depend on the Spanish language for comprehension logically would trust a brand they can understand. Others would judge the brand according to other elements. Cultural relevance is expected to be one of those elements that can build trust beyond language.

These data should not be surprising. It suggests that in their new cultural milieu many Hispanics, particularly those who are somewhat more acculturated, recognize the importance of being able to communicate in the language generally spoken in the United States. This does not constitute an argument to the effect that Hispanics have a lesser affinity with the Spanish language. The Spanish language can still be highly relevant and impactful to many Hispanics. Still, ignoring that English is part of the current life of many Hispanics would be unrealistic.

The study provides further information on the aspects of advertising that contribute to persuading Hispanic consumers, as shown in Table 4.6.

Responses to these questions were counts of the number of spontaneous choices (and choices could be multiple). Thus, someone could

Table 4.6

Aspects of Ads that Persuade Hispanic Consumers	
"Degree to which the following types of advertisements persuade you to buy or try a new product or service 'a lot' "	Percentage
Ads in the language I speak at home	38%
Ads that show reasonable competitive pricing	35%
Ads that show actual results from using a product	32%
Ads that convince me a new product is easier to use than my current one	29%
Ads that show me the benefit of a product over other I might use	25%
Ads that show my favorite brand offering a new product	19%
Ads that provide information about a new product	18%
Ads that feature a person like me using the product	16%
Ads that make me laugh	12%
Base	900

have checked all or only one, or none, of the answers. The most frequent response is that ads in the language spoken at home are persuasive. These ads could be in either Spanish or English depending on the language spoken in the respondent's home. Although linguistic considerations are important, they are not as salient as we would have expected. They are far from being overwhelming. Most marketers would have expected a clearer emphasis on language. Over 60 percent of respondents chose other attributes as having more persuasiveness. Price and information about the product are very important, and reasonably so.

A Complex but Flourishing Identity

Additional findings from this study further document that Hispanic identity is not weakening. On the contrary, U.S. society and its marketing industry seem to have reinforced a positive sense of self-esteem and value.

- 95 percent agree with "I am very proud of my Hispanic background"
- 91 percent agree that "It is cool to be Hispanic"
- 58 percent agree that "Hispanics are influencing everyone's point of view"

According to these findings, Hispanics seem to have reclaimed the pride that they could not openly express for many years. That is when children were punished in schools for speaking Spanish until about the 1970s. Now it is desirable to be Hispanic, and this renewed sense of popularity and acceptance serves to build bridges that for many years were blocked. This consolidating Hispanic identity reinforces Hispanic culture along with its language. The complexity of the duality of Hispanic existence in the United States requires recognition and understanding. This duality claims Hispanic pride on one hand and at the same time recognizes the importance of integration in the second culture.

A Schizophrenic Communication Environment

It would be false to claim that Hispanic popularity, recognition, and prestige is at its peak at this time, however. Additional data for the 2003 Yankelovich Multicultural Monitor shows that more needs to happen for inclusiveness to be more complete:

- 90 percent agree with "I think that the media should be doing more to portray Hispanics in a positive way"
- 70 percent agree that "there should be more television or other commercials directed specifically to Hispanic consumers"
- 61 percent agree with "Commercials that feature famous Hispanics as spokespeople are more likely to get my attention"
- 78 percent agree with "Discrimination is still a part of most Hispanics' day-to-day life"

Many Hispanics still struggle with a schizophrenic communication environment in the United States. On one hand marketers, politicians, many citizens, and some of the media welcome the diversity and contribution of Hispanics. On the other hand there are still strong remnants of discrimination, media absence and stereotyping, and some degree of hostility toward immigrants and their apparent differences.

These tendencies also highlight the importance of communication directed to Hispanics in their cultural context. That is, Hispanics do seem to wish for role models and portrayals that are culturally relevant, although they do not necessarily need to be in Spanish. The life of U.S. Hispanics includes an abundant experience that is in both Spanish and English. What seems to be missing are media programming and content strategies that provide Hispanic consumers with opportunities to see their life in its richness and current "reality."

Telenovelas largely reflect the life of people in Latin America, not of Hispanics in the United States. It is only very recently that efforts by some networks have begun to include aspects of U.S. Hispanic life. Mun2 is an example of this nascent trend. Several mainstream networks have also pursued new avenues to reflect Hispanics in the duality of their lives. ABC has been successful by featuring the George Lopez show. Also Nickelodeon has made an important contribution with Dora the Explorer and the Brothers Garcia. SiTV,[25] in 2004, is one of the latest contributors to this new Hispanic communication environment, where Hispanics see themselves as they are "here" instead of how they were "there."

The New Dynamic of the Hispanic Market

The Mexican contingent of the U.S. Hispanic market, being the largest, serves as a good weathervane of Hispanic market tendencies. The flow of people and money across the Mexican-American border has been a relatively underestimated source of social influence shaping the U.S. Hispanic marketplace.

- Large segments of entire towns in Mexico have moved to the United States. Aguililla, Michoacan has largely moved to Redwood City, California. A large part of Puebla, Puebla, has moved to Queens, New York. Substantive numbers of people from San Luis Potosi have moved to Chicago. The human settlements established in the United States continue to influence those who remain in Mexico through continued interaction.

- Parents in the United States send their kids to spend time with parents and aunts and uncles back in the home towns. These kids become influence brokers across the two sides of the border.

- Young people in Mexican towns have guidance from those who preceded them in moving to the United States. Visits and other modes of communication, including the Internet, shape expectations of those in Mexico and keep those in the United States close to their Mexican roots.

- Non-Hispanics in the United States increasingly have friends and relatives who are Hispanic. Many non-Hispanics are finding value in learning Spanish and venturing into the U.S. Hispanic market and Latin America.

- The border becomes increasingly artificial as more U.S. non-Hispanics accept the importance of the Hispanic migrant labor force. Commerce and the exchange of people will likely become more prevalent over time between Mexico and the United States, and perhaps other Latin American countries as well. A true

American union inclusive of the continent should not be a far-fetched dream.

- Hispanic households in the United States increasingly become functionally bilingual even if specific household members are predominantly monolingual in either Spanish or English. Many have different levels of fluency of both languages coexisting and evolving together. Because of this, dynamic children become increasingly important as cultural and market interpreters. And purchase decisions include multiple influences.

- The media increasingly is more open to cross-language programming and advertising, leading to the point where media and message planning includes a vast array of choices in formulating strategy. "Hispanic" media is not for Hispanics alone anymore, and "general market" media is not for non-Hispanics exclusively. What matters now is a cultural strategy that works across languages and delivers a consistent cultural message to Hispanic consumers in Spanish and English, as specific audience needs require.

Conclusions

One of the themes that plays out in this chapter is the duality of the Hispanic communication environment regarding language. Be it at home, at work, or in the media, Spanish and English are in a perpetual mix. Again, the dilemma for the marketer is how to grasp the needs of this target for English or Spanish communication, if the world they manage both functionally and emotionally is such a patchwork of two languages.

The temptation is to take a mechanical approach to the problem; that is, to look at the difference between languages as a matter of words, and conclude that the use of good translations will straighten out the whole confusing dilemma of how to address Hispanics. However, this chapter clarifies that language and culture are tied to one another, and that words are not "empty vessels" but carry meanings of a group's shared experiences loaded into them over time. Indeed, a "good" translation is not a word-for-word transliteration by a credentialed expert, but a cultural adaptation based on common understanding of the meaning of a message by the Hispanic target group.

Again, to come to a reasonable marketing approach it's necessary to look at the use of language and its impact on Hispanic consumers. In this chapter we cited statistics indicating that the U.S. Hispanic population includes well over 80 percent who speak Spanish at home. Yet, even a majority of those whose first language is Spanish also claim some proficiency in English, and 70 percent of those who speak Spanish at home claim to understand English very well. The question then becomes whether to market strictly to that Spanish-speaking segment in the language they speak at home, take a new direction and go after those who already are or are becoming English speakers, or go bilingual and face the challenge of maintaining one brand identity and associated messages in two languages.

To answer that question, a marketer may decide to target the Hispanic household as a unit. In one Hispanic household different generations may use Spanish or English almost exclusively, or both languages depending on whom they're conversing with, in and outside of the household. Children often navigate between Spanish and English, bringing ideas learned in English into the household. Many companies, including telecommunications and pharmaceuticals, have recognized this fact and have created bilingual communications that serve all members of the household.

Another way marketers can clarify language decisions is to look at the meaning that becomes attached to words and ideas in either Spanish or English, for Hispanic consumers. Depending on the topic, U.S. Hispanics may have learned their vocabulary in either Spanish or English. Topics that are close to their socialization experience in their home country typically are carried in the Spanish language; those that are related to what they have learned in their lives in the United States, which include many consumer products, tend to be associated with English. Marketers may then find it useful to look at their marketing objective and decide whether they should use the emotion-laden Spanish language to appeal to Hispanic consumer motivations, or the more functionally oriented English language to underscore relevance to their lives in the United States.

For those Hispanic consumers who code-switch in their communications between English and Spanish (commonly referred to as speaking Spanglish), marketers should tread very carefully. Spanglish is not a language with an organizational structure of syntax, so trying to replicate code-switching within consumer messages carries the risk of sounding ridiculous to those who create hybrid expressions. Only close contact with the consumer target group for a Spanglish message, often made up of Hispanic youth, can yield a credible and motivating message.

For the marketer, staying close to the reality of U.S. Hispanic consumers is key to marketing decisions, with the understanding that both

Hispanic cultural identities and the languages associated with them are in flux. Continuous contact with their countries of origin and other U.S. Hispanics in Spanish reinforces and refreshes their pride and love of being Hispanic, as they define it. At the same time, striving to learn and grow in their everyday lives in the United States brings them constantly closer to taking part in the English-speaking world, which they feel is so necessary for their own success and that of their children.

Implications for Marketers

- Language carries the cultural power of tradition, loyalty, and emotions of pride, success, and yearning; so don't assume you can just translate English to Spanish in order to include the Hispanic market in your marketing communications.

- Translation of materials can be an important element of relevant bilingual communication. Think of a translation as "cultural adaptation" and either begin fresh with an explanation of the topics in your message in Spanish, or go item by item, translating the idea vs. plowing through word for word.

  Always check the translation with intended Spanish-speaking consumers, to make sure that what they hear is what was intended. For a national campaign that will cover several Hispanic countries of origin, make sure through research known as translation verification that the Spanish terminology used is common and understandable to all groups.

- Remember that the introduction of a new idea or meme from the English-language general market into the Hispanic market may fall on a cultural landscape that is not fertile ground for its literal translation. You may need to introduce the same idea with a different set of symbols to make it relevant for Hispanics. Recall the Ameritech Caller ID campaign *El Aparato Para Sonreir* (The Smiling Device) discussed in this chapter. Consider carefully whether your product or service initially has been introduced to Hispanic consumers in Spanish or English. Many U.S. Hispanics spend their early years learning culture in a Spanish-speaking country and then become socialized as an adult in a second culture in an English-speaking country. Vocabulary in Spanish regarding soap or coffee may have strong emotional associations as part of growing up in their own countries; however, vocabulary regarding banking or computers may be familiar only in English.

- Be aware of the huge potential of the English-speaking Hispanic market. Some studies indicate that trust in a product is not necessarily related to that brand being communicated in Spanish. However, remember that the cultural experience of a Hispanic living in the United States is different from the mainstream. Therefore, communication to Hispanics in English must have cultural relevance to the lives they lead.

- Since Hispanics, even those who depend on Spanish, watch as much English-language as Spanish-language TV, consider carefully how you can best reach your audience through either or both. For more traditional products and those with strong cultural links to the Hispanic culture, Spanish-language TV is a cost-effective way to reach large numbers in concentrated urban environments. Even members of households who prefer to speak English watch Spanish-language television along with family members for particular types of programming.

  English-language media are a distinct possibility for reaching those not well-served by Spanish-language media, as well as for Hispanics who are bilingual or English speakers. As always, know your consumers and the types of shows they watch on English language media, always staying aware of the cultural elements that need to be taken into consideration. Consider which media will best speak to the type of product or service you are marketing. Again, high tech type products or those learned about in the United States may fit appropriately in English-language media.

- Both Hispanic pride and their success orientation may support the use of either Spanish- or English-language media or both for some marketing objectives. Corona Extra, already mentioned within the chapter, is an excellent example of the impact of a Spanish-language campaign. For other brands, their foray into English TV has brought them Hispanic clients as well as the interest of the more Hispanicized general market. For example, Coors took this route for their advertising with their *güey* campaign.

- If you are advertising on both Spanish and English TV simultaneously, targeting Hispanics with Spanish channels and the general market with English channels, be cautious that the ads, which, as you have learned in this chapter, will be watched in both languages by Hispanics, do not confuse or destroy the continuity and image of the product, service, or brand.

Case Study: *Español – Corona Extra*

Company/Organization: Corona Extra Beer, imported for western half of the U.S. by Barton Beers, LTD., Chicago

Advertising Agency: Español Marketing & Communications, Inc.

Campaign: Corona: *orgullosamente mexicana* (proudly Mexican)

Intended customers/clients: Mexican-American Males of Legal Drinking Age and older

Background:

For over twenty years, many domestic beers have been targeting Hispanic consumers in the U.S., and generating strong sales via cheaper-priced products, strong Hispanic market promotions, and strong Spanish-language advertising budgets. Many domestic beers attempted to take over the natural positioning of imported Latin American beers, tying in with Hispanic sports events, festivals, and music. Additionally, as marketing budgets grew, domestic beers frequently targeted their communications to U.S. Hispanics from key countries of origin, tailoring their messages, sponsorships, and spokespeople to particularly appeal to Mexican-Americans, Puerto Ricans, or Cuban-Americans.

Discovery Process/Research:

In the early 1990s, Barton Beers, the importer of Grupo Modelo beers in the western half of the US, conducted qualitative research (a series of focus groups) among target Hispanic consumers, particularly among Spanish-preferring males of Mexican origin. Based on the results of this research, and following discussions with Procermex, the Grupo Modelo subsidiary responsible for all U.S. operations, they hired Español Marketing & Communications, Inc. to grow sales and share in the Hispanic markets in their territory. Their marketing objective was to increase the number of occasions where consumers choose a premium Mexican beer— Corona Extra—over the cheaper domestic alternatives.

Over the past 10 years working with Español Marketing, Barton Beers has conducted both qualitative and quantitative studies to evaluate campaign and sales results, as well as to analyze consumer habits and beliefs.

These studies included:

- Positioning studies to test consumers' acceptance and likes/dislikes of positioning statements and copy claims for Corona communications
- Quantitative studies to determine the effectiveness of different television campaigns; packaging assessment studies to determine reaction to packaging initiatives
- Multiyear quantitative Awareness, Attitude, and Usage studies to assess frequency of consumption and consumer loyalty for Corona
- Snapshot qualitative research studies (primarily focus groups or mini-groups) to make sure that Corona's Spanish-language communications are relevant and have high appeal to all types of Mexican-Americans

Cultural Insights:

Following are the key conclusions from the 1990s' research:

- Hispanic consumers tended to be loyal to the beer they consumed in their country of origin. In particular, Corona consumers tended to be very loyal to "their" brand, having developed the preference for and loyalty to Corona in Mexico, and having made Corona their beer of choice upon coming to the U.S.
- While consumers professed loyalty to the beer from their country of origin, many consumed "their" beer for certain special occasions or in certain locations where image was important to them, while consuming domestic beers with great frequency during other occasions.
- Mexican beers were perceived to be premium beers, both in quality and price. Corona consumers believed that a premium price was justifiable for a premium beer, and would consume Corona with Mexican foods and snacks, in restaurants and bars, as well as at home with friends and family.
- Corona's popularity in the U.S., both among Mexican-Americans and among the general markets, was widely recognized, and was a source of great pride for Mexican-Americans.

Expression of Insights in the Campaign:

Español Marketing created a unique and relevant equity for Corona that allowed Corona to reclaim its rightful positioning as the "proudly Mexican" beer. All communications feature the equity tagline of Corona: *orgullosamente mexicana* (proudly Mexican).

Communications that have flowed from this equity positioning exploit many elements of Mexican culture, artisanship, natural beauty, food and customs, creating pride in the hearts of Mexican-Americans, and tying the pride that consumers have of being Mexican together with Corona's pride of being Mexican.

Television commercials have highlighted different states and regions of Mexico, featuring beautiful scenery, indigenous crafts, well-known and delicious foods, and types of music and dance, and tying Corona's heritage, quality, and pride together with the state or regional pride. Radio commercials have featured key insights of Mexican culture and customs, notable achievements of Mexicans, as well as fun executions about soccer, the passion of most Mexican-American men. Out-of-home executions feature beautiful Mexican landscapes, sometimes combined with tasty Mexican foods or beautiful Mexican elements.

Working with Barton Beers and Procermex, a compelling communications strategy was developed, which Español Marketing uses to guide Corona communications—Corona is the premium Mexican beer, as evidenced by its:

- Market leadership: both in Mexico and as the leading Mexican beer in the U.S.

- Distinctive, clear bottle: highlights its clean, pure look, demonstrating the high quality of the brand

- Delicious, refreshing taste: makes it the perfect accompaniment to traditional Mexican foods—both meals and snacks

Effect of the Campaign:

The sales and share of Corona Extra have grown in Barton Beers' territory, due in part to the successful communications strategy and relevant executions, increases in advertising spending, the continued growth of Mexican-origin Hispanics in the U.S., as well as increased distribution and marketing efforts by Barton Beers and their wholesalers and distributors.

Figure 4.2

Corona Extra campaign

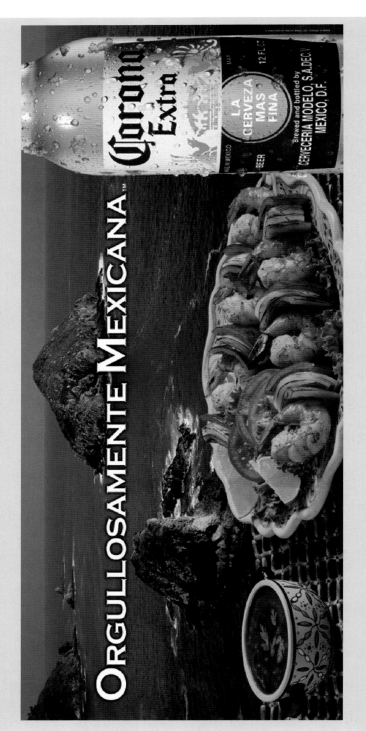

Advertising recall and likeability score very highly among Mexican-American males. In a category known for big-budget advertising using humor, scantily-clad women, and sports executions, the Corona campaign is truly unique in its approach, evoking great pride, nostalgia, and even gratefulness among Mexican-Americans for its exploitation of Mexican beauty. The communications campaign has resulted in displacement of domestic beers in exchange for increased consumption occasions for Corona, as well as solid increases in "beer consumed most often" and "preferred beer."

Case Study: *The San Jose Group – Ameritech Caller ID*

Company/Organization: Ameritech (pre-SBC acquisition)
Advertising Agency: The San Jose Group
Campaign: For Ameritech's Caller ID service.
Intended customers/clients: Hispanic telephone customers in Greater Chicago

Background:

The Consumer Services Division at Ameritech chose The San Jose Group as its agency in order to stimulate the purchase of its Caller ID service in the Greater Chicago market. Ameritech valued its Hispanic customers, who were heavy users of its local calling service. However, their sales data told them that these consumers in the densely Hispanic geographical market of Chicago had not been strongly attracted to the use of their value-added products and services, including Caller ID. In fact, many decision-makers within Ameritech were ready to give up on the Hispanic segment as a viable sales target for these products altogether. However, SJG and key marketing staff at Ameritech suspected that a key barrier to capturing previous Hispanic sales was driven by the fact that the company had traditionally only marketed these products to Hispanic customers by either using its English-language direct mail campaigns or, on occasion, doing straight translations of its English-language packages into Spanish. As such, both SJG and Ameritech believed that a new, culturally relevant approach, which captured the right sales message, would be more effective in piquing their interest and converting this interest into incremental units sold.

Discovery Process/Research:

SJG leveraged its own knowledge of Hispanic consumer attitudes and behaviors, combined with informal qualitative interviews with Hispanic telephone customers, to help Ameritech discover why this product had low acceptance in the Hispanic market.

Cultural Insights:

SJG confirmed its theory that cultural paradigms lay at the heart of Hispanic's perceived value of Caller ID. Through its interviews, SJG discovered that this consumer segment considered the caller ID apparatus impolite. Unlike general market customers, who have responded well to the convenience-based positioning of Caller ID, Hispanic customers subscribed to a social code of conduct that considers the act of prescreening someone's call without their knowledge as rude and disrespectful. (This cultural dynamic is often referred to as the "simpatía factor.") They also learned that the feelings associated with most phone calls that Hispanic customers received were pleasant and evoked a sense of connectedness with the family and friends calling in. As such, the "convenience" of prescreening calls was actually perceived as a cultural disconnect with this segment.

Expression of Insights in the Campaign:

To counter the impersonal impression of the caller ID apparatus, The San Jose Group created a direct mail campaign for Ameritech Hispanic customers in which they positioned the Caller ID box as *El Aparato Para Sonreir* (The Smiling Device). Instead of a device that was once viewed as something that put unwanted distance between them and their loved ones, Caller ID was now perceived as a relevant tool that helped the customer feel even more connected with their family and friends. As the direct mail copy stated, because the display unit could help them identify their callers before they actually started talking, customers could now greet them with more love and warmth because of it! In addition, SJG was given license to depart from Ameritech's traditional direct mail design palette (which featured mostly white space and the red and blue Ameritech logo) in order to introduce a more colorful, visually engaging package.

Figure 4.3

Ameritech Caller ID Direct Mail Package

Bilingual Brochure: Outside/Inside

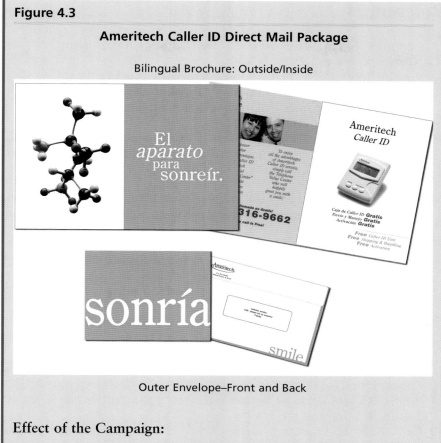

Outer Envelope–Front and Back

Effect of the Campaign:

After only three weeks from the launch of the direct mail campaign, the bilingual call center had 750 calls of interest, 375 Caller ID units were sold, and the Hispanic campaign outsold the general market campaign by 3 to 1. Subsequent campaigns from SJG that drew from a more integrated mix of direct mail AND direct response radio went on to perform even more successfully, outselling general market campaigns by 4 to 1.

References

1 Chomsky, Noam. *Knowledge of language: its nature, origin, and use.* New York: Praeger, 1986.

2 Roughly translated as that who wakes up early gets help from God.

3 Durance, Mike and Felipe Korzenny. "Focus groups for translation equivalence among Hispanics." *Marketing News.* September, 1989.

4 Voice over Internet Protocol.

5 Lucy, John Arthur. *Language diversity and thought: a reformulation of the linguistic relativity hypothesis.* Studies in the social and cultural foundations of language; No. 12. Cambridge: Cambridge University Press, 1992.

6 Bloom, Alfred H. *The linguistic shaping of thought: A study in the impact of language on thinking in China and the West.* Hillsdale, NJ: L. Erlbaum Associates, 1981: 73.

7 Korzenny, Felipe. "Acculturation vs. assimilation among Hispanics: E-mail self-reports." *Quirk's Marketing Research Review*, November 1999: 50–54.

8 Dry, Avis M. *The psychology of Jung, a critical interpretation.* London: Methuen, 1961.

9 "Walker there is no road, you make the road as you walk." This is part of a well-known poem by the Spanish poet Antonio Machado born in 1875.

10 Lynch, Aaron. *How belief spreads through society.* New York: Basic Books, 1996.

11 Brodie, Richard. *Virus of the mind: the new science of the meme*, 1st ed. Seattle, WA: Integral Press, 1996.

12 Gelb, Betsy D. "Creating 'memes' while creating advertising." *Journal of Advertising Research* 37.6 (1997): 57+. Questia. 5 Oct. 2004 <http://www.questia.com/>.

13 http://www.roslowresearch.com/studies/91.doc

14 Korzenny, Felipe, Rebecca Abravanel, and Adrien Lopez Lanusse. "Research uncovers Hispanic advertising impact." *Quirk's Marketing Research Review*, April 1997. http://www.quirks.com/articles/article.asp?arg_ArticleId=221.

15 Cherry, Colin. *On human communication: a review, a survey, and a criticism*, 3rd ed. Studies in communication. Cambridge, MA: MIT Press, 1978.

16 Stavans, Ilan. *Spanglish: The making of a new American language.* New York: Rayo, an Imprint of HarperCollins Publishers, 2003.

17 Homophily is the degree of similarity between communicators. See Rogers, Everett M., *Diffusion of Innovations*, 3rd ed. New York: Free Press, 1983.

18 Rodriguez, Richard. *Hunger of memory: the education of Richard Rodriguez: An autobiography.* Toronto: Bantam Books, 1983.

19 U.S. Census Bureau. Census 2000 Summary File 3. At http://factfinder. census.gov.
20 Vranica, Suzanne. "Advertising: Miller turns eye toward Hispanics— Univision deal is struck to solicit beer drinkers in fast-growing population." *The Wall Street Journal*. 8 October 2004.
21 See, for example, the report by the market research and consulting firm Cheskin. *The Digital World of the US Hispanic II*. Redwood Shores, California, 2001.
22 http://www.census.gov/popest/states/asrh/tables/SC-EST2003-04.xls
23 http://uscis.gov/graphics/shared/aboutus/statistics/Yearbook2002.pdf
24 Ibidem
25 http://www.hispaniconline.com/hh04/culture/sitv.html

The Processes of Enculturation, Acculturation, and Assimilation

5

The New Immigration Mix

The rate of immigration from Latin America has increased dramatically, when compared to other regions of the world over the past three decades. Figure 5.1 shows the pattern of legal migration from different parts of the world to the United States since 1925.[1] North America in this chart includes Mexico and Central America. Mexico has been the largest exporter of immigrants to the United States by far. Before 1970 Europeans were still the most common legal immigrants to the United States, and they dominated the landscape.

Now Hispanics literally and figuratively color the shape of cultural change in the United States. An interesting part of this puzzle, however, is that this is only part of the immigration equation because illegal immigration is difficult to calculate, and, as stated elsewhere in this book, illegal immigration has also been a major contributor to the growth of the U.S. Hispanic market. It would not be far-fetched to expect that illegal immigrants from Spanish-speaking countries outnumber those who are admitted legally.

This pattern of immigration has to have important consequences for:

- The immigrants who need to adjust to a new cultural and social situation. Immigrants experience a loss of identity and social structure that they need to rebuild in the host country. This happens until immigrants rebuild enough of the structure they need and until they acquire enough tools from the second culture.

- The receiving country, the United States, which absorbs new cultural patterns and becomes increasingly diversified. More and

Figure 5.1

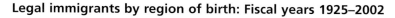

Legal immigrants by region of birth: Fiscal years 1925–2002

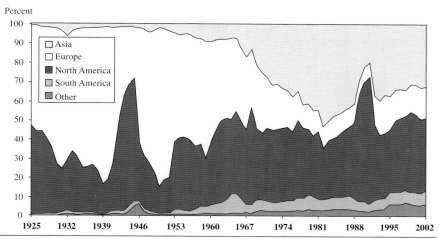

NOTE: See Glossary for fiscal year definition. Source: 1992-2002, Table 3; 1925-91, previous *Yearbooks*.

more U.S. citizens become involved with immigrants as neighbors, relatives, friends, coworkers, and learn new ways of doing things.

- Expatriates influence their countries of origin as they send information, cultural values, expectations, and money to relatives and friends. This flow of influence encourages further migration to the United States and creates a feedback loop that magnifies the cycle of migration very much like a positive feedback system.[2]

The United States is undergoing fundamental change as immigration from Europe and consequently Anglos in the United States shrink their ranks. The disproportionate growth of Hispanic consumers, compared with historical trends, sets the basis for a new cultural and economic paradigm. As Hispanics learn to be consumers in the United States, they are also influencing marketing practice. This mutual flow of influence highlights the importance of understanding how Hispanics acculturate and create meaning in their new society.

The Meaning of Cultural Change

Hispanics in the United States constitute a large-scale case study of cultural change. The process of change and adaptation happens for many reasons. One of the most common reasons why people adjust to new cultures is migration. This process involves large amounts of stress that come from the attempt to cope with uncertainty and lack of cultural support systems.[3] It is important to emphasize the amount of emotional and physical turmoil that immigrants experience because that struggle characterizes Hispanic life in the United States.

The scene of Hispanic men standing on street corners waiting for a pick-up truck to take them away for a day's work is a different experience depending on the onlooker's perspective. For many of the local residents these men are an eyesore that they would like to vanish. They don't like those poorly dressed men hanging around their neighborhood. They are considered a particular nuisance on weekends when these men have nothing to do but get drunk and sit around public places to talk about their loneliness. They look bad, smell bad, and many residents wish they would go away.

To those who hire their services for the day, these men are hard workers willing to do more work than anyone else and for less money. They are a blessing because they can get landscape, agriculture, and construction jobs done fast at reasonable prices; and these men do not object to doing more work. The more work the better for them, and they let their short-term employers know this.

They are generally honest and create a congenial work culture wherever they are. They smile, sing, joke, and have fun doing heavy work. It is difficult to find better workers. So, when manual work piles up the only thing one needs to do is go pick up a few "Mexicans" for the day. "Mexicans," in many locations where Mexican labor is abundant, has become the generic term for workers, pretty much like Kleenex has become the generic term for facial tissue.

The experience of these men is different. They have left behind their friends, their girl friend/wife, many times their children, their mother and father, relatives, and pastor. The images of those they care for stay vivid in their minds, day after day. They came to the United States to earn money to send back home. Many of the families of these workers would not survive without the support they receive from *el otro lado*.[4] After muscle-breaking work during the day, many hours under the sun, and nostalgia in the soul, these men face emptiness at the end of the day. They have nobody to go to, no real home, and, most of the time, they have nothing to do.

Some cry in the loneliness of their evening for those they left behind. Others get drunk with the other men anywhere they can sit and have some relaxation. Most can barely communicate in English, and some do not speak Spanish either. Many of those from Oaxaca, Yucatan, and other regions of Mexico and Central America do not speak

Spanish or English. They speak Mayan, Zapotec, and other native languages. These men are real oddities to Anglos and also to their Hispanic counterparts. But they strive and they work, and eventually they succeed at making some money and becoming residents of the United States, or they return to their homeland defeated by the loneliness and nights of anguish and tears.

These are very different perspectives from diverse viewpoints. It illustrates the give and take that occurs as individuals from one culture attempt to become adjusted to living in a second culture. This process and its relevance to marketers will be discussed in more detail later in the chapter.

Culture and Awareness

Many authors have defined culture.[5] A compromise definition of culture is the sets of designs for living that human groups pass on from generation to generation. These designs for living are both objective and subjective.[6] Objective culture consists of the external manifestations of culture that can be observed in food, dress, architecture, speech codes and patterns, interior décor, gestures, and so on.

Subjective culture consists of less concrete elements. These include values, beliefs, attitudes, ways of perceiving the world, social cognitions, norms, and so on. These subjective aspects are harder to pinpoint than the external or objective aspects of culture. Nevertheless, subjective culture can have profound effects on the ways in which people make choices and behave.

The vision of the cosmos that our parents taught us, which in turn they learned from their parents, is part of subjective culture. This perspective on the cosmos includes notions of what is right and wrong, and also of who is in our ingroup or outgroup.[7] This part of culture is metaphorically fluid because subjective culture for humans is like what water is for fish. The fish can hardly be aware of the water because the water is constant. Humans very rarely are aware of their subjective culture because it is constant and imperceptible. It is like the operating system of a computer. Subjective culture runs in the background.

Thus, just because someone is a member of a culture doesn't mean that he or she is aware of its subjective aspects. To assume that by hiring a Hispanic brand manager, this person will automatically understand Hispanic culture is a typical error of judgment. Members of cultures are not necessarily experts on their own culture. Many times the key problem with naïve members of a culture is that they assume that all other members of the culture are just like them. Many of the fiascos in Hispanic marketing happen just because of this. A more

"Americanized" marketer assumes most Hispanics are like him- or herself, and a more Spanish dominant marketer assumes most Hispanics share his or her perspectives.

Enculturation, Acculturation, and Assimilation

Enculturation

Authors and companies have defined these terms in varied ways.[8] A consensus, however, seems to have emerged. Enculturation is the learning of a first culture. This is the process that all humans born into a social group experience. They become part of their culture by learning the mores, values, orientations, and perceptual patterns of their social milieu. Enculturation tends to be pervasive and difficult to erase. Most people who have been raised in a particular culture tend to preserve aspects of it even if they spend only a few years in their original culture. The first culture a person experiences tends to leave an almost indelible pattern in the cognitive framework of people. Most people can think of someone they know who is still "very Mexican" or "very Cuban" even if he or she has been in the U.S. culture for many years.

McCormick & Company and their Hispanic Marketing Agency, K. Fernandez realized the emotional association that a food product can forge during enculturation. They built on the equity of McCormick Mayonesa from Mexico to introduce this well-known Mexican brand into the U.S. Hispanic market. They selected a target market of first generation Mexican females in densely Hispanic populated areas. They hypothesized that the Mexicans' love of lime, which differentiated this mayonnaise from the competition, and their longing for products from home, would create strong bonds to this well-known product. Their campaign took into account the importance of personal communication to the cultural background of these women, and used in-store promotions, booths, and community events to reacquaint them with this product that was part of their enculturation (see the K. Fernandez McCormick Case Study at the end of this chapter).

The National Pork Board, working with The San Jose Group, created a campaign for increasing pork consumption of Hispanics in the United States. The campaign dealt with Hispanic health concerns about pork including disease-related beliefs from their countries of origin and their worries about high fat and cholesterol levels. At the same time, the campaign played on Hispanics' love of pork as part of their traditional diets. To counteract health concerns The San Jose group created a campaign that was educational, informing Hispanics about the safe conditions surrounding pork in the United States and facts about its lower fat and cholesterol levels compared to other protein sources. To build on taste preferences, the agency linked pork with traditional Mexican dishes, some in which pork was commonly used, and others in which it could be substituted for meat or poultry for added taste enjoyment. Essentially, this campaign liberated Hispanic consumers to enjoy eating pork to a greater extent in the United States than in Mexico. Thus, the positioning re-established a Hispanic food-related tradition as an even more fully enjoyable norm in the adopted U.S. culture (see The San Jose Group National Pork Board Case Study at the end of this chapter).

The emotional depth of enculturation is expected to affect the way in which immigrants adjust to the second culture. Many Mexicans and Central Americans, when they first immigrate to the United States, tend to believe that they will go back home when they achieve their economic goals. Many avoid becoming citizens of the United States for some time because they feel they would be betraying their country of origin. Thus, enculturation imbues a strong loyalty to their country and the social lifestyle these individuals leave behind. The passing of time makes the return increasingly difficult. Those who give birth to children in the United States find it particularly difficult to return "home" because the children insist on staying in the United States.

John Berry[9] presents a compelling paradigm in which he considers the degree to which individuals value keeping their original cultural orientation, and the degree to which they find it valuable to maintain a relationship with the second culture. Those individuals who wish to preserve their culture and also relate to the second culture "integrate." Those who do not value preserving their original culture and value the relationship with the second culture "assimilate." Those who value their culture and do not care for the second culture tend to "separate." And, finally, those who do not value either culture become "marginalized."

Generally, these days, Hispanics in the United States tend to either integrate or remain separate but few seem to assimilate or to remain marginalized. That is because most tend to value their culture of origin, or their enculturation. Interestingly, Berry does not clearly articulate other forces that can have an important impact on how immigrants resolve their cultural identity. His paradigm does not address the acceptance of immigrants by the second culture. Because the United States has become much more welcoming of differences in the past 30 years or so, more Hispanics tend to reject complete assimilation. Now they have no reason for forgetting their original culture.

In fact, currently, there is much more social and economic value in preserving Hispanic culture in the United States.

An example of how Hispanic women build on their original sense of self is the Unilever's *Secretos de Belleza* marketing campaign. This campaign focused on reinforcing Hispanic women's confidence and self-esteem here in the United States. Unilever conducted extensive research to understand perceptions of beauty among Hispanic women and how they differed from non-Hispanics. They published this research in the Dove Report, which indicated that the majority of Hispanic women are happy with their looks.[10] Another research finding was that Hispanic women define beauty as both inner and outer beauty. Based on these cultural insights, Unilever created a national campaign for six of its brands: Caress, Dove, Pond's, Suave, ThermaSilk/Finesse, and Vaseline Intensive Care. They sponsored the TESORO Award events to honor top Latina role models in cities with large Hispanic populations, a key community-oriented component of their overall campaign.[11] By honoring Hispanic women role models in the United States, Unilever demonstrated their appreciation of the beauty both internal and external of Hispanic women, as well as forged a stronger relationship with their brands.

Acculturation and Assimilation

Acculturation and assimilation should be addressed simultaneously because these processes can be conceptualized as distinct alternatives for resolving cultural change. Acculturation can be described as the process by which individuals acquire a second culture in addition to their first culture. Assimilation, on the other hand, can be conceptualized as the process of abandoning one's first culture in favor of a second culture. Figure 5.2 illustrates these concepts.

Figure 5.2 illustrates how acculturation consists of enlarging the cultural repertoire of an individual, whereas assimilation keeps the repertoire constant by replacing one culture with another. Results from proprietary qualitative and quantitative research point in the direction of acculturation as opposed to the assimilation of Hispanics at this point in history.

The marketing of many products and services to Hispanics is contributing the building of capabilities in their second culture, while acknowledging the need to include elements of the first culture to maintain comfort level in this transition. Countrywide Home Loans, a leading residential mortgage lender, engaged Español Marketing & Communications to assist them in achieving their corporate commitment to bring increased opportunities for home ownership to the

Figure 5.2

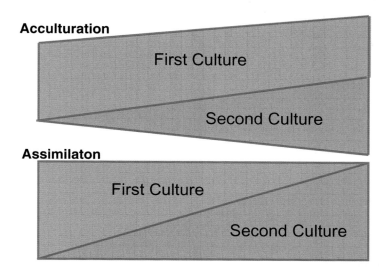

Acculturation/assimilation

Hispanic Market. They created an image of Countrywide as a company they could trust in getting a home loan, something that was not a part of their first culture, and then they promised to help them get the loan they could aspire to, and educate them to help themselves in the process. Through a system of bilingual and personally oriented assistance, Countrywide helped Hispanic consumers to negotiate this new step in their acculturation to their second culture (see the Español Countrywide Case Study of the end of this chapter).

A tendency toward acculturation or biculturalism is now the strongest emotional objective most frequently endorsed by Hispanics. Those who are relatively new to the United States understand the need to learn the second culture. Those who in the past had abandoned their Hispanic orientation are now reclaiming it themselves or through their children. That is because it is now a positive experience, in general, to be Hispanic in the United States. Despite remnant prejudice and discrimination, the overall balance of Hispanic experience in the United States is now more positive than it had been at other points in time.

Many marketers continue to ask the question of whether Hispanics will undergo the same experience as their predecessors from Europe experienced in the 1800s and early 1900s. Those immigrants eventually assimilated. They, however, had different immigration goals than those of today's Hispanics. European immigrants wanted to escape famine, violence, and turmoil. Many wanted to forget their bitter past.

Hispanics, in contrast, generally dream of going back "home" eventually. In addition, new immigrants refresh the ranks of Hispanics with vigorous constancy. Communities become heavily Hispanic, and remaining Hispanic is increasingly easy and achievable. Still, most Hispanics understand very well that their economic and social future depends on being able to succeed in U.S. culture. Thus acculturation becomes a most attractive outcome.

The best of both worlds describes the position of those who acculturate. They have the opportunity to select attributes of both cultures that they enjoy. Those who acculturate, as opposed to assimilate, have a more complex view on life. The bicultural view of the acculturated Hispanic is likely to bring about generations of individuals with a broader perspective on life. Bilingualism and biculturalism traditionally have been seen as transitional phases in the lives of immigrants. The complexity of new bicultural societies like Quebec in Canada and U.S. Hispanics makes biculturalism a way of being and not just a state of transition. There are studies that have documented both negative and positive aspects of bilingualism. The balance, however, appears to be positive.[12]

It makes intuitive sense that individuals who look at the world from more than one perspective would have an advantage over those who do not. Bilingualism, unfortunately, has been the label applied to many who are not only not bilingual but rather functionally illiterate in one or both languages. The fact that someone says a few words in Spanish and a few words in English does not make him or her bilingual. When someone has the necessary competence to communicate in an articulate and effective fashion in one language or the other, then that person can be said to be bilingual. These are the individuals who are socially advantaged by having a dual communication perspective and cultural outlook.[13]

A notion that derives from this line of reasoning is that if more Hispanics become increasingly educated in both English and Spanish, they will likely make increasingly important contributions to U.S. society. This will contradict the negativism that many ethnocentric writers have publicized when reflecting on the impact of Hispanic growth and bilingualism in the United States.[14]

Third Culture Individuals

An interesting phenomenon resulting from crossing cultures is that belonging to one culture or another becomes difficult. Mexicans in the

United States are often quoted as saying *ni soy de aquí ni soy de allá*, or "I am neither from here nor from there." That is part of the experience of cultural change. As immigrants move from one culture to another they find that their culture of origin becomes more and more distant. Unfortunately the second culture, for many, is also elusive. The reasons why the second culture is not adopted include the following.

- The individual rejects the second culture for not having the qualities he or she misses from the first culture. For example, the person may dismiss the second culture as a cold and unfriendly culture and may justify being in the United States for the economic advantage but not for the customs. The justification of economic benefit compensates for the suffering and social distance, thus the individual can rationalize being in the United States without integrating into the larger society.

- The individual aspires to be part of the second culture, but this receiving culture demonstrates itself to be unwelcoming. In this situation the individual may develop a "sour grapes" syndrome and express disdain for the second culture even though he or she originally wanted to be part of it.

A way to resolve these conflicts is to belong to a third culture of people who are not from one place or another any longer. Studies conducted on children of expatriates show that these children, even after they are adults, tend to feel most comfortable associating with others who share the third culture experience.[15] All those who "are not from here and not from there" share something important. They share being different, marginal, with no other salient identity but that of not belonging. This is a phenomenon that has not been widely recognized but that should help explain why there are communities of expatriates who do not mix well with their host culture.

The "third culture" is a metaphor for the process that many immigrants undergo. Many Mexicans, for example, after immigrating to the United States, find themselves affiliating with others who have had a similar experience. When they go back to Mexico they find out they don't belong. Their friends and relatives in Mexico accuse them of speaking "funny." But, in the United States they are accused of the same. Basically they stop belonging and become a "third culture." The third culture phenomenon becomes more pronounced among marginalized young people. They go through adolescence rebelling against their parents for one thing and society for another. They wind up being their own identity. The Chicano movement of the 1960s is a relevant example of this third culture phenomenon.[16] It was a movement of Mexicans in the United States in search for identity.

Marketing to individuals who experience a third culture as opposed to a more clearly defined heritage and perspective on life demands a different way of thinking. Marketing to groups of people who are in search of identity requires sensitivity to their needs in their real context. A typical error committed by U.S. Hispanic media is to assume that most Hispanic consumers in the United States would continue to relate to imagery and ideals of their countries of origin. It has not been until recently that Hispanic media began to recognize that reaching Hispanic consumers in the United States requires more than showing what Mexicans watch in Mexico City, or Venezuelans watch in Caracas. A new generation of shows has started to represent the duality and conflict that these consumers experience in their lives.

The development and positioning of products also need to address this conflict. Selling products to consumers as if they were still in Michoacán or in San Salvador would be irrelevant.

Acculturation Segmentation

Marketers have learned to segment groups of consumers in order to more accurately develop products and customized marketing programs. Segmentation, in some ways, has lost some of its allure with the advent of Integrated Marketing Communication (IMC). IMC advocates state that new marketing approaches should be based on one-on-one customization and not on segments. Some speak of aggregations of individuals as opposed to segmenting a population.[17]

There are different ways to segment customers. Many segmentation approaches rely on demographics. Others rely on demographics and psychographics. Still others use behavioral data to create segments of customers who exhibit similar behaviors. Clearly, if a segmentation approach is not pragmatically oriented to the needs of the marketers it can be useless.

In Hispanic marketing there have been several efforts to segment Hispanics. One of the most common approaches in segmenting Hispanic consumers has consisted of a linear division of Hispanics into categories like Spanish dominant, transitional, and English dominant. Clearly, Spanish dominant consumers exhibit certain common behavioral patterns associated with their language behavior. Those called transitionals or partially acculturated are those who are supposed to be between cultural worlds. Then, those who are English dominant are those who have technically assimilated. This perspective appears to address the concept of acculturation as a progressive process that goes from being "completely Hispanic" to being completely like whatever the majority of the United States is. For the sake of simplicity, that other extreme would be Anglo. This perspective points to the end process of acculturation as being assimilation. This type of oversimplification has been widely used and marketers have assumed that all those in one of these large categories show very similar behaviors.

Bidimensional Acculturation Segmentation

Clearly, there are variables in addition to language dependence that influence how people behave. In the mid 1990s, the authors of this book introduced to the marketing discipline the idea that acculturation is not linear but at a minimum bidimensional, if not multidimensional. It did not make intuitive sense that Hispanics would have to abandon their original culture to become increasingly acculturated.[18] Hispanics could keep their original culture, add elements of the second culture to their repertoire, or abandon their original culture in favor of the second culture. In addition, another option is that they could reject both the culture of their parents and the host culture at the same time.

In addition, acculturation should happen in a continuous and not a discrete fashion. There can be literally infinite gradations of culture acquisition. This means that individuals can vary quite a bit among themselves even in relatively homogeneous subgroups.

Figure 5.3 illustrates this bidimensional approach to acculturation segmentation.

This empirical classification generally is built through the creation of indexes that incorporate measures that reflect one or the other cultural orientation. In other words, the X axis represents language and behaviors that are strongly associated with Hispanic culture, and the axis itself is built through the addition of these variables. Similarly the Y axis represents English language dominance and behaviors typically associated with an Anglo orientation. It can be observed that individuals can vary in their degree of belongingness to each of the quadrants. That is possible because their endorsement of cultural behaviors is variable. Thus an acculturated person can lean more toward the Hispanic end, be equally Hispanic/Anglo oriented, or be highly Anglo and relatively low in their Hispanic orientation. Each quadrant allows for different degrees of the cultural orientation represented by the quadrant.

This Cartesian coordinate system shows that individuals falling in the upper left-hand quadrant are Hispanic Dominant. Clearly this

Figure 5.3

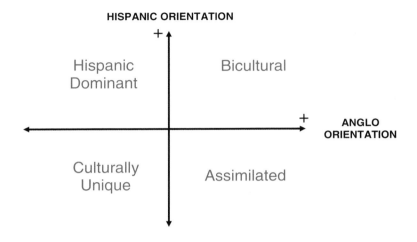

Bidimensional approach to acculturation segmentation

label is a simplification, but it is intended to refer to those Hispanics who are culturally and linguistically defined by their Hispanic origin. These are individuals who depend on the Spanish language for communication. Their attitudes are strongly aligned with the values of their countries of origin. They tend to be heavily dependent on Spanish language didactic information to make consumer decisions. These are individuals who tend to be quite open to commercial messages because they depend on them for learning about products and services. They have not adopted the cynicism that characterizes their "assimilated" counterparts.

Acculturated individuals combine their cultural repertoires to different degrees. These are people who can navigate between the Hispanic and Anglo cultures. They tend to make consumer decisions based on the relevance of the cultural cues of the situation and their reference group when making choices. They have a more ample repertoire of behaviors available to them. In many ways this quadrant represents what the bulk of Hispanics will be in the future. That is, individuals who do not give up their Hispanic culture but who learn how to navigate the mainstream culture, thus becoming bicultural.

They will become a dominant group if U.S. society continues to value Hispanic culture and allows for plurality to flourish. Otherwise, other quadrants will become more dominant in the future. At this time in history the United States has learned to appreciate Hispanic culture and Hispanics are led to believe that their culture and language are valued. That is why Hispanic music, food, fashion, and other cultural manifestations are increasingly popular. It has to be acknowledged, nevertheless, that things can change.

Assimilated individuals are those who have largely forgotten their Hispanic roots. These are individuals who may still have some emotional relationship with Hispanic cultural manifestations but who generally identify themselves as "Americans" as opposed to "Hispanic Americans," "Mexican Americans," or another national combination. They are likely to speak English almost exclusively, and they resemble non-Hispanics in their cynicism toward commercial messages. Individuals in this quadrant, however, are living through a period or "root" searching as they realize that their Hispanic background is now desirable and valuable. Many are prompting their children to learn Spanish and they, themselves, are increasingly attempting to learn the Spanish that either they have forgotten or never learned. A process of retro-acculturation is likely to take increasing importance among these individuals.

Culturally unique individuals are, in concept, those who have not allied themselves with the U.S. Anglo-dominant culture, and have not preserved to any large extent the culture of their parents because they do not identify with it. They are "not from here and not from there." They are those third culture individuals discussed earlier. They can be those who have identified themselves as Chicanos, Newyoricans, batos, and so on. These are individuals who feel pride in their unique identity and either reject or are unable to identify with their culture of origin or the dominant culture of the United States. In terms of consumer behavior, these are individuals who like to experiment and innovate because they have little to lose. Thus, they wear unusual clothing like baggy pants, or drive extravagant cars (low riders). Many of their innovations set trends that other groups pursue later. These individuals build a cultural identity out of the need for one.

This bidimensional segmentation helps the marketer in identifying acculturation subtleties that will impact interest in and purchase of products and services. Part of the usefulness of this segmentation approach is that product usage and other attitudes and behaviors can be plotted in the two-dimensional space. That would allow the marketer to visualize the acculturation status of current customers and prospects. Also, brand attitudes and related behaviors can be identified by subsegments in each of the quadrants. This approach can be very useful in guiding the marketer in identifying those more likely to purchase a product and also what beliefs and values are associated with specific subsegments. Clearly, the planning of the questionnaire used for any segmentation will heavily influence its usefulness.

A Multidimensional Acculturation Segmentation

This spatial model of acculturation can be expanded to include other cultural dimensions. In theory a third dimension could well be an African-American dimension. This is because individuals living in the United States are likely influenced not just by Anglo culture but also by African-American and other cultures. Assuming data and analytic sophistication, the model could be expanded to include multidimensional levels of acculturation for almost any individual living in the United States. This is an area of exploration that would constitute a useful and interesting doctoral dissertation and an ambitious marketing exploration of the multicultural United States.

Acculturation Segmentation by Life Stage

The variability found within each of these quadrants warrants combining this acculturation segmentation with other variables. The 2002 Yankelovich/Cheskin Hispanic Monitor introduced for the first time a Hispanic marketing segmentation that combined the acculturation segmentation with a life-stage breakdown, as shown in Figure 5.4.

The twelve resulting segments represent a finer view of Hispanic consumers. Note, however, that the sizes of the segments in the illustration are not necessarily proportional to their actual size in the Hispanic population. This study identified the specific characteristics that each of these segments has according to a large battery of questions. The study was conducted with individuals 16 years of age and

Figure 5.4

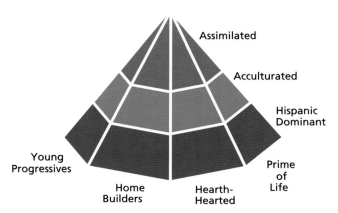

Acculturation segmentation by life stage

older. The Young Progressives are young people who are not in committed relationships, Home Builders are young couples, Hearth Hearted are families with older children, and Prime of Life are older Hispanics. This classification is useful because the marketer can empirically measure the characteristics of each segment and then decide which is most likely to be a primary, secondary, tertiary, and so on target for his or her product or service.

Thus, for example, Hispanic dominant Home Builders are likely to be the ones with most young children at home, and they are highly likely to be of Mexican origin. These characteristics alone make them important targets for baby products. Understanding how young Mexican families behave and think would then allow for specific targeting and positioning. As with the previous segmentation, this one also allows for the identification of multiple consumer attitudinal and behavioral issues to be included in the definition of each segment. Depending on the specific category, each segment could be made very relevant to the marketer's strategy.

La Agencia de Orcí created a marketing campaign for the Honda Accord in 2003 which segmented Hispanic car purchasers according to acculturation and lifestage. Overall, Honda's strategy at the time was to move toward a younger consumer. However, the Honda Accord had been a very successful sedan with older consumers. This segment was more acculturated, family oriented, and bilingual. The main benefits of the Accord for them were dependability, quality, and reliability. But in order to also appeal to a younger segment of the population, La Agencia de Orcí created a campaign with a more emotional appeal based on the style and performance features of the new Accord. Simultaneously they retained comfort and safety as part of the positioning for the older segment. By clearly understanding the consumer segments that made up the Hispanic market and using a creative combination of English and Spanish Language advertising, they made the Honda 2003 the leading model in mid-sized sedan sales and successfully positioned the Accord for a younger purchaser.[19]

Acculturation Segmentation and Cultural Tension

In 2004, Synovate[20] adopted the notion of Cultural Tension and combined it with levels of acculturation. A low level of cultural tension was conceptualized as lack of feelings of discrimination, close family ties in the United States, unlikely to attend Hispanic events, less traditional, seek opportunities to learn non-Hispanic aspects, and feel comfortable with others who are non-Hispanic. A high level of cultural tension was conceptualized as the opposite.

Synovate came up with four quadrants, combining a dimension of more or less acculturated with high or low levels of cultural tension. That resulted in six segments. One was a mostly acculturated segment. Three partially acculturated segments were labeled as American Latinos, New Latinos, and Traditionals. Two relatively unacculturated segments were labeled as Unacculturated Stable, and Unacculturated Traditional. This segmentation approach is useful as well because it takes into consideration the degree to which Hispanics struggle with their identity in the United States. The largest contingent, by far, was found to be the aggregate of the partially acculturated segments, accounting for almost 60 percent of their sample.

In a similar fashion to the Yankelovich/Cheskin segmentation, Synovate describes in their report the demographic and behavioral measures associated with each segment.

The Future of Hispanic Segmentation

If the goal of contemporary marketing practice is to establish relationships with individual consumers, segmentation aggregates likely will become smaller and more finely tuned. Although language and cultural data will continue to make the work of the marketer easier in product design and messaging, many other behavioral consumer variables will be incorporated in future segmentations. The more actionable the segmentation is the more it will be used and will result in marketing successes. A combination of finely tuned cultural, consumer, geographic, and demographic factors will make the marketer increasingly powerful. But this power will not be a power to manipulate but to establish relationships. Relationship building is based on better consumer understanding and also identification with their needs.

Allstate developed an 800-number campaign that allowed the segmentation of its target to emerge from Hispanics who responded to an ad on Spanish-language TV, including an 800-number to call for more information. From their research prior to the campaign, Allstate understood that Hispanic callers should have the opportunity to speak immediately in their language of preference with a bilingual representative. With a sophisticated routing capability, the incoming call from an interested Hispanic was sent to an Allstate representative in the area in which the caller was located. The Allstate representative took demographic information from the caller and noted responses to a few basic questions regarding insurance needs.

As a result of the 800-number campaign, Allstate built a detailed database on Hispanic callers, and what business actions the call led to, including sales completed. In this way they developed a keen understanding of how to target Hispanics who would be most interested in their services, what their demographics were, and where and how to reach them effectively. They added direct mail with more specific insurance information to this campaign, fulfilling the detailed information needs of these consumers for this new type of service. Interestingly, more than 85 percent of the callers conducted their calls in Spanish, and the Spanish preferred consumer had a close rate twice that of the English preferred.

This case study exemplifies a consumer-based segmentation, a culturally sensitive multimedia campaign, and a company whose marketing communication contributed to the acculturation of Hispanics in the unfamiliar area of insurance (see the Allstate Case Study at the end of this chapter).

Stereotypes and Acculturation

As discussed earlier in this chapter, acculturation is a two-way process in which society and the individual or group of individuals interact. Those interactions have different outcomes as seen in the segmentations presented earlier. Hispanics move in the acculturation space depending on their social fortunes and the general receptiveness of the overall culture in the United States.

Stereotypes are portrayed in the media, be it in programming or commercials. Stereotypes are also held by individuals and they are talked about and discussed. Hispanics see images of themselves in media portrayals or when they are told about the stereotypes they belong to.

Stereotype Stages

The media has been postulated to have gone through different stages in the portrayal of minorities.[21] At first the media tended to ignore minorities and made them largely invisible. As a second stage, that of ridicule, minorities tended to be portrayed as clowns and buffoons. Third, minorities have been portrayed in both sides of law enforcement, as either thieves or criminals or cops. Last, an era yet to be fully realized is that of respect, in which minorities are portrayed in diverse roles in different walks of life.

Media and other forms of social stereotyping can have important implications in generating reactions by the target, in this case Hispanic consumers.

Stereotypes and Their Impact on the Larger Society

One of the typical Hispanic reactions has been criticism and discontent with Hispanic portrayals, because of their lack of variability and depth. Hispanic consumers who have had the advantage of higher levels of formal education tend to be very critical of stereotypical representations. Many of these consumers tend to feel insulted by the popular Telenovelas, which typically cast Hispanics as rootless elites or suffering servants. Also, they tend to find programs like *Sábado Gigante* bothersome because of the ridicule to which audience members are subjected and because of the very homogeneous characterization of Hispanics as hypersexual or childish. These are similar to the audiences that took offense to the characterization of Frito Bandito in the 1970s and contributed to its demise. These audiences felt that perpetuating the imagery of Frito Bandito would hurt the public image of Hispanics.

Negative reactions to stereotypical portrayals are not the exclusive privilege of highly educated Hispanics. Many Hispanics with lower levels of education have expressed to these authors their dismay at the cheap and caricature-like quality of many Hispanic characterizations they still find in Spanish-language advertising. When Hispanic consumers compare what they see in the relatively more sophisticated advertising in English-language media with some of the stereotypical ads they still see in Spanish-language television, they object. These consumers object to the lower quality and refinement of Hispanic representations.

It should be noted, however, that advertising directed to Hispanic consumers has experienced a renaissance in the past few years. Guided by the discipline of account planning and research, as well as by an increasingly sophisticated industry, Hispanic characterizations are more varied, and have claimed a wider appeal and recognition. The stereotypical ads of a mother with children and husband who praise the qualities of products, are slowly disappearing. Marketers have been learning to establish a more ample array of characterizations that help him or her to establish better and more specific links with the Hispanic consumer. These newer characterizations capture Hispanic consumers in their more realistic variety, as opposed to traditional stereotypes.

Also, the wide appeal that Hispanic culture has had on the overall culture over the last few years seems to support the notion that an era of respect and Hispanic diversity seems to have flourished. Content and advertising geared to Hispanics has resonated with non-Hispanic audiences. Now Hispanic culture has increasingly become popular and desirable. Hispanics now appear to look at their own portrayals in the media with measured optimism. Because of newer media portrayals Hispanics are beginning to be perceived as sexy, successful, and attractive. Jennifer Lopez, Christina Aguilera, Marc Anthony, Jose Leguizamo, Shakira, Santana, Ricky Martin, Gloria Estefan, and many others have become aspirational not just to Hispanics but to society at large. An era of respect may be on the near horizon.

Stereotypical characterizations can produce limited, inaccurate, and negative homogeneous views of Hispanics. Some stereotypes can also produce positive impacts on society—think of groups of people considered to be attractive, hard working, and productive.

Stereotypes and Their Impact on Hispanics

A self-fulfilling[22] prophecy is part of the social phenomenon[23] that stereotypes and portrayals can produce. The low self-esteem that many Hispanics have experienced over the years can be traced back to the stereotypes they have seen in the media and also to those that they have heard proffered by others. The images of short, fat, lazy, sleazy, drunken Hispanics cannot have helped Hispanics' sense of pride.

Varied representations of successful Hispanics seem to be infusing Hispanics with a renewed sense of pride. Interestingly this phenomenon is closely related to the courting of Hispanics, in which large companies have engaged. As Hispanics feel courted and as they perceive their own images to be evolving for the positive, they testify to a renewed sense of vigor and cultural pride.

We seem to be at the verge of a new era in which the negative stereotypes of Hispanics are turning into positive images. This process seems to be affecting societal perceptions and also Hispanic perceptions of themselves. This trend can have only positive effects on the overall U.S. society at a time when Hispanics grow in size and the Anglo community shrinks.

Stereotyping is not necessarily negative and not avoidable, and perhaps there is no reason for even trying to avoid stereotyping.[24] It is not the stereotypes that do harm, but prejudice and lack of awareness that stereotypes are generalizations. Generalizations can help or hurt depending on the context and how they are employed. As images in the media and in the social milieu become more diverse and positive, Hispanics are likely to hold increasingly positive auto-stereotypes.[25]

Marketers appear to be in a privileged position in this historical moment with regards to the U.S. Hispanic market. This is a time when courting the Hispanic consumer with positive images can result in product trials and potential brand loyalty. The work of the marketer is part of the acculturation process of U.S. Hispanics. The consumption of products and services contributes to acculturation. Interestingly, marketing approaches that positively portray Hispanics also create a reciprocal positive attitude among non-Hispanics. When non-Hispanics see attractive and appealing portrayals of Hispanics and their culture they start having reasons for coveting Hispanic culture.

Now is the time when media images and advertisements can profitably cross language media boundaries. It is a time when the Hispanic consumer likes to see him- or herself in both Spanish and English language media, and also a time when non-Hispanics are more likely to enjoy Hispanic portrayals in English language media and to be more curious about Spanish language media images.

At the same time that Hispanics acculturate, non-Hispanics are also acquiring the Hispanic culture as a second culture. Clearly, Hispanics have more urgency to acculturate, but the process has become increasingly reciprocal. Cross-over marketing opportunities can now go both ways.

Conclusions

The process of social change implied by immigration and acculturation presents important opportunities to marketers. Acculturating individuals are open to new inputs and influences. They need to understand and participate in their new environment in order to succeed and reach an integration comfort level emotionally. However, they also need to maintain their own identity, formed in the early years of enculturation in their countries of origin.

Since the 1970s, Mexico has contributed the largest number of immigrants to the United States. Prior generations of immigrants, mainly from Europe, became part of what was referred to as "the melting pot," replacing an American identity for their own. In contrast, most Mexicans intend to maintain their own cultural heritage. Most came to the United States for the opportunity to earn enough to return and live comfortably in their own villages.

Marketers can best understand acculturation of U.S. Hispanics by using a two-dimensional model consisting on one dimension of the tendency toward being/behaving according to the Hispanic culture, and on the other dimension a tendency toward the non-Hispanic, U.S. Anglo culture. This model is useful to understand where groups of Hispanics and individuals are regarding acculturation. Past research by Yankelovich and others has indicated that U.S. Hispanics are more frequently dispersed between an identity with strong Hispanic–low

Anglo dimensions, particularly more recent immigrants; and an identity that incorporates both Hispanic and Anglo elements, and could be thought of as bicultural.

Marketers using this or even more complex segmentation to fit their own research objectives can develop a keen sense of Hispanic consumer needs. This will allow them to create appropriate products, advertising, and consumer communications that will benefit their sales and Hispanic consumers as well. It will also prevent the need to narrowly stereotype these consumers. In the past, restricted advertising and media have perpetuated narrow and even denigrating stereotypes. Now, with a deeper understanding of the Hispanic consumer, marketers can have greater success in reaching their target, and Hispanics will have the chance to develop pride in a broader, more diverse bicultural identity.

Implications for Marketers

- Refine your understanding of your Hispanic target according to their level of acculturation. This will provide a sense of the breadth of your appeal across the market as well as guidance on appropriate communication.

- Remember that success in the U.S. culture is critical for Hispanic consumers and your marketing communications can contribute to their acculturation. This chapter includes the case studies of San Jose Group National Pork Board, Español Countrywide, and Allstate as examples.

- On the other hand, give attention to the fact that Hispanics maintain pride and fond remembrances for their own heritage as they acculturate, and the non-Hispanic market also displays an interest in subjects Hispanic as well. The case study of K. Fernandez McCormick Mayonesa at the end of this chapter, as well as the Español Corona Extra Case Study "Proudly Mexican" at the end of Chapter 4 are excellent examples of successful campaigns directed toward people of Mexican origin.

- Avoid assumptions or stereotypes of the relationship between Hispanics and the U.S. culture. Use culturally aware Hispanic professionals as researchers, consultants, and advertising agencies. Be aware of the invisibility of subjective culture, even to those from within it, and don't succumb to stereotypic premises.

- Hispanics are the largest minority in the United States and are growing and fanning out across the United States at a rapid rate. This is a cultural phenomenon not only for Hispanics, but for the

U.S. culture itself. Marketers have the opportunity to provide leadership in the sensitive and informed communication of their products and services with a cross-over perspective. This will continue the trend toward greater cultural openness to the benefit of all parties—U.S. Hispanics, the broader U.S. culture, and the norm of learning about and enjoying others as a fundamental value.

Case Study: *K. Fernandez – McCormick*

Company/Organization: McCormick & Company
Advertising Agency: K. Fernandez & Associates
Campaign: Hispanic Mayonesa product launch in the U.S. Hispanic Market
Intended customers/clients: First generation in the U.S. Mexican female heads of household

Background:

With the passage of NAFTA, McCormick had the opportunity to bring its best selling Mexican mayonnaise product, McCormick Mayonesa, to the U.S. Hispanic market. Since this product was so well known in Mexico, McCormick realized that they had important ready-made brand equity with U.S. Mexican consumers. They also understood that this mayonnaise product was developed with the unique taste preferences of Mexicans in mind so that it could be introduced into the U.S. market without modification.

Discovery Process/Research:

McCormick and their Hispanic Marketing Agency, K. Fernandez, researched the demographics of Mexican markets for the development of their integrated campaign. They also conducted both qualitative and quantitative research. They developed target markets in the heart of densely Hispanic populated areas. From their long history in the Hispanic Market, K. Fernandez made use of a multiplicity of channels known to be effective in reaching the U.S. Mexican market. Their intent was to create a personal context for re-familiarization with a known product.

Cultural Insights:

K. Fernandez brought the cultural insights of Mexican shoppers to this U.S. campaign, recognizing that taste preferences, particularly the Mexican love of lime, and the longing for products from home would create strong bonds to this well-known popular product. They realized that the equity would be particularly strong among immigrants from Mexico who were living for their first time in the U.S. and were likely to be nostalgic for beloved products from their heritage. They were clear that building on brand and product equity would be an effective way to promote the purchase of this product to U.S. Mexicans, and to Central Americans who also grew up with this mayonnaise brand.

Expression of Insights in the Campaign:

K. Fernandez created a character named Marta Mayonesa to represent McCormick's typical Mexican female target. She is fairly new to the U.S., shopped at markets that were in high density Hispanic areas, she wants to make sure her family has fresh food products with the best taste and quality, she likes the taste of lime in mayonnaise not typical of U.S. brands, and she recognizes McCormick mayonnaise as the brand she grew up with that reminds her of home.

The Agency created a campaign focused on first-generation, Hispanic female primary grocery shoppers ages 25 to 54. Their market selection was based on product distribution channels and population profiles. The advertising emphasized the key benefits of the original Mexican campaign for McCormick Mayonesa: The taste of lime, the thick and rich texture, and that it was Mexico's favorite mayonnaise. They maintained the Mexican tagline, *Póngale sabroso*, because their research indicated it still had high recognition with Mexicans in the U.S. They promoted their product with radio, TV, and in-store promotions, including on-premise "grocery grabs" to gain trial and bring excitement in the campaign. In addition, they had booths at traditional community events and for in-store sampling. The advertising was phased in from introductory TV and radio commercials, to sustained media usage, and TV and radio to support promotional events.

Effect of the Campaign:

Sales grew from $300,000 to $8,000,000. The sales gains are driving distribution gains and product line expansion, and a 200% ROI was realized from McCormick's investment in the U.S. Hispanic market.

Figure 5.5

McCormick Mayonesa campaign

Case Study: *The San Jose Group – The National Pork Board*

Company/Organization: The National Pork Board
Advertising Agency: The San Jose Group
Campaign: El cerdo es bueno (Pork Is Good)
Intended customers/clients: U.S. Hispanics, particularly Mexicans

Background:

The National Pork Board decided in 2001 that the U.S. Hispanic market could provide an important niche for the expansion of pork consumption. They understood that the Hispanic population was growing at ten times the rate of the general market, and that there were large centers of market concentrations in key cities such as Los Angeles, Miami, New York, Houston, and Chicago in which this market reached close to 40% of the population. They also knew that pork was a meat product that had a consumption heritage in this market. They learned through existing quantitative data that although Hispanics make up only 8.4% of U.S. households, they account for 12% of pork spending.

Discovery Process/Research:

Working with its Hispanic agency, The San Jose Group (SJG), The National Pork Board conducted both qualitative and quantitative research in 2001 to develop their 2002 campaign launch strategy. They used qualitative research (focus groups) to probe into their initial questions related to suspected misperceptions that were blocking opportunities for the category. Once they understood the issues more clearly, they conducted quantitative research to find out how widespread both positive and negative perceptions regarding pork were in the broader population.

Cultural Insights:

Through their qualitative work, The National Pork Board and SJG discovered a dichotomy of attitudes in the Hispanic market about pork. They found that Hispanics love the taste of pork, which they use in many traditional dishes, and even favored the taste over other proteins. However, they also found that this segment had health concerns about eating pork due to cholesterol and fat content, which was wrongly perceived to be high in ALL cuts of pork. But even more concerning was the widespread fear of contracting not only trichinosis, but an even longer list of wives' tales, ranging from "worms on the brain," to convulsions, to even stunting your children's growth! These fears stemmed from experiences in their countries of origin, where pork-related illnesses are more likely in locations where meat is not maintained with proper refrigeration and in sanitary conditions. As a result, Hispanics felt a conflict in eating this meat that they loved in great quantities. Not surprisingly, the General Market slogan which referred to pork as "The Other White Meat" had little meaning for Hispanics, not only because meat is not typically categorized according to colors, but also because it did not address their main concern—food safety.

Expression of Insights in the Campaign:

The National Pork Board and SJG decided that they needed a strong educational campaign to give consumers the license to enjoy the pork they love, without guilt or fear. Campaign executions needed to strike a balance between an emotional appeal (typically required for Hispanic market food advertising) and a rational appeal (i.e., food safety and nutrition).

They moved away from the General Market campaign and created a slogan appropriate to the market: *El cerdo es bueno* (Pork Is Good). This tagline represents the centralized theme for the entire Hispanic marketing and communications platform. It is effective because it addresses all of the key barriers to pork consumption present in the minds of Hispanic consumers with a single, straightforward and simple message. "Pork Is Good" means U.S. pork is safe, delicious, and healthy.

This message was the basis for all creative executions, which offered the basic promise that "you can eat the pork you love 'guilt free'." The reasons to believe included: Pork is safe—modern methods of production have made disease from pork virtually nonexistent; pork is healthy—U.S. pork producers utilize improved genetics and production techniques to produce pork that is 31% leaner than 20 years ago; pork is delicious—pork dishes are a mainstay in the Hispanic culture. In print executions, a halo was placed over the "e" in cerdo (pork) to drive home the favorable image of pork.

SJG then leveraged The National Pork Board's well-established pork logo, which features the word "pork" inside of a pork chop-shaped icon, and added a subtext which read: *Calidad U.S. Pork* (U.S. Quality Pork). This new visual treatment provided reassurances by serving as a "quality seal of approval." This new logo, together with the slogan *El cerdo es bueno* (Pork Is Good), appeared in all of the campaign's visual materials.

INTEGRATED APPROACH

In 2002 they launched the program with an integrated campaign including magazine ads, outdoor advertising, radio, as well as retail promotions and public relations in three markets.

Advertising

The radio campaign consisted of a series of four 60-second commercials that leveraged humorous situations to poke fun at pork's "bad" reputation, while also providing consumers with important facts on the positive attributes of pork. Print ads and meat case signs featured authentic Latino dishes in colorful Hispanic table settings and provided health information with headlines such as "Feed Your Knowledge." These executions favorably and factually compared fat, calorie, and cholesterol levels for pork with other popular meat cuts. The outdoor execution highlighted the slogan, "Pork Is Good."

Public Relations

Extensive media relations efforts were conducted to support the advertising campaign messages and add credibility to the health/food safety claim. Dietitians were recruited and trained as spokespersons for on-air opportunities to educate Hispanics on the healthfulness of pork. In addition, they addressed Hispanic consumers' misperceptions about the safety of pork, by explaining that pork produced in the United States is of the highest quality and that today's pork is virtually disease-free. Comprehensive press kits, which included not only the health and safety information but also healthy pork recipes, were sent to media, who, upon receiving this information, were eager to spread the good news about pork into their communities.

In-Store Promotions

Retail sales promotions were set up in partnership with key retailers and other co-marketing partners to support pork sales through the development and execution of promotions leveraging the campaign messages.

Figure 5.6

The National Pork Board campaign

El cerdo es bueno™

Alimente sus conocimientos	
Corte Por cada 3 onzas, cocidas, con grasa recortada	Grasa
Cerdo Chuleta de lomo a la parrilla	6.9g*
Res Filete a la parrilla	8.1g*
Pollo Muslo sin piel al horno	9.3g*
*Datos tomados del USDA Handbook 8 Series	

pork checkoff © 2003 National Pork Board, Des Moines, IA USA

pork — Calidad U.S. Pork™

Effect of the Campaign:

The National Pork Board conducted tracking research at the conclusion of the 2002 campaign, which indicated that the campaign was successful at beginning to break down barriers and generating increased pork consumption.

- Perceptions toward pork improved (shows increase in average attribute rating scores):
  - "Pork is as low in fat as chicken" 22%+
  - "Pork is as nutritious as beef" 9%+
  - "Pork is good" 10%+
- The percentage of consumers who now believe the quality of U.S. pork is "very good" increased 38%.
- In fact, pork was the only protein to show an increase in favorability rating over the course of the study 6.5%+.
- 50% of all respondents said they were more comfortable purchasing pork as a result of hearing the campaign messages.
- And most importantly, Hispanic consumers reported purchasing pork more frequently and in larger quantities, resulting in a 14% increase in pork expenditures.

Since then, the campaign was expanded into 12 of the top Hispanic markets and TV was incorporated into the media mix. Attitudes toward pork and consumption indices continue to improve even more dramatically (results of the pre/post 2004 tracking study):

- Perceptions toward pork (shows increase in average attribute rating scores):
  - "Pork is as low in fat as chicken" 29%+
  - "Pork is low in cholesterol" 21%+
  - "Pork is safe to serve my family" 24%+
- The percentage of consumers who now believe the quality of U.S. pork is "very good" increased 64%.
- Pork was the only protein to show a statistically significant increase in favorability rating over the course of the study 16%+.
- 67% of all respondents said they were more comfortable purchasing pork as a result of hearing the campaign messages.
- And most importantly, the campaign generated a 31% increase in pork expenditures.

The success of this program has been recognized in more than six national communications awards, including IABC's Gold Quill; PCC's Golden Trumpet; PRSA's Award of Excellence; the Communicator Award; and two PR News' Platinum PR awards.

Case Study: *Español – Countrywide*

Company/Organization: Countrywide Home Loans, Inc.
Advertising Agency: Español Marketing & Communications, Inc.
Campaign: *facilitando sueños* (making the dream easy)
Target Audience: First-time homebuyers who prefer to communicate in Spanish

Background:

Countrywide Home Loans, one of the nation's leading residential mortgage lenders, made a corporate commitment to increase homeownership opportunities among previously underserved communities. The company hired Español Marketing & Communications to help in strategic development of Countrywide's marketing propositions for targeting members of the Hispanic market in these communities.

In the mid-1990s, few major residential mortgage lenders were targeting underserved communities that included Hispanic consumers. Those that engaged in Spanish-language marketing efforts at that time typically adapted their English-language messages to Spanish and frequently used terminology and images that were irrelevant or incomprehensible to members of the target audience who were often unfamiliar with the financial services category and reluctant to enter into a relationship with a mortgage lender without feeling comfortable in the home loan process.

Discovery Process/Research:

Since making its corporate commitment to historically underserved communities, Countrywide has conducted both qualitative and quantitative studies to determine and refine marketing strategies and home loan processes for Spanish-preferring consumers, to evaluate campaign and sales results, as well as to analyze consumer habits and beliefs.

Some of these studies included:

- Positioning studies to test consumers' acceptance and likes/dislikes of positioning statements and copy claims intended for Countrywide's communications.

- Commercial effectiveness research: Quantitative study of 1-on-1 interviews to determine the effectiveness of different television campaigns.
- In-house data collection: reports are generated to measure response to all types of communications, with precise logs of advertising dates/times, dedicated 800 numbers to monitor response to specific media campaigns, and correlation of contacts with Countrywide to actual loans generated.
- Multi-year quantitative Awareness and Attitude studies: to assess growth in advertising awareness and recall, attitudes, and consumer loyalty for Countrywide among all of Countrywide's key consumer segments.
- Strategic Partner research: Qualitative research (primarily focus groups) with strategic partners in the Hispanic market to determine tools that Countrywide can offer to educate consumers about the homebuying process and to generate new ideas for generating leads/business.

Cultural Insights:

Spanish-dominant (or preferring) consumers are less likely to contact mortgage lenders directly, due primarily to:

- inability to communicate well in English
- fear of failure (rejection and/or inability to understand the process)
- lack of category experience
- lack of established banking relationships

Instead, Spanish-dominant consumers tend to put their trust in a bilingual or Spanish-dominant real estate agent (typically referred to them by a friend or family member) to initiate and navigate the loan process for them.

Expression of Insights in the Campaign:

Based on consumer, real estate agent, and internal research, a system was created whereby consumers have opportunities to work in Spanish with a bilingual, bicultural Countrywide home loan expert—in person, by phone, or online. Countrywide strives to offer a flexible loan approval and delivery system, with pre-qualification or upfront approval processes and a wide portfolio of loan program options and qualification guidelines.

An illustrative Spanish-dominant consumer mindset that was identified by research was:

"I trust my real estate agent to know what price house I can afford and to get me a good mortgage. He's got lots of experience getting mortgages for people like me. Getting a mortgage is way too complicated for me to do myself, since I have never bought a house, I don't speak English well, and I'm not comfortable with the terminology or process."

In order to help educate consumers on the different functions of a lender and a real estate professional, as well as to help empower consumers to take charge of the home loan process without being entirely reliant on their real estate professional, Countrywide worked to establish the following selling proposition:

Countrywide is the company you can trust to help you select the ideal loan for which you qualify—and we can educate you to help you get it yourself!

In order to create an image of Countrywide as a reliable lender in which consumers could put their trust, the following benefits were reinforced through Spanish-language communications:

- Streamlined Process: Countrywide offers a streamlined loan approval and delivery system whereby virtually all verbal and some of the written communication can be done in Spanish. It begins with a Serious Buyer Certificate, which tells you and your real estate agent how much home you can afford, and helps to show that you are a Serious Buyer.

- A Leading Lender in U.S.: Countrywide is one of the leading residential mortgage lenders to the members of the Hispanic market. [Source: Based on a comparison of loans originated and purchased to African American, Hispanic, Asian/Pacific Islander and American Indian/Alaska Native homeowners, and reported in 2003 under the Home Mortgage Disclosure Act (HMDA) by individual reporters.]

- Loan Options: Countrywide offers a wide portfolio of flexible loan products at highly competitive rates, including some with no down payments (for those who qualify).

Working with Español Marketing, Countrywide created an educational campaign designed to educate target consumers about the homebuying process and to empower them to take the first step to buying a home by calling or visiting Countrywide. The tagline that has become the underlying theme of all Countrywide Spanish-language communications is *facilitando sueños* (making the dream easy), reinforcing Countrywide's commitment to increasing homeownership opportunities among members of historically underserved communities and helping them realize their dreams.

TV, radio, and print advertising initially ran in key local markets, frequently combined with educational public service campaigns created together with media outlets. Countrywide sponsored homebuyer fairs in many markets with on-air promotion and coverage by local television and radio stations and newspapers. Countrywide also created or sponsored many homebuyer's fairs, conducting educational seminars in Spanish for potential homebuyers, passing out first-time homebuyer handbooks, manuals on how to establish and improve credit, and brochures about loan products that were specially developed for first-time homebuyers that might not qualify in the traditional mortgage application process.

For five years, Countrywide sponsored a weekly homebuying show on the Radio Unica radio network, where consumers could call in and ask questions about the homebuying process, and a Countrywide home loan expert would answer them on air.

Countrywide has a relationship with Fannie Mae that led to the creation of an educational web site on univision.com for first-time homebuyers that has been very popular over the past several years. Countrywide also developed a proprietary Spanish-language web site—countrywide.com/espanol—that provides consumers with a great deal of information on homebuying process, types of loans, as well as information on refinancing and home equity line of credit products.

As part of its Hispanic marketing efforts, Countrywide currently advertises on network TV.

Effect of the Campaign:

Countrywide's internal research indicates that consumer awareness, trust, and market share for Countrywide have grown significantly in the Hispanic market, due in part to the successful communications strategy and relevant executions, increases in

Figure 5.7

Countrywide educational campaign

Su obstáculo: Creer que un solo sueldo no basta
La solución: El nuevo Préstamo Óptimo
de Countrywide

↘ Countrywide ha creado un nuevo préstamo...
para facilitar la compra de *su* casa

Con el nuevo Préstamo Óptimo de Countrywide®, muchas más familias pueden comprar su propia casa, incluso si no cuentan más que con un solo sueldo. Nosotros les podemos ayudar. Para empezar, hemos reducido los obstáculos relacionados con el pago inicial. Además, la flexibilidad de este préstamo les permite utilizar varios medios para calificar, como por ejemplo: su historial de pagos de renta y servicios, fuentes de ingresos de varios miembros de su familia y otros ingresos que normalmente no califican. No por nada somos expertos en encontrar soluciones.

Si usted ha soñado con tener casa propia, venga a hablar con los expertos de Countrywide y pregunte por el nuevo Préstamo Óptimo. Usted puede alcanzar su sueño, nosotros podemos ayudarlo.

SOMOS EXPERTOS EN ENCONTRAR SOLUCIONES

HOME LOANS
Facilitando Sueños℠

Countrywide Financial Corporation es un líder a nivel nacional en financiamiento de vivienda y uno de los miembros de los prestigiosos Standard & Poor's 500 y de Fortune 500. ⌂ Equal Housing Lender. © 2004 Countrywide Home Loans, Inc., 4500 Park Granada, Calabasas, CA 91302. Trade/servicemarks are the property of Countrywide Financial Corporation and/or its subsidiaries. Arizona Mortgage Banker License Number 0008805; Licensed by the Department of Corporations under the California Residential Mortgage Lending Act; Georgia Reg. #5929; Illinois Residential Mortgage Licensee; Massachusetts Mortgage Lender Lender License No. ML 1623; this is not an offer to enter into an interest rate lock-in agreement under Minnesota law; Licensed by the New Hampshire Banking Department; New Jersey (818) 313-6526, Licensed Mortgage Banker, NJ Department of Banking and Insurance; Licensed Mortgage Banker, NYS Banking Department; Registered with the Pennsylvania Banking Department; Rhode Island Lender's License. Some products may not be available in all states. This is not a commitment to lend. Restrictions apply. All rights reserved.

advertising spending, as well as to the continued commitment to streamlining the homebuying process for Spanish-preferring Countrywide customers throughout the country. Countrywide is currently one of the leading residential mortgage lenders to members of the Hispanic market.

Case Study: *Allstate*

Company/Organization: Allstate
Advertising Agency: Several agencies used
Campaign: Accessibility 800# Strategy
Intended customers/clients: Hispanic consumers in selected markets. *(One of the main purposes of this study was to create a system for reaching interested potential Hispanic customers as well as continuously refining Allstate's target.)*

Background:

Allstate formed a diversity action team in 1989 to assess the business potential of a market that was rapidly becoming more diverse. The general market in the insurance industry was maturing, providing diminishing opportunity for growth. However, the Hispanic market had a growing population that was underserved in the insurance category, and looked like a promising competitive niche. As a result of their initial information gathering and internal meetings, Allstate developed a comprehensive diversity strategy for the Hispanic market. The initiative was led by Allstate Hispanic Business Team. It was slated for implementation by Allstate agents in their direct service areas.

Discovery Process/Research:

The implementation of the 800# campaign facilitated the collection of data on the Hispanic market in targeted urban areas. Since interested Hispanics identified themselves by calling the 800# advertised by Allstate, the data that was collected supplied their demographics as well as their interests. This data allowed Allstate to continually refine its understanding of the Hispanic market, and to reapply the findings to the implementation of their 800# initiative.

Cultural Insights:

Allstate understood the needs of the Hispanic Market at the outset of this campaign from their qualitative research. They recognized the importance of face-to-face explanation of their products to Hispanic consumers, who often had little experience in this complex category. They knew that the key to success for this new campaign was to facilitate interaction between the potential Hispanic customer and the Allstate agent in the field.

Expression of Insights in the Campaign:

The Allstate Hispanic Business Team (HBT) implemented a holistic business approach to reach the Hispanic consumer. To maximize results, an integrated marketing model (Figure 5.8) was used to insure business strategies addressed key customer/consumer touch points and learning was proactive (continually seeking to understand) and ongoing.

This case study reports the approach, activities, and learning's for year 1997, on the Accessibility (800 Number) strategy as shown on the model. This strategy supported and improved the effectiveness of advertising investments and Allstate sales agency performance. The strategy delivered mechanisms that drove consumers, with no interim human interactions, to multilingual Allstate sales offices. The system geo-coded the callers' phone numbers, in real time, and delivered the caller to the nearest bilingual agency. See Figure 5.9 for a general description of the process.

The period covered by this case study is from February 1997 through December of the same year. During this period more than 50,000 calls were tracked for performance (conversation to sales).

Figure 5.8

Allstate integrated marketing model

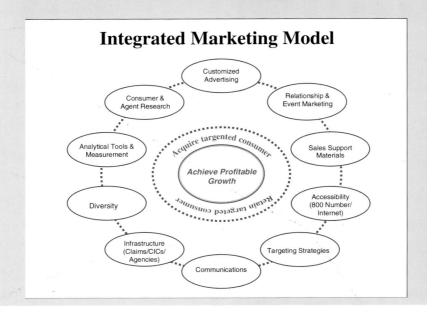

Integrated Marketing Model

Customized Advertising

Consumer & Agent Research

Relationship & Event Marketing

Analytical Tools & Measurement

Sales Support Materials

Acquire targeted consumer

Achieve Profitable Growth

Retain targeted consumer

Diversity

Accessibility (800 Number/ Internet)

Infrastructure (Claims/CICs/ Agencies)

Targeting Strategies

Communications

Figure 5.9

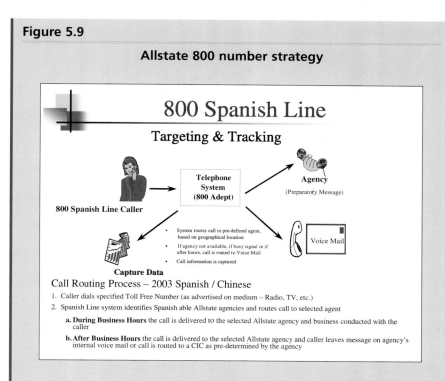

Allstate 800 number strategy

800 Spanish Line
Targeting & Tracking

800 Spanish Line Caller

Telephone System (800 Adept)

Agency (Preparatory Message)

- System routes call to pre-defined agent, based on geographical location
- If agency not available, if busy signal or if after hours, call is routed to Voice Mail
- Call information is captured

Voice Mail

Capture Data

Call Routing Process – 2003 Spanish / Chinese

1. Caller dials specified Toll Free Number (as advertised on medium – Radio, TV, etc.)
2. Spanish Line system identifies Spanish able Allstate agencies and routes call to selected agent

    a. During Business Hours the call is delivered to the selected Allstate agency and business conducted with the caller

    b. After Business Hours the call is delivered to the selected Allstate agency and caller leaves message on agency's internal voice mail or call is routed to a CIC as pre-determined by the agency

Mediums used were TV, radio, mail (ADVO—direct mail), and print (newspaper). The strongest driver of call volume was TV. This medium provided a constant call volume. However, with each introduction of direct mail (ADVO), peaks of intense calling took place. ADVO treatments were bilingual and designed to be culturally relevant, Hispanic-centric. Television created category and product awareness and ADVO functioned as a stimulant driving exceptional demand to the 800 Spanish line.

The 800 Spanish line metrics delivered insights on regional nuances to include brand preferences, channel preferences, and channel capacity. By tracking traditional operational metrics, calls by day and by time of day (Figure 5.10), Allstate was able to advise agencies on how best to deal with the demand. Many agencies extended their operating hours in response to these insights. Feedback flowed in both directions. Agencies and regional sales staffs provided the HBT ongoing local analysis leading to process changes. Changes included medium use and agency support processes. In the short-term, sales support materials were modified or created to deal with market needs. Early on these materials concentrated on educating the consumer on the insurance category. In

Figure 5.10

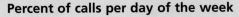

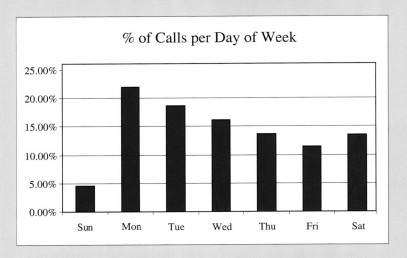

Percent of calls per day of the week

the longer term, the HBT engaged the regions and agencies in identifying support staff to improve language capability of the channel.

Initially we expected the large traditional Hispanic markets to deliver the greatest volumes of calls and sales, however, some secondary markets outperformed the primary markets. Subsequent research revealed that the brand and the agency channels' strengths, in these secondary markets, were behind the superior and unexpected performance.

A close look at call volumes revealed that consumers were anxious to reach an agent. Nearly 40% of the calls were duplicate calls, consumers calling the toll free number numerous times hoping to reach an agent after hours (after 7:00 pm) or on weekends. Of the calls received only 60% were unique callers. This volume was used to determine sales closure rates. As mentioned, insights on call patterns led to local initiatives to help agencies improve office performance to maximize consumer demand. In some instances regional offices set up pools of bilingual employees to deal with unique demands.

The sales closure rate of 8.8% exceeded the target of 6.0%. A ratio of 18:1 (premium to added cost) also exceeded the target of 10:1 for the program. A close look at sales by product mix provided insights used in future campaigns. As expected the Auto

Figure 5.11

Media and language preferences

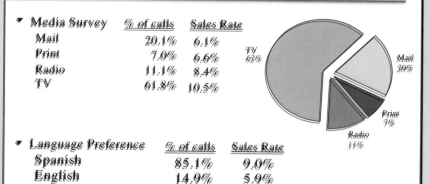

Measurements

Media Survey	% of calls	Sales Rate
Mail	20.1%	6.1%
Print	7.0%	6.6%
Radio	11.1%	8.4%
TV	61.8%	10.5%

Language Preference	% of calls	Sales Rate
Spanish	85.1%	9.0%
English	14.9%	5.9%

product was the dominant item sold. Auto tends to be the entry product for most new entrants to the insurance category.

The multi-medium effort provided significant "stick-tion" with the Hispanic consumer. This is demonstrated by the sales rate of 4.1% seven plus months after the launch of each marketing effort. The campaign delivered key insights on medium and language preferences (Figure 5.11). More than 60% reported that TV advertisements were the key reason for making the call to Allstate. Second was mail, primarily ADVO. Subsequent research revealed that TV created a high state of "awareness" and "consideration", but mail items, tangible by nature, moved many consumers into the "shopping and quoting" stage (see Marketing Funnel, Figure 5.12). A robust bilingual agency channel quickly solidified relationships leading to strong sales performance. More than 85% of the callers conducted their conversations in Spanish, with the balance, 14.1%, conducted in English. The Spanish preferred consumer had a sales closure rate nearly twice that of the English preferred consumer, 9.0% versus 5.9%. All messaging, MarCom, was delivered to the market in Spanish.

Figure 5.12

Marketing funnel and levers

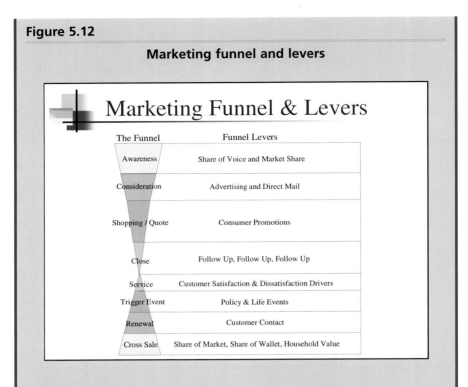

Marketing Funnel & Levers

The Funnel	Funnel Levers
Awareness	Share of Voice and Market Share
Consideration	Advertising and Direct Mail
Shopping / Quote	Consumer Promotions
Close	Follow Up, Follow Up, Follow Up
Service	Customer Satisfaction & Dissatisfaction Drivers
Trigger Event	Policy & Life Events
Renewal	Customer Contact
Cross Sale	Share of Market, Share of Wallet, Household Value

Effect of the Campaign:

Effects of the Allstate 800# campaign can be seen in the section above as realized during its ongoing implementation. In summary, The 800 Spanish line (Accessibility) strategy delivered extraordinary results. By leveraging insights gained, future campaigns continued to deliver high performance (high sales rates) for many years.

References

1 U.S. Department of Homeland Security, *Yearbook of Immigration Statistics, 2002*. U.S. Government Printing Office: Washington, D.C., 2003, page 6.
2 Wheatley, Margaret J. *Leadership and the new science*. San Francisco: Berrett-Koehler Publishers, 2nd ed., 1999, page 78.
3 http://www.usfca.edu/usfnews/03.02.04/fp2.html
4 A colloquial way of referring to the United States, that is, "the other side."
5 Lee, Yueh-Ting, Clark R. Mccauley, and Juris G. Draguns, eds. *Personality and person perception across cultures*. Mahwah, NJ: Lawrence Erlbaum Associates, 1999.

6 Ibidem

7 Triandis, Harry C. *Individualism & collectivism.* Boulder, CO: Westview Press, 1995.

8 Berry, John W. "Acculturative Stress." *Readings in ethnic psychology.* Pamela Balls Organista, Kevin M. Chun, and Gerardo Marín, eds. New York: Ruthledge, 1998. 117–122.

9 Ibidem

10 http://www.hispanicprwire.com/news_in.php?id=2292&cha+8

11 http://www.hwil.org/news/001269.shtml

12 Homel, Peter, Michael Palij, and Doris Aaronson, eds. *Childhood bilingualism: Aspects of linguistic, cognitive, and social development.* Hillsdale, NJ: Lawrence Erlbaum Associates, 1987.

13 Ibidem

14 Huntington, Samuel P. *Who are we: The challenges to America's national identity.* New York: Simon and Schuster, 2004.

15 Pollock, David C. and Ruth E. Van Reken. *Third culture kids: the experience of growing up among worlds.* London: Nicolas Brealey Publishing, 2001.

16 Keefe, Susan E. and Amado M. Padilla. *Chicano Ethnicity*, 1st ed. Albuquerque: University of New Mexico, 1987.

17 Schultz, Don E., Heidi F. Schultz. *IMC, the next generation: Five steps for delivering value and measuring financial returns.* New York: McGraw-Hill, 2004.

18 *Acculturation: Advances in theory, measurement, and applied research.* Edited by Kevin M. Chun, Pamela Balls Organista, and Gerardo Marín, 1st ed. Decade of behavior. Washington, DC: American Psychological Association, 2003.

19 Information provided to the authors by La Agencia de Orcí & Asociados.

20 Synovate. *2004 US Hispanic Market Report.* Miami, FL: Synovate, 2004.

21 Greenberg, Bradley S. and Jeffrey E. Brand. "10 minorities and the mass media: 1970s to 1990s." *Media Effects Advances in Theory and Research.* Bryant, Jennings and Dolf Zillmann, eds. Hillsdale, NJ: Lawrence Erlbaum Associates, 1994. 273–309.

22 Also called the Pygmalion effect.

23 Hilton, James L. and William Von Hippel. "Stereotypes." *Annual Review of Psychology*, 47, 1996: 237–271.

24 Yueh-Ting Lee, Lee J. Jussim, and Clark R Mccauley, eds. *Toward appreciating Group Differences.* Washington, DC: American Psychological Association, 1995, 3.

25 J.W. Berry. "A psychology of immigration," *Journal of social issues* 57.3, 2001.

Cultural Dimensions and Archetypes

6

Introduction

After you have explored the Hispanic market in many of its defining characteristics, this chapter's goal is to provide stimulating ideas for insightful and effective marketing and communication strategies. This chapter concentrates on the subjective aspects of culture that marketing professionals are less likely to be familiar with. These subjective aspects are those that lie under the tip of the iceberg, and make up some of the strongest cultural influences on the Hispanic target. This is an exploration into the mind of the Hispanic consumer with the aim to establish successful relationships.

Subjectivity is at the center of marketing, and cultural subjectivity is at the core of cross-cultural marketing. Hispanic cultural subjectivity defines perceptions, beliefs, and actions. Subjectivity is shaped by the culture that ancestors have passed on, by common experiences in countries of origin and communities, and by the amalgamation of original and adoptive cultures. Cultural dimensions and stereotypes are discussed here and elaborated to inspire marketers to open avenues into the Hispanic mind for successful cross-cultural marketing communications.

Going Beyond the Surface to Beat the Competition

Successful positioning is the element that makes or breaks an otherwise good product.[1] Marketing experts and managers need it. Advertising planners and creatives search for it. Consumers relate to it. It is a key element of differentiation that everyone in the marketing and advertising industry wants to arrive at. Winners and losers are differentiated by how a product, service, or idea connects with consumers. Yet, comprehending the subjective cultural domain where the key to successful positioning lies is one of the most elusive, most challenging, and most often missed arenas of the U.S. Hispanic market. This chapter intends to offer guidance to marketers on how to approach this challenge.

Successful Positioning

Positioning is generally considered a concept that elicits desired responses from customers.

> "Product positioning refers to the way the customer views a product or service in relation to all other products or services that would be considered as satisfying the purchase desire or need. The product or service is positioned to develop a certain image among potential buyers in relationship to other products or substitute products.[2]

Positioning is the communication garment that dresses the product or service to appeal to the consumer. Over the years multiple companies and authors have described positioning in different ways. Most of them seem to converge on the idea that positioning in advertising is a symbolic attempt at characterizing a product or service in a way that it connects with potential users. The most basic form of positioning consists of specifying a benefit and reasons that support that benefit. Currently in an environment in which multiple products within a category are almost identical the benefit is usually an emotional benefit to assist in differentiating the product.

This crafting of positioning is the crucial point at which knowing about the culture allows the marketer to establish an emotional connection with the consumer. This is the moment in the elaboration of the marketing communication strategy when going beyond psychological and sociological considerations becomes an imperative. As discussed in Chapter 1, this is because, when marketing across cultures, you need to have cultural understanding to make sense to the consumer.

Since U.S. Hispanic consumers bring the emotional connections from their countries of origin combined with the pull of the U.S. mainstream culture, they present U.S. marketers with the challenge of forging these dual influences in positioning. For example, The San Jose Group developed a new positioning of Ameritech's Voicemail 98 message retrieval service to increase its cultural appeal to Hispanic consumers. Ameritech had not achieved anticipated success with their

Hispanic bilingual direct mail materials, which were developed from their English-language campaign. The San Jose Group chose a well-known cultural symbol for Hispanics, the parrot, and used the associated phrase "Now you can talk more than a parrot" in a humorous campaign. They created the direct mail campaign to appeal to the Hispanic emotional need to stay connected, in this case to talk uninterruptedly with loved ones and not lose any other call even if they were still chatting. The San Jose Group's positioning for this campaign supported Ameritech in achieving their sales goals, and connected the Hispanic market with a relevant service (see The San Jose Group Ameritech Voicemail Case Study at the end of this chapter).

Cultural Dimensions and Archetypes as Means to Needed Differentiation in the Marketplace

There are values and patterns of thought that are transmitted from generation to generation within cultures. These patterned ways of thinking and believing can be used as anchors in the communication process with consumers that come from a different cultural perspective, Hispanic in this particular case. In any successful sales encounter we look for aspects in the prospect's life that will help us make a better connection. In the cross-cultural case the parallel is encountering cultural patterns that will allow the marketer to demonstrate that his or her product has emotional affinity with the Hispanic consumer.

The most typical and overused cultural dimension employed to market to U.S. Hispanics is that of individualism vs. collectivism. For a long time most ads directed to Hispanic consumers showed or communicated in different forms that Hispanics are family and friends oriented. In its most basic form this is one of the most primitive dimensions in which Hispanics rate very high on the collectivism end of the continuum. And it makes definite sense that Hispanic audiences will react more favorably to portrayals of family and friends than to more individualistic portrayals. Clearly, overusing one of these dimensions can lead to its wearing out and becoming less relevant and effective.

This chapter delves into these and other less known and used dimensions. Though some may argue that individualism and collectivism are ends of one continuum, it can also be said that they can represent two different dimensions. It may be counterintuitive, but it is possible to think of cultures that can be both individualistic and collectivistic to different degrees, as masculinity and femininity are not extremes of one dimension but separate dimensions on which individuals can vary. There will be further elaboration on these issues later.

Archetypes, in many cases, are ranges of dimensions that character-ize a culture. Thus, for example, on the individualism and collectivism dimensions, the high end on one and the low end on the other continua could be characterized as an orientation to friends and families. Figure 6.1 illustrates the quadrant in which the family and friends orientation resides.

This orientation to friends and family represents a cultural arche-type because this tendency acts as a mold for behaving, thinking, and feeling within a culture. These molds we call archetypes shape the way in which members of a culture look at the world. Archetypes can be said to represent syndromes of cultural thought and action.

Marketers who are able to identify important cultural dimensions and archetypes may claim important positions in the minds of mem-bers of a target culture. This is particularly true if these dimensions and archetypes have not been overused.

Bromley Communications was challenged with the creation of Hispanic advertising for BURGER KING® to support the overall brand positioning of their 2004 HAVE IT YOUR WAY® campaign. This campaign focused on individualization of the ANGUS STEAK BURGER to the consumer's personal liking, an emphasis not commonly associated with the more collectivistic Hispanic market. Through research, Bromley found that Hispanic consumers' awareness of the ANGUS STEAK BURGER campaign was lower than the main-stream market, and that their comfort level asking for individual

Figure 6.1

Individualism and collectivism dimensions

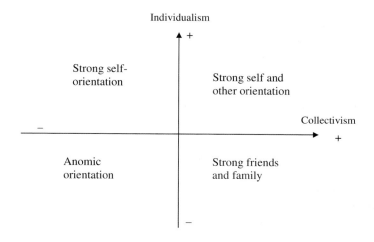

preferences in the predominantly English speaking restaurants was low. Bromley also recognized that within the collectivistic culture, there were numerous examples of self-expression tendencies among Hispanics, for example, in the arts. Bromley Communications created television executions to establish personalization and self-expression with Hispanics in everyday communication style. With this culturally tuned advertising, BURGER KING® exceeded Angus Steak Burger volume forecast sales projections for the Hispanic market by 20 percent (see Bromley Burger King Case Study at the end of this chapter).

Establishing a Cultural-Emotional Link with Consumers

Consider that historically Hispanics have been taught that loyalty to others in power positions has survival and advancement value. The assertion of power in Hispanic cultures traditionally has been a strong determinant of the social order. If sales personnel understand this notion of loyalty to persons in power positions their first chore is to establish themselves as authorities in their subject matter. The sale will be relatively easy once authority has been established.

This example shows the fundamental link between archetype use and connecting with consumers of different cultures. This process will become clearer as more examples are presented. This process is similar to that which lovers use to endear themselves to one another. The dedicated suitor will learn about what makes his or her beloved smile, cry, and enjoy, and then he or she will attempt to cast messages in ways that are relevant to his or her partner.

Enamoring in the marketing context, instead of being from one person to another, is the process of endearing members of a culture to a brand. Moreover, in many ways this emotional linking builds a relational experience that will not end with a sales transaction. As a result of establishing a strong relationship with the consumer, the marketer should aim at having it continue over time.[3] One of the most typical errors marketers make when marketing to Hispanic consumers is to assume that Hispanics share the same world view as they themselves or other consumers have. If this book achieves the aim of communicating to marketers and advertisers that the Hispanic consumer requires modifying and changing assumptions it will have succeeded in its mission.

Building relationships over time are emphasized in different ways in two case studies from earlier chapters (K. Fernandez McCormick's Case Study at the end of Chapter 5 and Enlace Macy's West Case Study at the end of Chapter 3). In the first case study, K. Fernandez and Associates created a California campaign to build on the Mexican equity of McCormick's mayonnaise in Mexico. The case study plays on the role of the woman in Mexico of pleasing her family with the food she puts on the table, and the taste of lime that characterizes the product, a taste of great importance in the Mexican culture. Macy's creates a store atmosphere and connects with cultural icons in the U.S. Hispanic culture to build on the history of personal comfort in Mexico, and the Hispanic leaders who now stand for their U.S. Mexican culture.

Cultural Dimensions

This section explains dimensions of culture that form the bases of archetypes. These dimensions deal with use of time, perceptions of leadership, salience of groups, gender, and attribution of causality. As we saw earlier, the intersection of dimensions provides the nesting place for archetypes to take root.

Monochronism and Polychronism

Edward T. Hall, in his multiple works dealing with time and cross-cultural communication, has identified at least two ways in which humans handle time. These two dimensions are polychronism and monochronism.[4] In his view these two dimensions differentiate well between cultures. Polychronic cultures are those in which individuals handle multiple events at one time, and monochronic cultures are those in which people manage time linearly, one thing at a time.

Cultural Perceptions of Time

Space and time are the most basic dimensions of knowledge.[5] Our knowledge is framed in them in an almost imperceptible way. We order things chronologically and spatially to compare, contrast, and order our worldly experience. Interestingly, it appears that the way in which humans handle time and space is influenced by culture.

If you have ever experienced travel in Latin American countries, you may recall seeing that clerks in stores talk to several customers at the same time. Similarly, hotel receptionists talk to different guests simultaneously and it seems natural. They seem to multitask quite seamlessly. In Western countries, particularly the United States and Northern Europe, people handle time more linearly; they do one thing at a time. Doing multiple activities simultaneously is confusing to monochronic people, and often considered impolite.

Think for a moment about a scene in which you have a mono-chronic and a polychronic person trying to establish common ground. You could anticipate that the monochronic person will become increasingly impatient with the polychronic individual, and conversely that the polychronic person will become bored with his or her counterpart.

Customer Care and Product Usage

These dimensions have interesting and subtle implications for marketing. First, they affect customer care in a very direct way. Customer care representatives need to understand the cultural perspective customers are coming from. Further, when considering product usage polychronic consumers are more likely to use products with less attachment to schedules and timeframes. Thus, product consumption occasions may need to be addressed differently when dealing with Hispanic consumers. Understanding this cultural pattern can be illuminating when attempting to understand life rhythms, work habits, product usage, and communication behaviors.

Media Habits

Given these considerations, a media planner could conclude that he or she should schedule complementary media channels for message distribution at atypical times. If, due to polychronism, Hispanics are more likely to watch television while reading the newspaper, then media buyers can advantageously place advertisements in both media at the same time to complement each other.

What these dimensions do is provide conceptual guidance. For most specific marketing problems, the marketer will understand that Hispanics are more likely to be polychronic, but the answer as to which media to schedule simultaneously, or specifics about product consumption will need to be addressed via primary research.

Monomorphic and Polymorphic Leadership

Leadership styles characterize different types of societies.[6] Societies that are more traditional have been found to have a higher prevalence of leaders that exert leadership in multiple areas. More Westernized or so-called "modern" societies exhibit a higher concentration of specialized leadership. The realtor is a realtor and the insurance salesperson is an insurance salesperson in a more differentiated society.

The meaning of diverging leadership styles and approaches in this context is that Hispanics tend to be more polymorphic than monomorphic. This phenomenon manifests itself in multiple forms:

- The Hispanic man that purchases a car from a car salesperson who happens to be particularly attentive and personable starts depending on this salesperson for advice in other areas. This customer may eventually approach the car salesperson for immigration information or for counsel on where to send children to school.

- The Hispanic woman who purchases a home from a competent realtor eventually depends on the realtor for advice on marriage issues and even on what life insurance to purchase for her husband.

- Hispanic students become dependent on the teacher's advice for many aspects of life outside school.

Although these behaviors are not unique to Hispanics, they are more prevalent among Hispanics than they are among non-Hispanics in the United States. These tendencies have important implications for marketing communication.

Polymorphic leadership shapes the ways in which brands diffuse and grow through Hispanic interpersonal networks. Once these polymorphic leaders start believing in a particular product, brand, or idea, they spread the word through their wide spectrum of influence. As Hispanics immigrate to the United States they depend on these types of leaders to learn about, for example, Folgers, Pepto Bismol, Charmin, Kix, Huggies, and other brands that are popular in the community. Refer to the Bromley Communications Charmin Case Study at the end of Chapter 2 for their care in establishing brand connection, and to the Español Countrywide Case Study at the end of Chapter 5 for leadership with the whole mortgage process and their understanding of the leadership of the real estate agent.

Influencing Hispanic leaders can be even more powerful among Hispanics than among non-Hispanics. However, this leadership is not by ascription. That is, someone who has a bureaucratic position does not necessarily have the people influence that a natural leader has. This is the point at which sociometric research can be very useful. Understanding who talks to whom about what becomes crucial in knowing who to influence in the first place. These dimensions provide conceptual guidance but they are not a substitute for specific research designed to answer tactical questions.

Individualism and Collectivism

These are the two most discussed dimensions when addressing the U.S. Hispanic market. Most marketers these days have heard that Hispanics are group or collectivity oriented.

It is not necessarily true that Hispanics are collectivistic by nature or that U.S. non-Hispanics are fundamentally individualistic. Folkways and human organization can largely explain these orientations. In most Hispanic societies, the interdependence of group or family members is basic for survival. In societies where there are no reliable institutions for its members' security one would expect that a system of social obligations would thrive.

Hispanic parents expect that their children and grandchildren will help support them in their old age. That is why planning for retirement is relatively alien to Hispanics. In addition, group interdependence helps achieve economic goals. For example, Hispanics are known for purchasing homes and cars collectively. Different families pool their resources and purchase a home; then, when they have enough additional resources they buy the second home, and so on, until all families have one. Hispanics use similar strategies for the purchase of other high-ticket items.

Social institutions like Social Security and financial credit substitute for group interdependence among non-Hispanics in the United States. These functions in our society did not originate with an individualistic orientation. They evolved as their culture created institutions on which people could rely as opposed to relying on others. Hispanics are likely to undergo a similar process over time as they are exposed to and come to trust social service type institutions.

The present state of the U.S. Hispanic market is that it preserves collectivistic values that are emotionally and functionally important to them. Still, in the clash of Hispanic and the non-Hispanic overall culture, Hispanic collectivistic values may prevent the adoption of functional practices prevalent in the overall U.S. society, like planning for retirement and utilizing credit for purchasing large ticket items.

In this context, the marketer has to deal with important disjunctives. He or she can try to persuade Hispanics that there are better ways to achieve their goals, or the marketer can adapt products or services to match Hispanic cultural patterns. The cost is high either way. The conclusion is not obvious, however, because the marketer has to make an evaluation of where trends will go. If trends veer toward less dependence on social institutions,[7] then adapting products and services to meet that structure will do better. If, on the other hand, Hispanics were likely to evolve toward more individualistic perspectives, then the marketer would be better off to accelerate the pace at which Hispanics adapt to U.S. society through consumer education. Allstate has a clear understanding of the importance of educating the Hispanic consumer on the new individualistic concept of insurance based on their extensive research and their history with the Hispanic market (see the Allstate Case Study at the end of Chapter 5).

The collectivist perspective of Hispanics makes a difference in other contexts. These contexts may include the simple representation of groups in tactical executions, or the more subtle inclusion of collectivist ideals in the values of the communication campaign. Considering the role of this dimension in strategy generation and execution can be of high importance.

Androgyny

The dimensions of femininity and masculinity characterize androgyny. These can be considered separate dimensions, as someone could exhibit different degrees of masculinity and femininity. The essential characteristic of androgyny is precisely the presence of relatively strong masculine and feminine traits simultaneously.[8]

Although this is not a well-explored or studied area, based on many years of market research and observation of the culture, the authors of this book hypothesize that Hispanic men and women are more androgynous than their non-Hispanic counterparts are. Anglo Saxons tend to have more defined gender-based behaviors. Hispanics, perhaps because of the syndromes of machismo and marianismo, tend to exhibit higher levels of both gender behaviors.

The typical macho states that he does not cry, does not care about womanly things, and so on. Still his music is heavily loaded with laments and crying for the lost love. The macho becomes highly emotional at the smallest provocation. Thus, this individual is highly masculine, but also highly feminine at the same time.

The typical Hispanic woman suffers, cries, lives for her children, and laments her unfortunate existence. At the same time, this woman runs the home with an iron arm. She orders the husband around; she confronts anyone who threatens the wellbeing of her family. She becomes a tough lion when put in a corner. She is very "macha."[9]

This orientation toward androgyny makes the typical marketing target less obvious in the Hispanic market than the 18 to 49 female head of household that the general market typically addresses. Many marketers have made the mistake of assuming that the decision maker for household items in the Hispanic home is the woman. Due to androgynous tendencies, the Hispanic male is many times involved in deciding what to buy for the home.

This is also due, in part, to the fact that Hispanic men are more likely to immigrate first to the United States and then bring their women after a period of time. Thus men have to learn about brands and products in the absence of women. Men influence the brand purchased for the home in many product categories. Moreover, these

categories may be somewhat unexpected because they include deter-
gents, toothpaste, food, and even shampoo.

Cultural Attributions

Humans tend to point to the causes of behavior depending on cultural tendencies derived from patterns of thinking that develop over
time. For example, there are cultures that emphasize that the individual is responsible for his or her destiny. Other cultures emphasize that
the group and society are responsible for the behavior of the individual. Attributions,[10] then, are made on two dimensions; one is internal
cause attribution and the other is external cause attribution.

Noteworthy cultural differences in attribution exist in the United
States between Hispanics and non-Hispanics. Hispanics are more
likely to point to others as the causes of behavior. The reason someone
succeeds or fails is because someone helped or someone placed obstacles in the way. U.S. non-Hispanic cultures are more likely to point to
their successes and failures as their own responsibility. Self-reliance
indeed is a highly prized value stemming from internal cause
attribution.

Making external attributions has implications for Hispanic marketing in different ways. For one thing, word-of-mouth and grass roots
marketing is more effective because the reasons for using products or
endorsing ideas originate from the outside, from the social group.
What others say or do is more influential among Hispanics, a product
used by many is more appealing than a product used by a select few.
In response to the question, "why do you use Colgate toothpaste," the
typical response is "because everyone uses it." Among non-Hispanics
it is more common to hear something like "I use it because it leaves my
teeth feeling cleaner." In the Hispanic case it is the decision of the
group that gives impulse to the behavior. In the other case it is the
internal decision-making process that mobilizes the behavior.

Marketers who understand this differentiation will emphasize an
external locus of influence when communicating with Hispanic consumers. The Hispanic target aspires to conform and be like others. As
David Riesman indicated in his classic book, *The Lonely Crowd*,[11]
societies can be differentiated by the orientation of people. Hispanics
are more "other oriented" and non-Hispanic Anglo Saxons are more
"inner oriented."

It should be obvious that collectivism, as discussed earlier, is related
to this "other orientation." Using a metaphor, Hispanics seem to
behave like the tentacles of an octopus, inextricably linked to each

other. U.S. non-Hispanics, metaphorically, behave more like cats by asserting their individuality.

Attribution in this context is the way in which humans explain their behavior. If Hispanics tend toward external explanations, then advertising and communications need to be informed by this perspective. A Hispanic consumer is more likely to buy a Chevy if many of the people in his or her social circle own one. A non-Hispanic Anglo is more likely to buy a Porsche if he or she has made the decision to stand out from the crowd. These are two very different perspectives. Social pressure in marketing to Hispanics can be a more powerful tool than when marketing to others.

MendozaDillon, a Hispanic Advertising Agency, exemplified a high level of awareness of the importance of the social influence of attribution in their campaign for Galderma Laboratories' Tri-Luma® Cream. This health product is effective in treating melasma, blotchy discolorations on the face and arms due to hormone changes from pregnancy, use of oral contraceptives, or hormone replacement therapy. MendozaDillon created a multipronged socially-oriented education initiative in which they provided in-language materials and face-to-face information on melasma and their product to both Hispanic females and to health care providers in the Chicago area. These included community seminars, health care fairs, as well as materials for the offices and clinics that service Hispanic women. TV, print, and radio advertising were used to promote Hispanic community and health care events. In essence, MendozaDillon's campaign included a socially oriented educational, large-scale community initiative to the benefits of Tri-Luma® Cream and the Hispanic market affected by this health problem (see the MendozaDillon Galderma Case Study at the end of this chapter).

Cultural Archetypes

At the start of this discussion, we saw that archetypes are portions or intersections of dimensions that characterize a culture. Archetypes in this context relate to those cultural beliefs and molds that guide behavior within a culture. Different assumptions guide different aspects of life and many times these are unconscious but nonetheless powerful.

An extreme example of an archetype is the attraction that humans have for sweets. Sweet foods are rich sources of instant energy. Our ancestors were constantly deprived of high-energy foods so when they found them they ate them right away. These had high survival value.

In the United States, however, there is an overabundance of food and eating sweets nowadays becomes dysfunctional as they contribute to obesity and other health problems. Other examples are sweet drinks for Hispanic women in particular. Marbo was highly aware of this craving for sweet drinks among Hispanic adults and children in their creation and marketing of Tampico (see the Marbo Tampico Case Study at the end of Chapter 2).

Many cultural patterns behave in similar ways. They are part of people's cravings, drives, and attractions but it is not clear why they are so to the individual; they derive from long-term processes of cultural adaptation to the environment. Archetypes are driving forces that come from inside the culture. Stereotypes, however, are generalizations based on insufficient data that outsiders impose on a group of people to characterize them. It is critical for marketers to distinguish between the two, to develop powerful positioning and advertising based on the former, and to avoid deadly errors resulting from the latter.

The prototype is an abstraction of a class of objects to characterize them based on their key elements. However, this chapter is mostly concerned with archetypes as they are likely to influence consumer behavior in ways that are not obvious to the casual observer and not even evident to the members of the culture under consideration.

Identifying Archetypes

The identification of cultural archetypes can be achieved by engaging in one or both of the approaches detailed next. Popular culture and literature can provide a great number of insights into the folkways of Hispanics that can allow for better communication and marketing. In-depth interviewing and ethnography are other ways in which the marketer can identify patterns of culture that otherwise could not be determined by more casual observations.

Popular Culture and Literature

Listening to the music, observing rituals, and reading literature generated within the culture constitute a rich source for the identification of archetypes. For example, understanding the celebratory meaning of death in some pre-Hispanic cultures can be gleaned from looking at what happens in a cemetery on the day of the dead.[12] Seeing people around graves consuming food and drinking alcoholic beverages in celebration of the person lying in the grave provides a deep perspective on the meaning of death for Mexicans. At the same time, reading Octavio Paz's *Labyrinth of Solitude*[13] provides a rich perspective on how members of the Mexican heritage think and feel about death.

A cultural perspective that challenges death and in many ways makes light of it can be a challenge for insurance companies and healthcare providers. Only understanding this archetype, a syndrome of beliefs about death, can help communicate effectively with Hispanics of Mexican backgrounds. Physicians understanding of these tendencies would then be able to design their messages in terms that are more likely to touch the emotional cords of the patient; for example, "don't take the medicine just to help yourself but to protect your children." Compliance with doctors' instructions tends to be very low among Hispanics and this may be one of the main explanations for that lack of obedience.

In-Depth Interviewing and Ethnography

On many occasions, cultural archetypes can be derived from in-depth questioning of individuals or groups. In addition, insights about cultural archetypes can be derived from ethnographic interviews and observations. Ethnographic interviews and observations in marketing are short episodes of talking with and observing the behaviors of consumers in their own environments. An example that became a major cultural insight for a manufacturer of diapers was obtained from a laddering exercise conducted in focus groups.

The objective was to understand how to position diapers among Hispanic mothers. The laddering exercise took the form of repeated "why" questions to attempt to reach an emotional element that could differentiate a brand of diapers from another. Hispanic mothers in this context talked about diapers in this approximate sequence:

Diapers keep my child dry and without rashes
(Why is that important?)
Because as a mother I want them to be comfortable
(Why is it important to you that they are comfortable? (even if this question sounds strange and with an obvious answer))
Well, because my children are the most important things in my life
(Why are they the most important things in your life?)
Mhm . . . because they represent my future . . . a continuation of me
(Why is that important?)
Because I see myself as a line of people coming from my ancestors and extending to my children

> *(Why, then, is it important to keep them dry and without rashes,*
> *when thinking about their being your extension to the future?)*
>
> *By keeping them dry and without rashes I am giving them the*
> *right start in taking the first steps toward their future*

The archetypal thinking found was a belief in generations as temporal extensions and continuity. The marketing finding was that helping the mother give the right start to the child would be highly motivational. The campaign based on this finding was very successful.

The rest of this chapter will address several areas of archetypes that can be important when marketing to the Hispanic market. These are intended as thought and research provoking avenues.

Selected Archetypes That Make a Marketing Communication Difference in the Hispanic Market

Money

Although money and wealth are important to members of most cultures, how these are conceptualized can vary in important ways. In conjunction with the cultural pattern of machismo, having money among many Hispanics is seen with defiance. As the masses of Hispanics, particularly mestizos[14] and Native Americans (Indians), have endured slavery and endemic poverty over the past 500 years, the meaning of wealth typically has been associated with the experience of powerful others, not oneself.

Latin American popular culture is filled with examples of "being poor but proud" type statements. These are most common in the lyrics of music. Being poor is seen as a better alternative to being wealthy but corrupt, as if both were natural opposites. One accepts suffering and deprivation as one's lot in life. Thus, money has less of a positive connotation. Enjoying life, on the other hand, has a very strong positive tone. Multiple manifestations in literature, music, drama, and film have idealized this paradox. Enjoy the moment because the future is elusive, and money does not matter as long as you are happy!

Given this archetype, it is difficult to sell financial services with the sole main argument that the customer will make more money. The positioning in this market, then, has to emphasize other aspects of finances that make enjoyment of life more possible and fuller.

Related to this issue are the concepts of debt and mortgage. Interestingly, given eight centuries of Arab domination of Spain,[15] the idea of lending with interest permeated the culture with the belief that lenders are evil. This explains why borrowing money in most of Latin America is something you do when there is no other choice. In the United States, borrowing money is a way of life. Reconciling these two perspectives is a major subject in need of much re-education.

Lenders advertise in Spanish that they have low interest mortgages without realizing that they are committing a double mistake. First, emphasizing the interest part has a negative connotation. Second, the term mortgage in Spanish is *hipoteca*. In Latin America, you rely on a *hipoteca* only when you are in real trouble.

Placing a *hipoteca* on your home for Hispanics means you are endangering the future of your family. In contrast, a mortgage in the non-Hispanic United States is a common and accepted thing; that is, having a mortgage is simply enjoying the opportunity to have a home. However, when lenders use the term *hipoteca* to Hispanics, they are referring to an unpleasant association. Things would be so much easier if translations were just so simple!

Happiness, Life, Religion, and Death

Being alive represents happiness among Hispanics, and is not to be taken for granted. That is why enjoying every day is important, and that is also why delay of gratification is weak vs. immediate pleasure. This archetype comes from lessons learned over the many years of subjugation first in the Native American kingdoms that dominated Latin America, and later with the foreign dominance, destruction, and enslavement of the peoples of the continent.

The Roots of Fatalism

Since life is ephemeral and unpredictable, a deep sense of fatalism is strongly rooted in many of the Native American and Mestizo groups of Latin America. Although immigration to the United States is paired with the ambition to leave behind the uncertainty that leads to fatalism, this philosophy of life persists for a long time in the United States as well. It is linked with a worldview pervaded by the unpredictability of life and the events surrounding it. Saving for tomorrow is less important than throwing a great *quinceañera*[16] party today.

Mañana

Saving and many other "preventive" types of products and behaviors fall in this domain. If activities don't provide some type of immediate gratification then the behavior is less appealing. Thus, the joy of saving for one's kids must be positioned within this context. The typical *mañana* does have an important element of truth. *Mañana* is safe because by tomorrow many things will have happened; thus enjoy today and let us worry about tomorrow when it comes.

Celebration of Life

Happiness, life, and death are related as contrasts and different faces of the same coin. A successful insight that helped a major coffee brand took advantage of in-depth Hispanic consumer understanding some time ago. The brand, in its overall positioning, owned the morning occasion of coffee drinking. To learn about how to connect with the Hispanic market this brand conducted an in-depth study of Hispanic beliefs, not about coffee, but about the morning.

Repeated in-depth probing of respondents from most countries of origin told the same story time and time again. They explained that the morning is a time for celebration, because when you open your eyes you know you're still alive, and being alive is an occasion for celebration. You celebrate being alive in the morning because at night, when you go to sleep you do not know if you will be alive in the morning. In part due to Catholic tradition, a person is supposed to pray before going to bed so that God does not take the soul away during sleep. Being spared by God and awakening in the morning is a joyful moment in the day. The coffee brand enthusiastically embraced the discovery of this archetype and positioned its brand as the coffee brand that helps Hispanic consumers celebrate the morning. That campaign evolved into a great success.

Life Is a Valley of Tears

From ancient Native American traditions and the life of misery under the conquest that the people of the Americas have had to endure, there has emerged a unique view of life. This perspective presents life on earth as being less valuable than the next life. Life in this world is many times referred to as a valley of tears—*un valle de lágrimas*. This contributes to living for today as opposed to tomorrow and explains why death is celebrated. In the collective mind of the culture death has the redeeming qualities of being the end of suffering. In addition, death has the promise of a better life. Not that enjoying life now is unimportant, but death and destiny are seen as being closer to life itself than U.S. non-Hispanics perceive it. Marketing in this context presents special challenges for products such as life insurance. Obtaining consumer insights that will allow the circumvention of these beliefs and make the product meaningful is of the highest relevance.

Guilt vs. Shame

Catholicism has strongly imparted a sense of existential guilt among Hispanics. From the original sin to the notion that there is something wrong with the individual who transgresses, Hispanics live with a constant need to atone. Statements like *me remuerde la conciencia* (my conscience bothers me) and continual references to *culpa* (guilt) are the staple of popular culture in telenovelas (Spanish-language soap operas). Ruth Benedict[17] in her differentiation between Western and Eastern civilization argues that the West is more characterized by guilt, an internal driver that attributes responsibility to the individual. She states that Eastern cultures like the Japanese are shame cultures where the group is responsible for social behavior, not the individual.

U.S. Hispanics represent an extreme in the guilt continuum. Marketers who understand this can position brands and products in ways that guilt reduction occurs. Hispanic mothers are in constant search for ways to reduce guilt for not doing more for their husbands and children. Helping the consumer alleviate guilt can be beneficial to both the consumer and the marketer by establishing a symbiotic relationship.

Parent-Child Relationships

In Hispanic families, children are highly prized and considered to be a blessing from God. Hispanics tend to have large families, which are a matter of pride to parents, and a great deal of attention is provided to their care, upbringing, education, and well-being. Children are an integral part of the family as a group, thus all the family spends much of their time together: They shop together, play together on Sundays in the park, eat together, and have strong bonds with larger groups of family and friends. Extended family members often contribute to childrearing, particularly grandmothers and aunts who actively help mothers caring for their large numbers of children.

There are specific roles in the family that guide these interrelationships. The mother has primary responsibilities for tending to the children making sure that they are healthy, nicely dressed in clean and as attractive clothes as the family can afford, and that they eat healthy and tasty foods. Mothers are very affectionate with their children and want to please them. They find reconfirmation in their identity as a mother when their children love the things they provide for them. Conversely, mothers tend to feel enormous guilt when they can't give their children the things they want.

The father is also dedicated to his children but his role tends to be more along the traditional male norm of working for their economic well-being. However, he is seen as the head of the family so that he has the final say in major decisions regarding his children. He may also become involved when there are more serious discipline problems with children because fathers generally insist on respect, although the mother is almost always a part of these matters. In cases where fathers may be more strict and authoritarian, "The mother often acts as mediator between an authoritarian father and the children."[18]

Hispanic fathers are generally very loving and affectionate with their children. They revere their daughters, hug and caress them, and are typically easy touches for their wants. They also tend to be somewhat protective of their daughters, particularly as they enter adolescence and attract young men. Fathers also highly value their sons, who are seen as providing for the future of the family. Hispanic *papa's* share their love of sports with their sons, and can be seen playing soccer in the park or watching sports on TV with them. As the key disciplinarians they demand that their children show respect to them as the head of the family and to their elders. As the sons grow older, they may be expected to work, often in the same profession as their fathers, to help pay for the expenses of the family.

Children are very close to their mothers and admire their devotion and sacrifice for the happiness of their sons and daughters. The children are influential in choices their mothers make, a fact that can be observed in supermarkets where Hispanic children are present on family shopping expeditions. This is an important fact for Hispanic marketers to realize. It's also important for marketers to recognize that mothers often get caught in dilemmas; they want to satisfy both the demands of their children as well as provide food and services that are good for their health.

Even though children have the love and attention of their mothers and the dedication of their fathers to provide for their needs, they also have their own responsibilities and behavioral norms. They are socialized to be loving, sociable, and respectful of others in the family. Older siblings are expected to help out with younger family members. Often, in terms of the household, girls are asked to help their mothers with cooking, taking care of younger children, and carrying out other household chores. However, these chores, fulfilled in the company of mothers or grandmothers, are often remembered as happy times in the lives of these young women. The California Milk Advisory Board Campaign, *Generations*, developed in 1997 by Anita Santiago Advertising, the Board's Hispanic advertising agency, highlights the relationship between daughters and their mothers and grandmothers in cooking together with milk. This image portrays the relationship between women in the family—mothers, grandmothers in traditional household chores.[19]

Boys, in contrast, tend to be catered to more in the family than girls, continuing in some ways the patriarchal structure and machismo of their Hispanic heritage. They may work with their father on weekends in gardening or construction or have responsibilities consistent with those of other male family members.

There are some aspects of child-rearing that receive less emphasis in Hispanic vs. non-Hispanic families such as toilet training and weaning from nursing from the breast or the bottle milk. These behaviors are seen as part of nature and being a child, which will end according to nature's own timing. Indeed, it is not unusual to see Hispanic children drinking from their bottles or sucking on pacifiers at three or four years of age.

Hispanic parents pay strong attention to symbolic religious and coming of age ceremonies for their children. Even for Hispanics who may struggle economically, it is considered extremely important to have celebrations for baptisms, first communions, coming of age *quinceañeras*, the 15-year-old coming-of-age parties for their daughters, and weddings. After the religious rites in the church, large parties are organized for relatives and friends, elaborate clothing is purchased for the children honored, and food and drink are served in abundance. These occasions are used to reconfirm the bond that their children have with the extended family and community, and to solidify the place of each child and the family in the eyes of others. Families will spend lavishly on these celebrations, even though they may have to sacrifice in other areas to afford them.

The connectedness of generations of Hispanic families is a deeply emotional element of the culture. The San Jose Group supported their client, ATA Airlines, in developing their positioning for the Hispanic market drawing on this archetype. The San Jose Group recognized that the escape focus on vacation used for the U.S. general market positioning (On ATA, You're On Vacation) had little to do with Hispanics who largely wanted to use their vacation time to get together with family members whom they couldn't see on an everyday basis. They also discovered through research that ATA had low brand awareness with Hispanic consumers, who needed not only to have name recognition but trust in the airline they would choose for flying their family. They created a direct-response integrated marketing program branding ATA as *Su Aerolínea Oficial de Vacaciones* / Your Official Vacation Airline. The campaign moved the ATA from a relatively unknown airline among Hispanics, to receiving strong monthly in-call volumes and revenue from this growing consumer segment (see The San Jose Group ATA Case Study at the end of this chapter).

Machismo and Marianismo

Earlier in this chapter under a discussion of androgyny the topic of macho was brought up. There, it was considered in its more common stereotypical understanding as the tough, dominant, insensitive Hispanic male. The female counterpart to that concept, *marianismo*, a lesser-known stereotype referring to the compliant, powerless woman who responds to the demands of her husband in a traditional wifely role, was also raised. In this section, the two concepts will be addressed as structures underlying the role relationship between Hispanic males and females. We will look at both the negative and positive dimensions of *machismo* and *marianismo* to understand how their interpretation differs among U.S. Hispanics.

Both *machismo* and *marianismo* have deep historical roots for U.S. Hispanics, originating in Europe, passing to Latin America in the conquests of Spain and then developing deeper meaning in the revolutions that formed modern Latin American countries. Now, these concepts continue their evolution in the cultural changes occurring among U.S. Hispanics as these immigrants confront and become acculturated in their new environments. In all cases these two concepts have been counterparts perpetuated by the perceptions, imagery, and behaviors associated with each.

The European concepts associated with *machismo* developed from male-dominated religions, male divinities, male leaders of the church, and male heads of state. *Machismo* emphasized the strong, indomitable male who ruled others with an unswerving iron will. The concept of *marianismo* was the flip side of the coin defining the female as the powerless, compliant, and suffering counterpart of the male, circumscribed by religion, law, and social norms, and referred to by the pure name of the Virgin Mary. The conquerors of Spain brought their sense of dominance and male-female relationships to the new world. Alan Riding sees this as deeply rooted in the Mexican history of male-female dominance: "Mexico's mestizaje began with the mating of Spanish men and Indian women, thus immediately injecting into the male-female relationship the concepts of betrayal by women and conquest, domination, force, and even rape by men. Just as the conqueror could never fully trust the conquered, today's macho must therefore brace himself against betrayal."[20]

Although these early explanations of *machismo* and *marianismo* are heavily laden with negative connotations, they also historically have had their positive dimensions. The macho male image has been associated with leaders who were victorious in battle and in life, who always showed a confident face and dared not show emotions lest their enemies take advantage; who were valiant and benevolent with those less powerful, particularly women and children (perceived as lesser beings); and who were among equals only with males of their society with whom they could celebrate their manhood. The woman according to *marianismo*, modeled after the purity of the Virgin, comes from "the cult of feminine spiritual superiority, which teaches that women are semi-divine, morally superior to and spiritually stronger than men."[21]

Coming to conclusions about what is the current balance between *machismo* and *marianismo* of U.S. Hispanics is not within the scope of this book. Suffice it to say that this is an element of culture going through change, a trend that can also be said of the male/female relationships in the wider U.S. culture. Knowing the history of these interlocking concepts—*machismo* and *marianismo*, as well as the more paternalistic tendency of the Hispanic culture—suggests that marketers need to be sensitive to research questions around gender, raise issues particularly around decision-making in Hispanic families, and construct strategic directions in tune with cultural and emotional realities of men and women.

Though there are weaknesses that can be encouraged in the extremes of *machismo* and *marianismo* from male boorishness to female weakness, there are important strengths inherent in them. These strengths may include male responsibility and pride in providing leadership for his wife and family; and female strength, tenderness, and devotion in caring for her husband and children. Marketers need to understand these terms and their implications for male-female relationships from within the Hispanic culture, and be careful not to develop campaigns based on the potent and often judgment-laden gender perceptions within their own cultures.

Health Beliefs, Remedies, and Modern Medicine

Healthcare for U.S. Hispanics is an area full of frustration. Hispanics often go without the care they need for themselves and their children, or, if they succeed in getting treatment, they are often dissatisfied with their care. Access to healthcare in the United States is very different for most Hispanics than in their countries of origin. In many Latin American countries healthcare is an overall benefit for workers and their dependents, and healers are available with traditional remedies to deal with everyday illnesses and types of health problems that doctors or nurses do not treat. In the United States, many Hispanics are without health insurance and even those with it feel uncomfortable in the predominantly English-speaking health institution environments. They complain that there are impersonal administrators or health professionals with whom they have difficulty communicating their problems even if they do speak English, and whose remedies they may not trust.

However, it is also important to note that experts, particularly doctors, are highly respected in the more hierarchical Hispanic culture so that Hispanics in the United States also feel it is important to take their opinions into consideration. In addition, Hispanics respect many aspects of their new life in the United States and are striving to learn as they become a part of the new culture. Feeling between the health norms from their past in their countries of origin and the modern healthcare systems in the United States creates a stressful situation. This is particularly critical because they need their health so they can work and take care of their families economically and physically, and they are devoted to keeping their children, who are the center of their lives, healthy.

U.S. doctors, nurses, and other healthcare givers express their exasperation in trying to understand what the real health problems of Hispanic patients are and why these patients frequently do not follow the health care treatments that they prescribe. In addition, Hispanics who are sick often do not come in for health treatment until they are extremely ill and need to go to the emergency room.

U.S. health professionals realize that there are some health beliefs among Hispanics that differ from the non-Hispanic U.S. patients. These beliefs often appear to the medical profession as superstitious and based on nonscientific premises. The traditional remedies related to cultural theories about disease, to U.S. healthcare givers, do not seem to have the same benefits as the prescription drugs they utilize. In obtaining modern medicines, Hispanic patients also have difficulty understanding why they need to have a prescription for medicine from the pharmacy. Indeed, in many Latin American countries, pharmacists are professionals who directly prescribe medicines for those who are ill and no intermediary in the health world is needed. Beyond what the pharmacists offer, Hispanics often prepare their own home remedies—frequently herb teas, brews, and pomades—made from recipes handed down over generations from their mothers and grandmothers.

There are basic differences in the way Hispanics traditionally understand the causes of illness. Modern medicine in the United States attributes illness to more scientifically described origins, whereas

Hispanic culture tends to assign the routes of an illness to many different levels of experience.

"Many Hispanics believe that illness can be caused by:

1. Psychological states such as embarrassment, envy, anger, fear, fright, excessive worry, turmoil in the family, or improper behavior or violations of moral or ethical codes;
2. Environmental or natural conditions such as bad air, germs, dust, excess cold or heat, bad food, or poverty; and
3. Supernatural causes such as malevolent spirits, bad luck, or the witchcraft of living enemies (who are believed to cause harm out of vengeance or envy)."[22]

The extent to which U.S. Hispanics both maintain their traditional healthcare and incorporate the innovations offered them by their new culture should be of keen interest to marketers in this area. Felipe Castro, Pauline Furth, and Herbert Karlow conducted a study of Mexican, Mexican-American, and Anglo-American women to understand the relationship between cultural beliefs about health and their reactions to Western healthcare directives. They found that even though Mexican women tend to maintain their traditional cultural beliefs, they also take directives of modern health givers into account. "These results suggest that Mexican-origin women have a dual system of belief which tends to weaken but not disappear with increasing acculturation. The dual system however would not appear to interfere with their ability to accept and comply with prescribed biomedical health regimens."[23]

Refer to The San Jose Group National Pork Board Case Study at the end of Chapter 5 for health-related beliefs among Hispanics, which inhibited their purchase of pork, a well-loved protein source. In addition, read the MendozaDillon Galderma Case Study at the end of this chapter for causal attributions of Hispanic women to melasma as well as their willingness to get medical help and use Western medicine for this "embarrassing" condition, once educated about it in a community-related health setting.

Curanderismo

In order to comprehend how Hispanics experience U.S. healthcare institutions, it is of interest to understand a vital community healthcare institution that exists in many Latin American countries. *Curanderos* or healers have been a traditional part of Mexican culture and have counterparts in other areas of Latin America. These are people in Latin American communities who treat illnesses through their power over the healing process and with various types of medicines, such as herbal remedies, handed down to them through the culture. They handle the physical and emotional problems that attend illnesses in the context of the family and the community. Curanderos operate within the belief system surrounding health, which is part of the heritage of Mexicans, in contrast to modern health institutions that bring new knowledge and practices to these immigrants.

Robert Trotter II and Juan Antonio Chavira conducted ethnographic research on *curanderismo* in the Lower Rio Grande Valley of Texas. "The simplest and most common gift of healing among *curanderos* is the ability to work on the material level . . . The objects (healers use) include herbs, patent medicines, common household items (eggs, lemons, garlic, and ribbon, for example), and religious or mystical symbols (water, oils, incense, perfumes, and so forth). The ceremonies include prayers, ritual, sweeping or cleansings (*barridas* or *limpias*), and other complex rituals using all or some of the special objects."[24] Trotter and Chavira found that it was not uncommon that those they studied would use both *curanderos* and institutional health care for the same illness. *Curanderos* also work on the spiritual and mental levels, bringing special powers to bear that involve the supernatural.

These broad healing interventions in the lives of the Hispanics *curanderos* cover treatment areas that would ordinarily include family doctors, psychiatrists or psychologists, and priests in their newly adopted U.S. cultural context. Interestingly, these authors found that Mexicans in their study, in a "polychronic" style, not infrequently had both a family *curandero* as well as a family doctor for the same illnesses. This tendency to be able to hold both an appreciation for traditional cures as well as for the expertise of the doctor in their new culture can be important for marketers involved in the U.S. healthcare industry to understand. Developing insights regarding the emotional appeal of products or services can be of key importance, whether these are seen as linked to their traditions or based on the expertise inherent in their new environment.

Hot and Cold Theory of Illness

One of the most elaborate frameworks for the conceptualization of disease in Latin America is the "Hot and Cold" philosophy. Although this has come down through generations in Latin America as folk remedy, it had its origin in early scientific medical thinking brought to the Americas from Spain and Portugal in the 16th and 17th centuries. There were originally four dimensions to the Hippocratic theory: dry, cold, hot, wet, or a combination of these. "Illness . . . is believed to result from a humoral imbalance which causes the body to become excessively dry, cold, hot, wet, or a combination of these states. Food herbs, and other medications, which are also classified as wet or dry, hot or cold, are used therapeutically to restore the body to its supposed natural balance."[25]

The general idea that has evolved is that diseases and remedies fall into either hot or cold categories; wet and dry were dropped over time, depending on how the diseases are described. The prescription is that "cold" remedies are given for "hot" ailments and vice versa, in order to restore the balance of health to the sufferer. For generations, Hispanics have received treatment according to these categories, and have continued to treat their children under the same philosophy. Since this theory is alien to most U.S. healthcare providers they are baffled when they suggest, for instance, that their patients drink cold fruit juices as treatment for a cold, but their patients end up not following this advice. They miss out on the understanding that a cold drink is not considered an appropriate cold remedy, a cold disease in the hot-cold classification system. More typically, a hot ginger tea would be given for a common cold.

Physicians and other health care professionals who understand this system can work within it so that they do not have to disrupt deeply held beliefs in order to achieve the treatment they believe is important. Since the classification of remedies changes with the different forms in which they are given—for instance vitamins are considered hot remedies and can be taken for colds or other cold diseases such as menstruation—doctors can prescribe them instead of insisting on cool drinks and formulas. Thus, marketing communication strategies can encompass sensitivities from traditional beliefs in order to achieve acceptance and viability with Hispanic consumers. Again, the use of in depth interviews and ethnographic research in understanding these deeply held traditional beliefs is vital.

Conclusions

Successful Hispanic marketing efforts are those that connect the brand with these consumers at the emotional level to create enduring customer relationships. To make that emotional connection it is important to discover what makes these Hispanic target consumers laugh, cry, love, grieve, decide, and act to commit to a product or service. Marketers who are outside of the culture of U.S. Hispanics need to develop an understanding of the subjective level of these consumers, an area which cannot be queried directly. This is the core of the U.S. Hispanic culture, which has been shaped by ancestors and early socialization in their countries of origin, as well as their adoptive culture in the United States.

This chapter suggests that through understanding dimensions of culture and cultural archetypes marketers can discover the fit of their products or services within the emotional drivers of Hispanic consumers. This will make their brand meaningful to the lives of their Hispanic target, and position it competitively among the array of other products in their category. With an initial awareness of the cultural dimensions of Hispanic consumers, marketers working with experienced Hispanic researchers can use in-depth interviewing and ethnographic research methodologies to reach deep emotional levels related to their brand.

Marketers can take advantage of understanding cultural differences between the Hispanic and non-Hispanic markets in the United States in considering the positioning and marketing of their brands. Through knowledge of these differences, marketers can think through why conceptual development of advertising must be done from within a culture basis, and the inherent problem of translating a U.S. non-Hispanic campaign for use with Hispanic targets. Among the cultural dimensions mentioned are:

- The polychronic nature of the Hispanic market, which makes many things happening simultaneously comfortable in the media or in customer service vs. the monochronic preferences of the non-Hispanic market for in-depth one subject treatment and orderly processes.

- Hispanic consumer preferences for polymorphic leadership styles, in which one trusted expert can provide guidance in a wide variety of areas vs. the monomorphic non-Hispanic consumer who trusts experts with a deep level of knowledge and experience in one field.

- The strong inclination of Hispanics to collectivism, thinking of the family and the groups to which they belong as essential elements to the functioning and enjoyment of their lives vs. the U.S. non-Hispanic pride in achieving on one's own merits and competition to get ahead of others.

- The Hispanic tendency to attribute causality to sources outside of themselves—to other people or other forces vs. the non-Hispanic belief in the power of self-reliance to create one's own path to success.

Marketers also discovered cultural archetypes in this chapter, which can be powerful tools for deep cultural understanding of Hispanic consumers. Cultural archetypes are parts of dimensions of culture that come to bear on certain discrete areas of Hispanic consumers' thinking, feeling, and behaving. Each of these archetypes forms a cultural mold with the potential to shape Hispanic reactions to a marketer's product or service. The marketer has had the opportunity to read examples of marketing success stories linked to archetypes.

The archetypes mentioned in this chapter could easily affect marketing decisions on a wide range of consumer products from automobiles to diapers, to banking, insurance, or healthcare. The marketer can use these examples of cultural archetypes to further comprehend subjective level influences on Hispanic consumers. Three of the archetype examples mentioned are:

- There is an archetype that links happiness, life, religion, and death in the Hispanic market. Historically it flows from the difficult, often cruel history of oppression in Spanish-speaking countries. It manifests itself with an emphasis on enjoying life in the present because it can be taken from you by forces unknown at any moment, and looking to death and the peace and joy promised by religion in the afterlife. Yet, archetypes for U.S. Hispanics are an amalgam of the culture of their home country as well as their adopted culture. So, in this complex motivational mold Hispanics also hold a belief that they can make a better life in the United States for themselves, and especially for their children. This archetype strongly impacts marketing of future-oriented products such as insurance and savings plans. It also comes into play in the marketing of present-oriented festivities and indulgence.

- For Hispanic parents, children are their ultimate blessing and the key to their future. There is an archetype that shapes Hispanics' parent-child relationships, preserving the culture of their past and yet fitting well with their functioning in the U.S. culture. Fathers are the heads of the family, responsible for its well-being economically and with the external world, and have authority over children. Mothers have daily responsibility for the children's health, well-being, and happiness. Both parents indulge their children, hold them close to their family in their social life, and stress the importance of education. Yet, children have norms of respect, performing family household tasks appropriate to their gender, and participating in the rituals of their heritage. The continuous closeness of the Hispanic family, working or playing, weekdays or weekends, is in contrast to the "doing your own thing" norms of the more individualistic U.S. non-Hispanic society.

- Traditional Hispanic health beliefs, remedies and their attitudes toward modern medicine forms an archetype that differs markedly from U.S. non-Hispanic culture. Hispanics tend to see health in a holistic way, and treatment of illness involves physical, psychological, and spiritual frameworks. In this chapter we have discussed *curanderos* or healers who use a wide range of herbal and traditional medicines to treat patients in their own community and home environments. The familiarity and comfort in this treatment is in strong contrast to the bewilderment Hispanics face in Western medicine. Doctors' appointments, prescription medicines, impersonal clinics, and non-Spanish speaking administrators are barriers to the use of modern U.S. healthcare systems. Marketers of healthcare services, over-the-counter remedies, and pharmaceuticals need to take this archetype into consideration as they position their hospitals, clinics, brands, and attendant services for success in the Hispanic market.

Implications for Marketers

- Overt differences in cultural behavior and artifacts are easier to observe and chronicle than hidden, subjective differences. To have success in the U.S. Hispanic market, marketers cannot paper over a general market initiative and expect to win the hearts and minds of this target. They need to go to the heart of the culture and grasp its meaning relative to their marketing objectives.

- Cultural dimensions and archetypes, the intersection of cultural dimensions around a topic, hold the molds that affect the attitudes, feelings, and behaviors of U.S. Hispanics. Marketers should strive to learn about these dimensions and archetypes through exposure to Hispanic literature, art, cinema, and music as well as in-depth research. In order to touch Hispanic emotions, marketers need to position their products and services with attention to these cultural influences.

- The U.S. Hispanic culture is a unique amalgam between the influences of home country heritage and their new culture in the United States. There is a striving on the part of Hispanics to be successful in this country and yet hold on to what is dear to them from their own country and language. Marketers should endeavor to find the balance for their product and service in the particular cultural condition of the U.S. Hispanic market.

- Marketers need to suspend the comfort level of their own invisible subjective culture and make their personal and professional decision to move into the unknown, yet fascinating space of another culture, in this case the U.S. Hispanic culture. You need to understand that this is *the* way to latch into the emotions of the Hispanic market with the positioning of your brand. Make sure to have a culturally trained research and marketing companion from the Hispanic culture to act as a guide for your journey. For a while, you will need to rely strongly on them, but well-crafted campaigns, based on solid cultural understanding, should be the result, and your increasing sophistication will continue to lead you to future Hispanic marketing successes for your brand.

Case Study: *The San Jose Group – Ameritech Voicemail 98*

Company/Organization: Ameritech (pre-SBC acquisition)
Advertising Agency: The San Jose Group
Campaign: For Ameritech's updated voicemail product, Voice Mail 98: Ahora Puedes Hablar Más Que Un Perico (Now You Can Talk More Than a Parrot)
Intended customers/clients: Hispanic telephone customers in Greater Chicago

Background:

Ameritech's Consumer Services Division asked The San Jose Group to develop a direct mail campaign directed to the Hispanic market for their Voice Mail 98 Message Retrieval Service. Voice Mail 98 incorporated new features, which made it easier to receive and retrieve telephone messages, including a Spanish-language prompt system. Given the high telephone usage of Hispanics, Ameritech anticipated an increased opportunity for their new service in this market. However, previous Ameritech direct mail campaigns, which featured either English-language/general market creative or straight translations from English to Spanish, failed to capture Hispanic sales of any of its value-added services.

Discovery Process/Research:

The San Jose Group found that quantitative data supported an overindex of both Hispanics per household and long-distance calling incidence, yet, a significantly lower use of answering machine technology. They supported their client's perception of potential for this product in the market, with the right approach.

Cultural Insights:

Given their knowledge of the market from their history of research in this category and the quantitative data at hand, The San Jose Group recognized the importance of developing a campaign that had cultural appeal to this market. They not only wanted to make Hispanics aware of the benefits of Voice Mail 98 for capturing personally important calls, but also to catch their attention by using an engaging and culturally relevant graphic.

Expression of Insights in the Campaign:

SJG chose a visual and colorful icon that is well-known in Latino culture for being cheerfully talkative—the parrot. From a message standpoint, SJG developed a fully bilingual direct mail package and incorporated a common saying about these talkative creatures into their headline, "Now you can talk more than a parrot." The copy emphasized the dual benefit of capturing the important long distance calls that might otherwise be missed, while not having to interrupt their current conversations, which was widely perceived as rude and disrespectful among Hispanic customers. By positioning this benefit within the amusing visual context of a parrot, SJG was able to build the relevant association between Voice Mail 98 and Hispanic customers' ability to keep on talking as much as they needed, wanted, and loved with family and friends.

Effect of the Campaign:

As a result of this campaign, The San Jose Group informed the Hispanic market in their target area of the usefulness of the new Voice Mail 98 in a culturally relevant and clear manner, achieved the sales goals of Ameritech for the Hispanic niche market and addressed the Hispanic consumers' cultural need of keeping in close contact with family and friends.

Figure 6.2

Ameritech Voice Mail 98 bilingual direct mail brochure

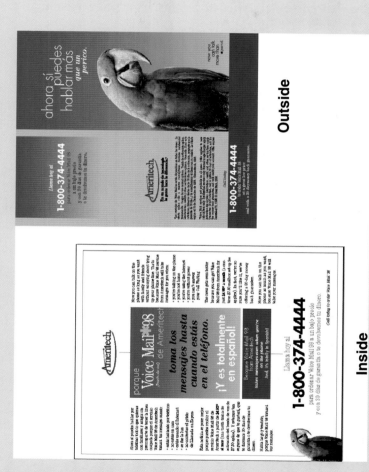

Outside

Inside

Case Study: *Bromley – Burger King*

Company/Organization: Burger King Corporation
Advertising Agency: Bromley Communications
Campaign: HAVE IT YOUR WAY®
Intended customers/clients: Spanish Speaking Hispanic Fast Food
  Hamburger Users

Background:

American eating habits shifted dramatically in the late 1990s
and early 2000s. In addition, expansion of the competitive market
began tapping into fast food turf. Fast casual restaurants such
as Chipotle Mexican Grill, Fazoli's, Panda Express, Baja Fresh
Mexican Grill, and others have introduced consumers to a new
eating experience: fast food without all the plastic.

Burger King Corporation's attempts to increase sales and restaurant traffic in light of these developments have proven to be challenging. While the fast food hamburger leader, McDonald's, has
repositioned its "food, folks, and fun" branding and introduced
innovative products such as their premium salads and McGriddles
to consumers, the BURGER KING® existing brand equity continues to focus on one thing, the fire grilled Original WHOPPER®
Sandwich. Although consumers rank BURGER KING® restaurants tops for their burgers, they perceive a lack in brand and product innovation, which consumers are increasingly seeking from the
restaurant industry. (1)

While the U.S. health craze has affected visitation to fast food
restaurants among general market consumers, Hispanics, particularly Spanish-speaking Hispanics, continue to drive overall consumption of the fast food category and the business of BURGER
KING® restaurants. In fact, when it comes to fast food, Hispanic
consumers typically over-index the general market in consumption
and average spending.

Bromley Communications research showed that Hispanic
BURGER KING® Loyals tend to be less acculturated (Spanish-
language dominant and maintain strong ties to their Hispanic culture), while fast food Switchers are more acculturated to the U.S.
mainstream. Research has demonstrated that as Hispanics become
more acculturated to the U.S. market and its practices, they
become more perceptive about their restaurant needs. They look
for choice: a variety of taste, brands, and price. As consumers

become more comfortable with the language and experimentation, they become more open to trying new brands. (2)

In August 2004, as an attempt to reinvigorate its brand image and product line across consumer segments, Burger King Corporation launched a new burger, The Angus Steak Burger, to continue its reign as the "king" of burgers, while becoming an innovator in the restaurant industry. The challenge was to capitalize on learnings from their research and to increase brand awareness by further differentiating the BURGER KING® brand from the competition in ways that would result in increased sales and brand preference.

Discovery Process/Research:

In order to reinvigorate and further differentiate the BURGER KING® brand, Burger King Corporation launched a MAINSTREAM campaign focused on its HAVE IT YOUR WAY® brand equity in March 2004. Shifting their focus on a younger audience, the Generation X and Y segments, Burger King Corporation intended to gain brand loyalty through its customization principal, which stresses the importance of customization and individuality among a consumer group yearning for these emotional connectors (3).

In order to craft messages that were synergistic with the mainstream efforts and yet resonated with target Hispanic consumers, Bromley Communications and Burger King Corporation conducted exploratory qualitative research related to its HAVE IT YOUR WAY® brand equity. The purpose of the research was to attain a deeper understanding of consumer habits and attitudes in order to best interpret the brand platform among Hispanics. The learning generated key insights that directly influenced creative development of the Hispanic campaign.

In the spring of 2004, further in-depth qualitative research (including one-on-one interviews, dyads, and triads) was conducted in New York, Los Angeles, and Miami. This wave was also designed to deep dive into food preference motivators for both Spanish-dominant and bilingual/bicultural Hispanic fast food consumers.

Cultural Insights:

While Burger King Corporation had strongly established its HAVE IT YOUR WAY® brand equity among the General Public in the 1980s and 1990s, the Company's establishment among Hispanics lagged behind the other segments. In research conducted among Hispanics, both English- and Spanish-speaking consumers, the basic perception of the HAVE IT YOUR WAY® brand correlated well with the established customization equity of "getting what you want," "getting things your way," and "like the way you like them." (4) When it came to connecting HAVE IT YOUR WAY® to BURGER KING® in the Hispanic consumer market, awareness levels were lower than in comparison to the general market. (4)

In addition to the HAVE IT YOUR WAY® and BURGER KING® disparity among the Hispanic market, cultural beliefs and language also affected the connection to customization in a fast food restaurant environment. (4) The core target Hispanics for Burger King Corporation claimed that there was a lack of comfort in customization at BURGER KING® restaurants. They cited the inability to communicate their needs to employees largely because of the language barrier. They also felt there was a tendency to exemplify disrespect, which kept them from asking employees to go above-and-beyond to fulfill their special request. Hispanics tend to customize in their everyday life as an essential component of self-expression. For example, they express a unique, personalized voice through their cars, tattoos, music, and clothing. However, they do not have this same level of comfort to express their unique needs and interests outside their homes and personal space, and this creates a barrier. (4)

Expression of Insights in the Campaign:

In the development of Hispanic-targeted creative under the mainstream campaign of HAVE IT YOUR WAY®, Bromley Communications felt it was key to position BURGER KING® restaurants as THE place for customization through self-expression. However, they recognized that for their bulls-eye Hispanic target, BURGER KING® and other fast food restaurants are *not* naturally perceived as an environment which allows self-expression. They learned from their research that awareness of customization at BURGER KING® restaurants is lower among the Hispanic consumer group. (4) They decided that to achieve their key objective, they needed to make Hispanics feel welcome to customize and "self-express" themselves at BURGER KING® restaurants.

In August 2004, Burger King Corporation launched the Angus Steak Burger under the HAVE IT YOUR WAY® campaign. The launch of the premium Angus Steak Burger was the brand's answer to creating product innovation and reestablishing the BURGER KING® brand. While the Angus Steak Burger tested well among the general population, Spanish-speaking consumers did not understand the benefit of "Angus"—tasty, quality beef. (5) Needing to establish customization equity and educate consumer on the quality of Angus beef, the brand challenged the agency team to emphasize the sheer enjoyment of customizing their very own high quality Angus steak burger to their liking only at BURGER KING® restaurants.

Bromley Communications produced five television executions supporting the Angus Steak Burger Launch, including three Spanish and two English language spots. They developed each execution to communicate the importance of self-expression through food at an environment, BURGER KING®, which had been outside of identified "comfort zones."

In each execution, Bromley used talent to play an essential role in establishing and communicating self-expression through food. They developed a spot entitled, "Baby Shower" where an urban Hispanic male, Lyric Less, invites his mother to a BURGER KING® restaurant to try the new Angus Steak Burger. In this spot, Bromley expressed not only the educational aspect of the Angus, but visually and lyrically the individuality important to the Hispanic market. With each spot for the Angus Steak Burger they took an individualistic route to establish personalization and self-expression with everyday Hispanic people. In each, Bromley did not use scripted copy, but everyday language familiar to the Hispanic consumer market.

Effect of the Campaign:

As a result of the creative and promotional elements, Hispanic-identified BURGER KING® restaurants beat the forecasted comparable sales figure by 18%, exceeding Angus Steak Burger volume forecast by 20%. The "Best Place for Burgers" rating for BURGER KING® restaurants continues to be dominant versus national competition (by 8.7 percentage points over McDonald's and 13.3 percentage points over Wendy's).

(1) National Adult Tracking Study: Burger King Corporation Secondary Quantitative Research
(2) Agency Primary Qualitative and Quantitative Research/ Analysis
(3) Burger King Corporation Qualitative Research Analysis
(4) Agency Primary Exploratory Research
(5) Agency Qualitative Concept Testing

Figure 6.3

Burger King® HAVE IT YOUR WAY® TV commercial

Figure 6.4

HAVE IT YOUR WAY® graphic choices

Figure 6.5

Burger King® HAVE IT YOUR WAY® product wrapper

Case Study: *MendozaDillon – Galderma*

Company/Organization: Galderma Laboratories, L.P.
Advertising Agency: MendozaDillon
Campaign: Melasma Awareness Campaign
Intended customers/clients: Hispanic females, particularly those suffering from melasma, and the medical community which treats Hispanic females.

Background:

Galderma Laboratories, L.P. licensed a new product, Tri-Luma® Cream, to treat melasma, a dermatological problem which widely affects women of various ethnic origins, including Hispanics. This condition consists of blotchy discoloration of the face and forearms and is attributed to an imbalance of hormones due to pregnancy, use of oral contraceptives, or hormone replacement therapy. Galderma decided to focus a campaign on Hispanic females because of the large size of this population and the commonality among these women.

Discovery Process/Research:

Galderma conducted qualitative research with Hispanic females, doctors, and health practitioners in three major Hispanic markets—Miami, Los Angeles, and Houston. They conducted focus groups with Hispanic women who had melasma and mini-groups with those general practitioners and dematologists who treated Hispanic women.

Cultural Insights:

In their research Galderma found that there was a lack of knowledge about the disease both among Hispanic women and the healthcare community which treated them. The Hispanic women who suffered from this problem attributed it to a variety of causes including birth control pills, pregnancy, and liver problems. Many of the women in the focus groups reported feelings of low self-esteem, and not wanting to go out in public because of the marks on their faces. Since Hispanic women are known for their strong motivations to appear attractive, this was an especially depressing problem for them. Those afflicted with melasma reported using home remedies such as lemon, salt, garlic, oatmeal, and other whitening creams to try to get rid of the facial marks.

Compounding the problem, healthcare providers for these women, i.e., general practitioners and dermatologists, had low awareness of melasma and often misdiagnosed their condition.

Expression of Insights in the Campaign:

MendozaDillon developed an integrated communication campaign which focused on creating an awareness of melasma and its treatment for Hispanic consumers. The Agency developed a strategy which was primarily educational, intended to inform Hispanic women about melasma, and to give their healthcare professionals an understanding of how to recognize and treat the disease. They presented Tri-Luma® Cream as the effective and time-efficient treatment for melasma. The Agency guided all aspects of the campaign with sensitivity toward Hispanic women's feelings of loss of esteem when they had melasma, and their need for appearing attractive and presentable in their social world.

Galderma and MendozaDillon put together an integrated educational communication campaign in Chicago. They created professional education classes for health practitioners and doctors for which they received continuing medical education units. They delivered in-language materials to local Hispanic family health practices and general practitioner offices about the disease and Tri-Luma® Cream. They also focused on Hispanic consumer health events across the city, at which Hispanic females could receive free health screening. In addition, they provided information to Hispanic women's organizations and medical students on the topic of melasma. They developed awareness for all these events through branded TV, print, and radio advertising, which drove people to the events and generated interest in the Hispanic healthcare community at large.

Effect of the Campaign:

The results of the campaign were widespread in the Chicago area. Galderma, working with MendozaDillon, interacted and distributed information to 852,000 consumers, educated over 32,000 attendees during community seminars and health fairs, provided CME credits to approximately 100 doctors and health professionals, received 1,105 inquiries from TV ads after first three flights and 1,130 from print ads after first insertions, and created new Hispanic distribution relationships/accounts for sales follow-ups. Throughout this campaign the agency generated over 5 million media impressions.

Figure 6.6

Galderma Tri-Luma® ad

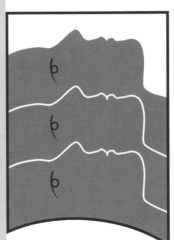

Tri-Luma®
Cream

(fluocinolone acetonide 0.01%, hydroquinone 4%, tretinoin 0.05%)

Case Study: *The San Jose Group – ATA*

Company/Organization: ATA Airlines
Advertising Agency: The San Jose Group
Campaign: Branding / Direct Response Campaign
Intended customers/clients: Hispanic Families / Hispanic Travelers

Background:

By the mid-1990s, ATA Airlines had been in business for more than 24 years and had become synonymous with vacation travel. It boasted ironclad brand equity, an efficient direct response-marketing model, and low-cost fares offered to approximately 40 destinations throughout the U.S., Mexico, and Puerto Rico. It was about this time that ATA also began to recognize a growing number of Hispanic surnames in its ticket database. Intrigued with the idea of a possible new revenue stream, ATA wanted to explore how a targeted marketing approach toward the Hispanic segment could help to strengthen its market position and achieve its growth objectives. ATA chose The San Jose Group to develop and implement its first-ever comprehensive advertising/marketing program geared exclusively at the U.S. Hispanic consumer market.

Discovery Process/Research:

SJG helped ATA to undertake a thorough market analysis with the agency's proprietary strategic planning and research model (Inside Out™). The assessment included both secondary and informal qualitative consumer research; in-depth competitive profiling; ATA brand, core competencies, and infrastructure auditing; travel agent community research and upside potential modeling.

Cultural Insights:

SJG confirmed its theory that the escapism-based general market positioning (On ATA, You're On Vacation) did not resonate with the Hispanic family, who travels on vacation *with family and friends* to visit *more family and friends*. Furthermore, SJG discovered that ATA enjoyed no brand awareness or name recognition among this segment, making it difficult to instill trust in the Hispanic traveler, who has a propensity to fear air travel. (Many actually confused ATA with the long-distance telephone leader, AT&T.) Lastly, Hispanics were open to purchasing airline tickets via telephone, yet the Indianapolis-based airline had no bilingual in-bound customer service resources to manage the calls.

Expression of Insights in the Campaign:

To build trust and simultaneously drive phone volume, a direct response-driven, integrated marketing program was conceived, branding ATA as: Su Aerolínea Oficial de Vacaciones/Your Official Vacation Airline. Visuals utilized in the campaign's launch featured this new slogan placed inside of a logo treatment that resembled a colorful "seal of approval" and conveyed to the consumer, "if you are traveling for vacation, you are on the right airline." SJG utilized TV, radio, outdoor, and print advertising to effectively target

Figure 6.7

ATA Airlines campaign

key segments, and helped ATA to establish a Hispanic customer-friendly infrastructure by creating an in-bound bilingual call center to exclusively manage the response for the Hispanic program. SJG also registered a new toll-free number, 1-800-VUELA-ATA (Fly ATA), and provided sales training and scripting for consistent messaging at every point of contact. The initial phase of the program piloted in Chicago and focused on the most popular vacation destinations, low fares, and direct flights. Based on the effectiveness of the pilot, SJG expanded ATA's advertising program into multiple markets not only throughout the U.S., but also to Guadalajara (Mexico), a new route added by ATA in 2001 and an important homeland destination visited by many Mexican-Americans every year.

Effect of the Campaign:

ATA became successfully positioned as the Official Vacation Airline among its new Hispanic target—a segment who had little to no previous awareness of the carrier, and seamlessly communicated its general market positioning in a culturally relevant way. In the first few months of the program, monthly in-bound call volume (tracked directly from the 1-800-VUELA-ATA #) increased from 5 to 500. It is now soaring above 14 K per month. According to client sales reports, the Hispanic program has generated over $420 MM in revenues for the airline—most of which had been achieved even prior to the addition of Guadalajara. Needless to say, what began as a mere "hunch" among a few enterprising ATA marketing executives has grown to become one of the airline's most embraced initiatives throughout all levels of its sales and marketing organization.

References

1 It should be emphasized that if a product does not live up to the expectations of consumers, no communication will make it succeed.
2 Michman, Ronald D. *Lifestyle market segmentation.* N.p.: Praeger Publishers, 1991, 12.
3 McKenna, Regis. *Relationship marketing: Successful strategies for the age of the customer.* Reading, MA: Perseus Books, 1991.
4 Hall, Edward Twitchell. *Beyond culture.* New York: Anchor Books/Doubleday, 1989.
5 Kant, Immanuel. *The critique of pure reason; The critique of practical reason, and other ethical treatises; The critique of judgment,* 2nd ed. *Great books of the Western world.* Chicago: Encyclopædia Britannica, Inc., 1990.
6 Rogers, Everett. *Diffusion of innovations.* New York: The Free Press, 1986.
7 This alternative may be realistic as certain institutions appear to falter, e.g., social security.
8 Dean, Carolyn, *Andean Androgyny and the Making of Men,* in Cecelia F. Klein, ed., *Gender in prehispanic America,* Washington, D.C., Dumbarton Oaks Research Library and Collection, 2001.
9 The feminine term for *macho.*
10 *New directions in attribution research.* Edited by John H. Harvey, William John Ickes, Robert F. Kidd. Hillsdale, N.J.: L. Erlbaum Associates, 1976.
11 Riesman, David. *The lonely crowd.* Studies in national policy, 3. New Haven: Yale University Press, 1950.

12 The day of all Saints, also the occasion for the U.S. Halloween.

13 Paz, Octavio. *El laberinto de la soledad*. 3rd ed. Colección Popular 107. México: Fondo de Cultura Económica, 1989.

14 Mestizos constitute the majority of people in Mexico and a large proportion in Central America and South America. Mestizos are the progeny of Spanish and Native Americans. Native Americans in this context are the native peoples of the American continent, not just the United States.

15 Ar-Riba is the Arabic concept indicating lenders are unethical if they charge interest.

16 *Quinceañera* parties are celebrations of coming of age of young women at age 15. It is traditional to spend large amounts of money on these celebrations that can last several days.

17 Benedict, Ruth. *The chrysanthemum and the sword*. New York: World Publishing, 1967.

18 Slonin, Maureen B. *Children, culture, and ethnicity: Evaluating and understanding the impact*. New York and London: Garland Publishing Company, Inc., 1991, p. 166.

19 Roberta Maso-Fleischman: "Archetypal research for advertising: a Spanish-language example," *Journal of advertising research*, Vol. 37 No. 5. Sept–Oct 1997, p. 81(4).

20 Riding, A. *Distant neighbors*. New York: Vintage Books, 1985, p. 10.

21 Stevens, Evelyn. *Marianismo:* "The other face of machismo in Latin America," *Female and male in Latin America essays*, Ann Pescatello, ed. University of Pittsburgh Press, 1973, p. 91.

22 Molina, C., R.E. Zambrana, M. Aguirre-Molina. *Latino health in the US: A growing challenge*. C. Molina and M. Aguirre-Molina eds. Washington, DC: American Public Health Association, 1994. http://www.apha.org/ppp/red/LatinAmeric.htm.

23 Castro, Felipe, Pauline Furth, Herbert Karlow. "The health beliefs of Mexican, Mexican American and Anglo American women," *Hispanic journal of behavioral sciences*, Vol. 6. No. 4., 365–366.

24 Trotter, Robert T. and Juan Antonio Chavira. *Curanderismo, Mexican American folk healing*. Athens: The University of Georgia Press, 1981, pp. 62–63.

25 Harwood, Alan. "The hot-cold theory of disease: Implications for treatment of Puerto Rican patients, *JAMA, the Journal of the American Medical Association*. Vol. 216. No 7. May 17, 1971, p. 1153.

Culturally Informed Strategy Based on Grounded Research

7

Because subjective culture is largely invisible, the marketer needs to make extra efforts to uncover the internal reality of the consumer. Marketing across cultures is particularly vulnerable to overlooking aspects in consumers' lives that can make the difference between marketing success and failure. The perceptions of the marketing message encoder and the perceptions of the Hispanic consumer message decoder can be quite dissonant.

The Cultural Research Paradox

In doing market research within a different cultural context, an important problem arises. In order to better understand the consumer's culture, the marketer tries very hard to measure all the variables he or she can think about. He or she diligently thinks of the different angles that can potentially deliver the consumer insights needed. The typical marketer mindset is to try to cover "all the bases" to make sure the Hispanic consumer is truly understood.

Unfortunately, and paradoxically, the more the marketer keeps digging the less he or she finds that provides the needed cultural insight. This is because to conduct cross-cultural marketing research the marketer needs a good amount of cultural information. Without enough cultural information the marketer would not be able to figure out even how or where to start asking questions that can lead to constructive cultural understanding. This paradox is reminiscent of the blind person that actually hurts him- or herself by being too careful.

This is why a psycho-socio-cultural approach can be extremely useful in crossing cultural marketing boundaries. Participants in the design of the research need to include at least some individuals who are "contexted" in the Hispanic culture. These contexted individuals can help shape the research in a way that it provides the insights that bring about a connection with the consumer.

The typical naïve questions include a heavy emphasis on attitude and usage: Do Hispanic consumers like and use a product? In the simplest case a negative answer to both the attitudinal and the usage question can lead the marketer to conclude that there is no hope that the Hispanic consumer will ever use the product. For example, when asking Hispanic consumers about their liking and use of refrigerated dough products, the consumer is very likely to state she does not like that kind of product and has never used it. The consumer may state she does not like the product because the description "refrigerated dough" may not sound appealing, but the consumer does not know what the product is like. Simply stated, a vast number of Hispanic consumers have passed by the refrigerated dough section in the supermarkets but have never known what those cardboard cylinders are for. Thus, lack of familiarity with the concept and the product may produce a negative reaction that should not guide marketing decisions.

Someone who understands where the consumers tend to come from in Latin America, and the nature of their shopping environments, can help guide the inquiry in a way that can produce actionable results. Simply put, the typical A&U (Attitudes and Usage) study could be a waste of time and money for certain categories and products. A contexted marketer/researcher would be more likely first to understand how Hispanic consumers consume bread, cookies, and so on. Then he or she would conduct taste tests and actual demonstrations of the product to assess potential. Also, the contexted marketer would likely place the new products in the homes of consumers after having instructed them about how to use them.

This culturally contexted approach is more likely to indicate the issues involved in attracting the interest of Hispanic consumers and the potential appeal of the product. Once the consumer bakes the product at home and the kids and spouse try it and enjoy it, then the consumer would be likely to purchase the product in the future. Replicating this in the real world would take the shape of store demonstrations and sampling. It could also take the shape of baking demonstrations at consumers' homes. Thus, if the marketer understands the background of the consumer to begin with, he or she is likely to go about asking questions in different ways, and interpreting the data in alternative ways as well.

Clearly, there are cases that are more complicated. For example, the product could be a product that contains baking soda. A contexted marketer would have some hypotheses about the importance of baking soda in the culture and would inform the research with questions that would lead to the discovery of affective/emotional issues associated with this ingredient. That would be very different from asking the consumer about the appeal of toothpaste with baking soda. The questions would deal with issues related to cleaning products and ingredients, and the evaluations of these products and ingredients along with their uses and associated beliefs. The associations and memories related to baking soda would be a stronger indicator of appeal and potential purchase than direct questioning. In this case direct questioning could actually lead to answers that could discourage further inquiry. If the consumer imagines that the product would taste bad because of the baking soda, then that could lead to the erroneous conclusion that baking soda is of no interest to Hispanics. This would be wrong because in practice Hispanics use baking soda to clean their teeth and believe that it has great cleaning and health attributes. Getting to understand the latter should be the aim of the marketing research effort.

The Paradox of Linguistic Equivalence

Another important issue in cross-cultural market research is the issue of translation and adaptation of instruments. An instrument is the more general term used to denote a questionnaire or any other tool used for data collection.

Typically, marketers ask for a questionnaire that has been used in the general market to be translated into Spanish for administration to Hispanics. This request sounds fair and reasonable. What is not generally considered is that translation of instruments is problematic most of the time. This is because language is not just a code that can be exchanged for another code. As we have seen elsewhere in this book, language is a living entity that has strong cultural and experiential connotations. Translators typically look for close word equivalents. Equivalence, however, is also subjective. Translation is likely to result in messages that resemble the original but the margin of variation is quite ample depending on the person doing the translation. Despite the objections of very competent and professional translators, translation cannot be perfect.

The simple question, "Can you please check your background among the options below?" is difficult to translate into Spanish. Several items in this question can be problematic, but the word "background" is specifically difficult. There is no direct equivalent of "background" in Spanish. A translator may use the term *antecedentes*, but this term has the connotation of legal history for many Hispanics. The translation needs to take into consideration the meanings embedded in people's minds.

Cultural Adaptation and Transculturation

Cultural adaptation of a question is perhaps one of the best options when converting a questionnaire from one language into another. Cultural adaptation requires that the adapter understand the idea in English and then recast it in Spanish "from scratch"—that is, without having the limitations of vocabulary obfuscating the process. Here the concept of understanding is crucial because if the adapter does not understand the idea very well, then the new message in Spanish will reflect such misunderstanding.

Transculturation is a term that some have used as an equivalent of cultural adaptation. Overall, the important idea behind these concepts is to have a bilingual individual understand an idea originally cast in one language and then imagine the same idea, in an optimized expression, in the second language.

Back Translation

Back translation has also been an approach that many in academia and industry have endorsed as a way of ensuring equivalence of translation between languages. Back translation consists of a professional translator translating some text into the second language; then another translator translates that text back into the original language. If both versions are judged to be equivalent then the translation is considered successful.

This approach, despite its logical allure, has important drawbacks. Since language use is highly subjective and dependent on the experience of its users, the two translators involved in back translation would have to be quite homogeneous. That is a very difficult task to accomplish. Further, even if the original and the back-translated version look equivalent, that is not necessarily proof that the translation into the second language actually conforms to the spirit of the original. In particular, what is difficult to achieve is that the gist of the communication be conveyed in a way that sounds as if it had been originally encoded in the target language.

Most likely a good cultural adaptation is more likely to result in accurate communication. The nagging difficulty will always be the subjectivity involved in deciding if the culturally adapted text is perceived by the target as it was intended in the first language. That is why the human receiver, the consumer, the respondent to the questionnaire, is the ultimate tester of the encoding.

The Paradox

This section started with the subtitle "The Paradox of Linguistic Equivalence." This paradox is involved in every translation and cultural adaptation effort. The gist of this paradox is that the more conceptually equivalent a translation of an instrument is to its original, the less likely it is for the researcher to find differences between the populations that use those languages. The converse is that the less conceptual, but more literal a translation is, the more likely it is for the researcher to find differences between two linguistic populations.[1]

This paradox highlights one of the most important problems in cross-cultural research. Marketers many times hypothesize cultural differences, and other times hypothesize cultural homogeneity. The paradox of equivalence goes to the core of inscrutability of measurement across cultures. Although equivalence is desirable, the more we work on making an instrument in a second language equivalent to the original in the first language, the more homogeneous the populations will appear to be. This happens because the more we strive for conceptual equivalence, the more likely we are to use terms that have more universal relevance, as opposed to culturally unique meaning.

Thus the marketer must live with uncertainty when planning marketing research across cultures. The obsession with truly knowing if two cultures think the same way about something can be only partially satisfied, if at all.

The Emic and Etic Perspectives

Globalization and localization have become important themes in the business world. These concepts have become increasingly salient in international marketing. The dictum "think global, act local" has become part of marketing wisdom. Many marketers talk about globalization as parallel to strategy and localization as parallel to tactic.

Many human patterns of behavior are general to all humanity. The expressions of fear, surprise, interest, surrender, and others are quite general. Most humans love their children. And as you know, there are many other aspects of being human that are quite general. What varies is the way in which behavior is enacted and interpreted.

An emic perspective on human consumer behavior would be to examine each culture individually without attempting to establish a mold for comparison across cultures. An etic perspective on consumer behavior would establish metrics to apply to several cultures so that they can be compared and contrasted. In 1954, Kenneth Pike published definitions and a discussion of the two terms.[2] An analogy of the emic and etic approaches to language and culture can be exemplified with objects. In the case of housing, the emic approach could consist of examining a home as a complex set of structural interrelations and character. The etic perspective would look at many homes in a comparative chart of homes by their traits. Thus, homes could be compared with respect to their number of bathrooms, bedrooms, and so on.

The emic approach would look at how the home feels, its feng shui, its Gestalt. The etic approach would look for a comparative examination of elements that exist across homes. It could be argued that one could develop a feng shui or Gestalt scale and compare homes across those dimensions. Although this is potentially feasible, the subjectivity involved makes this exercise a very complicated endeavor.

The typical cross-cultural marketer generally would feel much better if he or she could conclude how diverse cultures are similar or different across dimensions. Other marketers feel better understanding a culture on its own, independent of other cultures.

Most likely the etic and emic approaches need to coexist. This is because to get to know anything, we need to start from what is known, perhaps by comparing visible elements of culture. Then, once particular inconsistencies or discontinuities emerge, we need to delve deeper into a culture without further comparison to other cultures.[3] A typical impulse is to talk about Hispanic culture as being collectivistic and Anglo culture as being individualistic. At first glance this is a useful differentiation, but both cultures include collectivistic and individualistic patterns. It is the context and the way in which these patterns are exhibited that makes a qualitative difference. Burger King,® with its Hispanic advertising agency, Bromley Communications, maintained the individualistic theme of their non-Hispanic campaign, HAVE IT YOUR WAY® in their communication with the more collectivistic Hispanic market. Through qualitative research they found that Hispanics also have personal expression tendencies, which, when approached in a culturally sensitive way, could link them into the more collectivistic motivation of the overall campaign (refer to the Bromley Burger King® Case Study at the end of Chapter 6).

Marketers will likely continue to want to compare cultures and hope that they exhibit similarities so they can capitalize on economies of scale in marketing and communication efforts. Still, positioning and touching the soul of the consumer will happen with an approach that has particular resonance to the individual in the context of his/her culture. Thus, the dictum of "think global, act local," as if strategy were at the general scale and tactic at the specific scale, should be reconceptualized. Success will likely come from thinking globally and also thinking locally, with strategic approaches at both levels, thus answering the question of how my local strategy contributes to the global one.

Understanding the uniqueness of a culture from its own perspective gives the marketer a unique edge because it provides a platform from which a close relationship with the consumer can be achieved. Obtaining information about cultural commonalities can produce economies of scale. The paradox of equivalence in translation and measurement cannot be resolved but only transcended. Both the uniqueness and the common attributes of cultures are important. The common attributes allow for a wide-scope approach. The uniqueness of cultures provide the most important opportunities for marketers to make unique connections with consumers.

Cultural Bias and Standardization

Western marketers live in a world of numbers and are used to the assumption that almost everyone they deal with has numeric skills. Yet quantitative research, in particular, is very sensitive to cultural variability; not only the wording of questions, but the scales used for them. This is an issue that will come up several times in this chapter.

Related to the issue of numeric skills and the use of scales is the issue that Hispanics tend to use scales in ways that differ from non-Hispanics. Many marketers become mystified when they see statistically significant and consistently higher rankings and ratings by Hispanics as compared to others. In some cases, Hispanics also consistently rank and rate certain items lower than others.

Generally, this tendency toward using the extremes of scales has been associated with the idea that Hispanics are more passionate about their opinions. Thus, they really love or hate "things." This seems to be a good cultural explanation as Hispanics are more emotional, in general, about the products and services they use than their non-Hispanic counterparts.

This tendency seems to materialize across methods of administration, be it in person, phone, mail, Internet, and so on. This propensity to use extremes results in lower variance in Hispanic samples as compared with the variance found in non-Hispanic samples. That is because Hispanics tend to more uniformly respond to items.

There is a school of thought that argues that this tendency to answer items differently constitutes a bias.[4] This is said to be a bias in scale usage depending on culture. The argument is that collectivistic cultures, for example, would answer items worded in a collectivistic way more highly or favorably than individualistic worded items. This line of thought and research emphasizes that the language used in wording questions influences the answers obtained. But that is true in any study, be it cross-cultural or not. As stated earlier in this chapter, there is a need for culturally informed study design precisely to guide the creation of items that are likely to be answered differently depending on wording.

The key argument is that if two cultures or subcultures that are known to vary on a cultural dimension answer an item worded in two ways differently, on the average, then there is a cultural bias in the questions. So, members of a collectivistic culture would agree more with an item such as, "We decide to purchase product X based on my family's request," than with an item stating, "I decide to purchase product X based on my family's request." The subtle difference in this example is the use of the pronouns "we" vs. "I."

There are different solutions for this postulated bias. There are those who argue that first of all, items need to be submitted to a pilot test and reworded as necessary.[5] There are others who argue for some type of standardization. For example, it has been suggested that the distribution of a specific culture be standardized with the mean and standard deviation of the entire distribution. Others have suggested alternative approaches but most of them use some type of distribution modification to remove the variability attributable to the specific cultures and leave only the variability due to individuals.

This cultural bias phenomenon has been most keenly observed in Hispanic populations in positive responses to items. Observers have attributed these positive responses to a strong tendency of Hispanics to be nice to others. That is to say, Hispanics are hypothesized to be more prone to social desirability.

These observed tendencies have important elements of truth. What is in question is the degree to which they represent biases or actual cultural differences. If they represent actual cultural differences, it is the contention of these authors that attempting to remove that variability is in fact the elimination of the differences that we would want to know about in marketing to specific groups. What cannot be negated is that the development of questions needs to be informed by cultural knowledge. The absence of cultural expertise in interpreting data can be a hindrance when observing data differences that can be attributed to culture.

Nevertheless, in an "etic" quantitative approach the marketer or researcher may want to have some way of determining whether or not different cultures are actually answering an item in different ways, and may wish to have some way to "control" such variability. In the opinion of these writers, the best approach is to include one or more items that would obviously assess the degree to which a scale is being used differently. Such an item might be "What do you consider to be an acceptable grade for a child in school on a scale from 0 to 10?" Members of different cultures have different perceptions of what is an acceptable grade. If the means on this scale differ significantly, then the researcher can use these scales as covariates in the statistical analysis.

This action removes the variability due to the perception of phenomena on the scale and makes "etic" comparisons more plausible. Still, observed differences are what they are. It is the duty and responsibility of the researcher and the marketer to be informed as to what cultural issues may be at play depending on wording, order, place of administration, and other factors. The fact that one can control for cross-cultural variability does not mean that the marketer must do so. In fact, cross-cultural variability is the element that can provide the marketer with specific insights for his or her brand's advantage.

Use of Scales

The use of scales in market research is one of the most difficult issues marketers and researchers encounter. This issue is related to the previously discussed considerations of standardization. The choice of scale will influence the types of responses obtained.

The typical marketer and market researcher is used to administering measurement instruments to consumers that have been answering multiple choice tests and similar data collection instruments since their early youth. Many Hispanic consumers, particularly those coming from rural and poor backgrounds in Latin America, are not used to such devices.

Likert-Type Scales

Likert-type scales that rate a respondent's agreement appear innocuous to the observer. So, for example, "How much do you agree or disagree with the following statement: I prefer Spanish-language Television—READ: STRONGLY AGREE, AGREE, NEITHER

AGREE NOR DISAGREE, DISAGREE, AND DISAGREE STRONG-
LY," can produce interesting unanticipated responses, as follows:

- The respondent answers, "Yes, I prefer Spanish language television because I understand it better." The interviewer, as all good
  interviewers are instructed, restates: "Thank you, but would you
  say that you STRONGLY. . . . " At which point the disoriented
  consumer starts doubting the intelligence of the interviewer and
  responds, "Didn't I tell you I prefer Spanish-language television?"
  Clearly, this exercise can become very complicated because the
  respondent believes he or she has complied with the interviewer's
  request but the interviewer must get the response as demanded by
  his or her trainers and supervisors. The interviewer is supposed to
  obtain a response in the strongly agree to strongly disagree
  Likert-type scale. In practice the interviewer would likely try a
  roundabout approach, restating the response scale by saying
  "would you say you strongly prefer or prefer" until he or she gets
  an answer. The problem is that the respondent is being forced to
  respond on a scale he or she is not used to. When the respondent
  states that he or she prefers Spanish-language television, this is
  his or her answer, without gradations on a strongly agree to
  strongly disagree scale.

- Another Hispanic respondent answers "I agree" to this question
  using the scale provided. Due to the pattern discussed earlier, the
  interviewer is usually uncertain as to whether or not the answer
  is "agree" or "strongly agree." In practice we have found that
  this happens often. The Hispanic respondent confronted with an
  unusual questioning situation responds with agreement, but he or
  she is reluctant to elaborate by adding the adjective "strongly"
  because it seems unnecessary to represent his or her position. A
  solution that has been used to address this problem is to probe
  and ask "do you just agree, or strongly agree?" This additional
  probe brings about further issues. From the research designer perspective the clarification is very useful after having found that
  many respondents economize words and state either agree or disagree without qualification even when they actually meant to.
  Nevertheless, Hispanics appear to have a higher than average
  desire to please others, including interviewers. At the probe of
  whether the agreement is simply or strongly, the Hispanic respondent may feel that he or she is being asked for something else
  because he or she did not provide the "right" answer, and thus
  may answer "strongly agree." This "strongly agree" may be
  somewhat false because the respondent just meant "agree." Also,

the "strongly agree" may be inherently invalid because the respondent does not differentiate between levels of agreement. For many Hispanics degrees of agreement are unusual as in their lives they either agree or disagree.

- The respondent may just not understand the logic of replying to "agree – disagree" Likert-type scales. The logic of such scales is highly idiosyncratic to Western social science. Most Hispanics in the United States, we have found, appear to be more comfortable with questions that ask for a reply. After all, that is what questions are for. Many respondents have answered this type of question with a "yes," or "no," with the consequence of a tedious and uncertain dialog with the interviewer. Thus, the respondent needs to be educated into the logic of many scales conventionally used in Western social sciences. The researcher should not assume that the respondent will understand how to use these scales. That is why in many surveys researchers find that the high end of the scale is used much more than any other point. The respondent is using the scale as a dichotomous bipolar scale as opposed to using it as gradations of agreement. Training the respondent is not impossible, but it does take survey time. As the U.S. Hispanic population grows in the United States and as more surveys are administered, more respondents are becoming used to the utilization of Likert-type scales.

The marketer and the researcher not only need to understand the cultural perspective that the consumer brings to the consumption occasion, but also the measurement situation. In both cases they need to learn from the consumer.

Ratio-Type Scales

In measurement theory there are at least four different types of scales that have different attributes and restrictions. Nominal scales are those whose scale points do not have a quantitative meaning. That is, nationality, religion, race, football team preference, and so on are scales that simply attach labels to groups and they do not imply a quantitative value.

Ordinal scales, as their name indicates, are the types of scales that suggest that one item has more of an attribute than another. An ordinal scale can be one used for socio-economic level such as low, medium, high.

Interval scales are more sophisticated because in contrast with ordinal scales, the difference between any two adjacent points on the scale is supposed to be the same as the difference between any other two adjacent points in the same scale. Thus the difference between the points 1 and 2 on the scale is supposed to be the same as the difference between points 3 and 4 on the scale. The great advantage of interval level scales is that numbers on the scale can be added and subtracted, and the resulting figures have accurate meaning.

Ratio scales are the same as interval scales but possess an absolute zero. When a scale has an absolute zero it can be used for multiplication and division, beyond addition and subtraction. This is an important attribute because this type of scale can be very powerful for mathematical and statistical manipulation. The presence of an absolute zero is important because of interesting properties that this number has. Anything multiplied by zero remains zero, and anything added to zero leaves the original number as it was.

With this background on measurement scales, the discussion of ratio scales in measuring Hispanic marketing behavior can be pursued. A marketer or market researcher generally wants to have the highest level of measurement achievable—the ratio level. Using this higher level scale, the data can be analyzed in many different ways. The more detail and discrimination possible with the data, the finer the distinctions the marketer can make between types of consumers.

An ideal ratio scale would be something like "if the difference between the colors green and red is 10 units, what is the difference between Pepsi and Coke?" The answer to this question can be any number, including zero. Because the scale allows for the possibility of zero, and does not anchor the scale at more than one point, then, technically, the scale is a true ratio scale. However, a scale that has a true zero, but is anchored at more than one point is a simpler alternative. This would be a scale from 0 to 10, for example. In this case, zero is true in the sense that if someone has zero of something he or she has none of it. Also, the intervals can be assumed to be equal in the scale. This type of scale has proven itself to be particularly usable with Hispanic populations.

When conducting quantitative studies these writers discovered that Hispanics had a particularly good aptitude to use a 0 to 10 scale. The discovery of this was somewhat serendipitous. The explanation for this phenomenon is that in many school systems in Latin America, and particularly Mexico, teachers use a 0 to 10 scale to grade students. This type of scale then has become part of the culture and intuitive to a large extent.

When a Hispanic consumer is asked to rate a brand on a 0 to 10 scale, the responses tend to be less ambiguous and troublesome than when using other types of scales. So for example, instead of asking the consumer to agree or disagree with a statement, one can simply ask, "On a scale from 0 to 10, where zero means no preference at all and 10 means absolute preference, how much do you prefer to watch TV in Spanish?" It is sound practice to state the scale, with both anchors (zero and ten) and their "meaning," for the first couple of question-naire items; then respondents learn the logic and continue without much difficulty. The respondent usually has a much easier time under-standing this task and answering the question than with other types of scales. This scale may appear to be complicated because the inter-viewer may have to exert extra effort to explain the meaning of zero and 10. The extra effort, however, is seldom needed because Hispanic respondents usually understand that the implicit quality or "prefer-ence" in this case is the attribute being quantified.

The understanding of the rationale for the use of this scale has been a very important contribution to Hispanic research in the United States. Findings using this scale tend to render more discrimination between behaviors and preferences than almost any other scale. After conducting many Hispanic market research studies, it has been found that the face validity of this measurement scale appears to be as good as is attainable.

Validity is the degree to which the scale measures what it intends to measure. The intuitive validity of the scale after thousands of observa-tions has been demonstrated to be highly satisfactory. When compared with Likert-type scales this quasi-ratio scale appears to produce increased variability consistently. This is important because when con-ducting statistical analysis the existence of variability is fundamental in detecting differences and similarities.

Semantic Differential Scales

Charles Osgood[6] devised a scale type that is known as the Osgood Semantic Differential Scale. It is a simple and elegant scale, which he originally used in an attempt to uncover universal or cross-cultural dimensions of meaning. By means of the use of this scale in different countries he found that most cultures judge objects in three main dimensions: evaluation, strength, and activity. This has been a partic-ularly important finding in the social sciences because it documents underlying ways in which humans perceive elements of knowledge. These are dimensions as fundamental as time and space.

Still, the more relevant aspect to our current subject of Hispanic marketing is that these scales can be very useful for specific measurement problems. The Osgood Semantic Differential Scale is bipolar, with opposite adjectives on each end such as:

Angular _ _ _ _ _ _ _ _ Rounded
Weak _ _ _ _ _ _ _ _ Strong
Cold _ _ _ _ _ _ _ _ Hot

The respondent's task is generally to place an X on the line that is closer to the meaning that a particular word has. Thus, subjects can evaluate "flower," "burro," "love," "computer," "Coke," "Pepsi," and so on. Clearly scales like this can be very useful when attempting to identify the meaning of certain objects of knowledge such as brands. Since the meaning of objects is one of the most important aspects that marketers are interested in, the semantic differential presents a particularly attractive option.

Hispanic consumers have generally grasped this scale quite readily and do not seem to have the types of difficulties associated with Likert type scales. It is likely that the spatial relationship and the lines in between the two extremes make the logic of the task easy to understand and act upon.

Little Faces

Another more limited approach that has also been shown to work well with Hispanic populations is the use of the "little faces" or *las caritas*. This scale has direct denotative value that can be easily understood by almost anyone. The limitation is, of course, that the little faces only show affect and no other dimension; that is, from liking a lot to not at all (see Figure 7.1).

Most consumers we have had experience with have been able to identify the meaning of each face. The number of faces can be five or

Figure 7.1

Little faces scale

three. We recommend the use of five to allow for more variability in responses. These scales work particularly well with illiterate or functionally illiterate populations. Their major limitation is that the administration has to be in person, mail, or online.

Choice of Data Collection Approaches

The choice of a data collection approach is usually at the forefront of considerations. Marketers and market researchers usually find this step to be one of the most difficult moves when confronting research in a new culture.

The Wrong Question

The wrong question in doing research with Hispanics or with anyone is to ask whether to do qualitative or quantitative research as if they were just different modalities. Qualitative research should never be conducted to replace quantitative research, and quantitative research should never be done in place of qualitative research.

The criteria for selecting a research approach or method should be dictated by the research question being asked, and by the needs of the marketer at the time. Generally speaking, qualitative research should be conducted when the marketer needs to obtain in-depth insights and hypotheses about the nature of the consumer, or to test ideas, concepts, commercials, and other stimuli. Qualitative testing should be geared to uncovering specific aspects of meaning or "red flags" that could hurt the marketing objectives. It takes only a few consumers to tell you that "the emperor has no clothes." Qualitative research is not for obtaining statistically generalizable data.

Quantitative approaches generally are used in order to test hypotheses and obtain data that can be generalized to target populations. A quantitative survey usually is designed to obtain data that describes a phenomenon in the consumer population of interest. For example, "What is the likelihood that Hispanic consumers will purchase a new and improved toothpaste with baking soda?" or "What are the best predictors of Hispanic subscribership to satellite TV service?" or "How many Hispanics in the United States prefer Corona Extra as their top imported beer?"

A fundamental error made by some decision makers in the marketing industry is to assume that these approaches are options that achieve the same objectives. They are not. In many cases it is preferable to start with a qualitative study and then follow it up with a quantitative effort. This happens when the marketer wants first to find out subtleties about the issues and consumer language, then to follow up with a generalizable approach. Sometimes qualitative research is done after a quantitative effort. That happens when the researcher wishes to have consumers explain some of the quantitative findings. In Hispanic marketing, in particular, following quantitative research with a qualitative phase can be very useful because some of the findings may not be self-explanatory. As we have seen, cultural explanations can be difficult and not obvious.

Qualitative Approaches

Qualitative research takes on many forms. Generally, these modalities depend on a variety of factors that a qualified researcher will take into consideration. Some of the questions that determine answers in this decision making process include:

- How in-depth is the exploration?
- How much does one want to know about individual consumers?
- How important is it that respondents interact to create synergy through discussion?
- What are the objectives of the research:
  Is the research about idea generation?
  Is it about testing concepts?
  Is it about understanding specific behaviors in context?
  Is it about concept development?
  Is it about products in the design stage?
  Is it about brand imagery?
  Is it about creating meaning?
  Is it for testing translations or other types of text?
- What approach to data analysis is expected/desired?
  Is quantitative information going to be mixed with the qualitative data?
- Is the study about decision making processes?

And so on.

As you can tell, there are multiple considerations in the choice of qualitative approach. Some of the most common qualitative data collection approaches include:

- Focus groups
- Mini focus groups

- One-on-one in-depth interviews
- Dyads and triads
- Ethnographic interviews

Focus Groups

In the 1940s, Robert Merton[7] developed and published the concept of the "focused interview," in which a group of respondents were given a topic to think about before attending a group discussion. The discussion was guided with semi-structured questions. The main reason behind the focused interview was to have the synergy of the interaction among participants evolve into information that would not have been obtained by interviewing individuals. Thus, if the objectives and purposes of the research can be enriched by group discussion, then the focus group is the right approach.

Many marketers equivocally use focus groups as a series of one-on-one interviews. They ask a series of questions from each respondent in the group, one at a time. This is a waste of a focus group session. Shorter one-on-one interviews would much better serve the purpose of such individual questioning. Focus groups are for participation, discussion, and challenge. Focus group participants are expected to enrich the knowledge of the marketer through point-counterpoint, debate, and analysis.

In Hispanic research there has been debate as to whether or not Hispanics like to debate topics in a focus group environment. Some marketers and others have typecasted Hispanics by national origin. They have argued that those of Mexican origin are much less likely to discuss and tend to be quiet in focus group sessions. They have also said that Cubans and Puerto Ricans are great in focus groups because they are opinionated and animated.[8] It is true that Mexicans tend to be more deliberate in expressing their opinions and Cubans and Puerto Ricans more extemporaneous, however, all these Hispanics can produce a high amount of rich information under the right conditions.

Key Considerations in Making a Hispanic Focus Group Productive

The moderator is probably the most important aspect of a focus group. A great moderator needs to be a social scientist, a great group facilitator, a marketing consultant, and have a great disposition for enjoying people. As a social scientist the moderator understands and practices the logic of scientific inquiry. He or she understands the rules of evidence and understands how to exclude alternative explanations. A social scientist understands the logic of causality.

As a group facilitator, the moderator allows the group to flourish and produce rich insights and information. A facilitative rather than a directive type of moderator does the best job in general and in particular with Hispanic consumers. A facilitative moderator is almost invisible and lets the consumers shine in their discussion. This facilitator becomes a cultural interpreter between the back and the front rooms in a typical focus group facility.[9]

The moderator needs to have an understanding of marketing theory and practice. Without this he or she is not likely to provide the clients with actionable recommendations based on the research.

Also, the moderator must enjoy people and conversing with them. This seems obvious, but a stiff, unfriendly moderator can easily find his or her way to the front a focus group and have the group freeze. The ability to make people enjoy the moment and the discussion is crucial to good Hispanic focus group moderation. For this the moderator must understand the culture quite well, otherwise he or she may experience difficulties making people relax due to a lack of things in common.

The moderator does not have to be of the same national origin as the respondents. This is a typical concern expressed by marketers who hire focus group moderators. It seems as if there is some underground mythology perpetuated by moderators and others who claim that only Mexicans can moderate Mexicans and only Cubans can moderate Cubans. This is not true. As discussed earlier in this book, the core of the Spanish language is quite homogeneous across national groups. The "common places" are much more prevalent than the differences. Even when differences arise, a moderator can simply ask for clarification and this becomes a finding in the research as opposed to a problem. Idiosyncrasies exist even between villages in the same area and there is nothing wrong in asking for clarification. What matters is that the moderator be a native Spanish speaker if the participants in the groups are native Spanish speakers, or a fluent English speaker if the group participants prefer to communicate in English.

Depending on the purpose of the group or groups, the participants may prefer to communicate in Spanish, English, or have no preference. It is important to note that those who prefer to communicate in Spanish should not be mixed with those who prefer to communicate in English. The simple reason for this is that these two sets of people will not understand each other. This happens more often than one would like to imagine.

If a marketer indicates that he or she wants to have bilingual Hispanics in a group so that he or she can understand what they are saying, beware! That is not a good reason for having bilingual respondents. First of all, bilingualism comes in gradations, from very little English much Spanish to much English very little Spanish. People in that continuum are not equivalent in their attitudes, beliefs, or even communication skills and preferences. Two individuals who claim to be bilingual may not understand each other just because one is more dominant in Spanish and the other in English even though they may both claim to be bilingual. The Spanish or English proficiency of the respondents needs to be taken into consideration in the design phase of the research.

For a specific project a marketer may be interested in Hispanics who prefer to communicate in Spanish because he or she is designing a strategy to introduce an existing product to Spanish speakers. In another case, the marketer may want to reach with culturally relevant messages Hispanics who prefer to communicate in English.

In a more complicated strategy the marketer may want to include those who prefer to communicate in Spanish but who are exposed to both Spanish- and English-language media. For this same campaign the marketer may also wish to include the perspectives of English-preferred Hispanics who are exposed to English- and Spanish-language media. This latter case would be one in which the message needs to be relevant to both segments of the market who are exposed to the media in both languages. Still these two types of respondents should not be mixed in the same groups, but should be segregated into homogeneous groups for the discussions.

Marketers are also concerned about whether to mix nationalities of origin in the same groups. As a rule, the groups should remain as homogeneous as possible to obtain clear readings. For specific purposes the groups can contain mixed nationalities. For example, for translation verification, mixing nationalities can be an asset because the individuals in the group will debate the acceptability of the terminology right there, in one place. For food that represents regional preferences, mixing nationalities is likely to be unproductive. For cars and television sets, however, mixing nationalities may be acceptable, depending on the level of affluence of the consumers. As a rule, the more affluent the consumers the more they can be mixed. Less affluent consumers tend to be more idiosyncratic about their preferences and cultural orientations, as we discussed earlier.

Another issue of debate and continued concern is whether or not men and women can be mixed in the same focus group. As in most cases in the social sciences, it depends. For gender-specific issues, the groups ought to be divided by gender, for example, when the group deals with venereal disease. Men and women are likely to feel more comfortable talking about these issues in gender-segregated groups. Regarding other issues, segregating men and women is also dependent on social class and affluence. More upwardly mobile and affluent respondents have little difficulty debating issues in gender-mixed groups. In lower socio-economic segments, it generally works better to segregate genders just because men may be more dominant than women. Still, the key consideration in deciding whether Hispanic men and women should be mixed in the same group is the purpose of the research. If the purpose of the research is to investigate decision making about food consumed by the family, then it may be relevant to have at least some mixed groups to better understand the dynamic of the decision-making process between men and women.

In doing cross-cultural marketing, as seen earlier, many marketers make the assumption that the decision-making process is individual because that is the model they have used in the past. In a collectivistic culture, the unit of decision may not be the individual, but the couple or the entire family. It seems crucial that marketers suspend assumptions when planning research across cultures. Just think, by interviewing men and women individually regarding a process that is likely to be collective, the marketer may be excluding the interaction itself. Understanding the interaction between men and women in some decision-making processes can be more important than the fears of male domination, and so forth. That is why it is crucial to understand the culture in order to even start asking the appropriate questions in a research situation.

The venue where the research is conducted constitutes another consideration. When researchers and marketers started to use focus groups over 50 years ago, these research sessions generally took place in the homes of consumers who invited others to participate in a discussion session. As the industry became more professionalized, a series of facilities sprouted throughout the United States. These were meeting rooms with a one-way mirror behind the moderator so that observers could unobtrusively watch the discussion. These facilities tend to be located in modern office buildings in most major metropolitan areas. Very few home-like environments for focus groups remain in the United States.

When focus groups took place in homes of members of the community, respondents had little apprehension in attending such meetings. These days respondents are recruited to attend sessions in modern facilities by means of lists of people who have shown an interest in participating in such sessions. Sometimes respondents get invited to participate as a referral from someone else.

After much recruitment and focus group participation over the past 20 years, many Hispanics have become acquainted with the concept of focus groups and get recruited as do other members of the general public. Still, given the fast growth of Hispanic communities due to immigration, and given that Hispanics are not yet included in research sessions as often as others, many Hispanics are still suspicious of invitations to attend such meetings at a formal office location. This is particularly true when friends and relatives have not had any experience doing so. As an example, not long ago in Phoenix, AZ, recruiters could not get Hispanic women to attend a series of focus groups. On the phone women said they would attend, but they did not show up. To find out the reason for the lack of attendance, the moderator personally called the homes of the women who had failed to attend. The reason cited most often was that the husbands had found it very suspicious that their wives were invited to a gathering where they would be paid for their participation. They just found this not to be credible. The moderator asked them to come with their wives and many did attend once they were told the husbands could accompany them to the venue.

In other instances, we have held focus group sessions in church halls, community centers, and other known public locations. Having a venue that the respondents can relate to establishes credibility and trust. This is particularly useful in cases where the respondents are unfamiliar with marketing research and procedures.

Another reason why Hispanic respondents who are unfamiliar with market research may be reluctant to attend is when they are undocumented or illegal in the United States. This happens when the target is of recent immigrants. In this case, having the invitation come from a trusted source and the venue being a well known and trusted place can be of great importance. An example of a failure of this type of respondents to show was when in Houston, Texas, the recruiter chose a facility that was located across the street from the offices of the immigration and naturalization service.[10] No recruited respondent showed up.

Recruiting Hispanics for focus groups requires special efforts. Facilities around the country have been learning how to recruit Hispanics for focus groups. As Hispanics become more abundant in more cities around the United States, more facilities become sensitive to the issues surrounding the recruitment of Hispanics.

Since most focus group facilities in the United States are owned and managed by non-Hispanics, the sensitivity necessary for recruiting them is often absent. When recruiting Hispanics who prefer to communicate in Spanish the recruiter should have native fluidity in the Spanish language, and should understand the culturally based objections that respondents may pose when being recruited. If the supervisor is also a fluent Spanish speaker he or she will contribute to a better recruitment. If the needed respondents are fluent in English they can be recruited by English speakers. A Hispanic recruiter can usually be more effective in recruiting, other qualifications and skills being equal.

The screening instrument is another aspect of the recruitment effort that should be addressed. If respondents are going to be recruited in Spanish it is highly recommended that the screener be in both Spanish and English, on a side by side design. This is important because having the Spanish version available ensures that the recruitment is done in a homogeneous and consistent way, instead of relying on idiosyncratic interpretations by the recruiter. Further, if the supervisors do not understand Spanish, having the English version helps the management of the recruitment process.

When the respondents prefer to communicate in Spanish there should be a host at the facility who is a native speaker of Spanish. This person should be very welcoming and warm to create the right environment. Clearly, respondents of any background will appreciate a warm reception and hosting. In the case of Hispanics this is more important because the respondents are less likely to be cynical about the research situation, and may feel vulnerable in the strange environment. Anything that can be done to make the respondents feel at home will result in a better research experience.

It was already stated that Hispanic focus groups, particularly if they are in Spanish, require specific skills on the part of the moderator. Respondents may utter expressions that may be translated by the interpreter in the back room in ways that may not be either accurate or in context. Thus the moderator has to sometimes paraphrase or explain what he or she has understood so that the clients in the back room get the right idea.

Interpreters are a definite aspect of the orchestration of Hispanic focus groups that can make or break the experience. Focus groups that are conducted in Spanish usually require the services of a Spanish-to-English simultaneous interpreter in the back room. This interpreter may use a system of headsets so that those in need of interpretation into English can listen to the English language. Those in the backroom that prefer to listen to the Spanish language should have the opportunity to listen by means of headphones or via speakers in the backroom to the original Spanish conversation.

No matter how many certifications an interpreter may have, their ability to simultaneously interpret Hispanic focus groups cannot be taken for granted. We already discussed that translation and interpretation, in general, can be fraught with problems. Interpreters in the back room should be formally educated in both languages and ideally should have native fluency in both languages. As a minimum, the native fluency should be in English besides a very good ability in Spanish. The reason why native fluency in English is so important is because this is the version that the clients will be listening to in the back room. Discriminating clients should not accept mediocre fluency in English because then they miss a lot of the meaning of the conversation.

A good simultaneous interpreter does not just speak words as they are uttered in the room but even gestures to convey the connotation of the expressions. He or she uses the inflection of the voice to enrich the clients' understanding of what is happening.

A poor interpretation experience brings about misunderstandings between the clients and the moderator because each is listening to a different version of the same event. Starting out with a good simultaneous interpreter should be complemented with a good briefing of the interpreter so that he or she becomes familiar with the topic and issues that will be discussed.

Debriefing in the backroom is a very important element of any focus group, and fundamental when the focus group project is cross-cultural. After a series of focus groups the moderator and clients must get together to debrief what they have learned and to clarify any cultural nuances and ideas that emerged during the groups. It is a good practice to audio-record this debriefing session so the moderator and/or clients can have a record of the immediate impressions they obtained.

This is not an exhaustive list of issues that can enhance or detract from the success of a Hispanic focus group project. These, however, provide a good basis for thinking about major issues that need to be considered in obtaining Hispanic consumer insights and understanding.

Mini Groups

Mini focus groups are affected by most of the same issues just addressed. Mini groups can take multiple forms in terms of numbers of participants and the time allocated for the sessions. A regular group is usually conformed by 8 to 10 respondents and lasts about two hours. A mini group can be any variation that has either less respondents or lasts less time. A mini group can consist of three respondents for one hour, five respondents for two hours, and so on.

The decision on the configuration should be conceptually based. Usually mini groups tend to be organized when it is necessary to have each respondent elaborate on issues and have enough time to debate. Many red-flag advertising testing situations benefit from smaller groups because that way the client will have more in-depth observations from the discussion. More observations should generally be favored when time and budget allow them. Mini groups are a good way to obtain more observations in a particular project.

Dyads

Dyads also benefit from the synergy of the conversation and discussion. Productive examples of dyadic qualitative interviews are, for example:

- Mothers with a child
- Spouses
- Friends
- Individuals who have something either in common or in contrast

As indicated earlier, when trying to understand decision-making processes that are collective, this type of configuration could be productive if it is carried out properly. Dyads can produce rich information to enlighten how people feel about issues or how they go about deciding courses of action.

In-Depth One-on-One Interviews

When the synergy of the interaction is not important, then in-depth one-on-one interviews can be very productive. These sessions are less vulnerable to the process of social influence that tends to take place in groups. Interviews are best for understanding deep emotions and ideas that take a long time to express and understand. During this type of interview it is common to use projective stimuli that will encourage the respondent to express emotions that would otherwise be difficult. The respondents can turn very productive by means of the elicitation of metaphors and narratives.[11] The majority of the logistic issues associated with focus groups and mini groups hold true for one-on-one interviews except that group dynamics are not an issue.

The marketer should be aware of cultural issues that may make one-on-one interviews less productive than a group discussion. There are marketers that claim that one-on-one interviews are best, and there are others who are enamored with groups. The choice should not be based on preference or emotion, it should be made based on what is needed as a product of the research. This should also consider the cultural impingement that will make one configuration better or worse than another will.

Ethnographic Interviews

In market research the concept of ethnography has gained popularity. Ethnographic methodology is a qualitative approach used by anthropologists.[12] It consists of observing and recording aspects of everyday life as they occur, including the symbolic interaction that takes place among humans.

Marketers and market researchers usually conduct ethnographic interviews that are of short duration compared with the length of time that an anthropologist may spend in a community. In market research an ethnography may take up to six hours, whereas an anthropologist doing field work could spend months observing how a particular group of people live and behave.

The usefulness of observing and interviewing individuals in their own space and surroundings is that we can observe much more than an individual can describe in a contrived interview environment. People remember more aspects of their own behavior when they are in their own environment. Also, they can point to objects and show artifacts and ways of living that are very difficult to replicate in a facility.

In cross-cultural marketing research these interviews have even more value than when conducting intra-cultural research. The researcher typically videotapes and/or photographs the home environment or the shopping situation at the same time that a respondent addresses questions and issues. The marketer and/or researcher become a guest in the environment of the respondent and can then appreciate the richness of behavior in its own context.

As an example, this type of research has shown itself to be extremely useful in product development. When the marketer has the opportunity to watch consumers prepare a type of food in their own environment he or she can obtain much more valid and vivid information as to what is appealing and palatable to the consumer. Also, the marketer learns the context of consumption so that the tone and execution of communications capitalize on the nuances that make consumers relate to the food under consideration.

Depending on objectives, the observer(s) may start the ethnographic interview at the home of the consumer and then continue it during a shopping trip to the local grocery store. If the study is about automobiles, observer(s) may ride along with the respondent and talk about cars and the issues that impact their car preferences. Observing the actual driving behavior is so much more powerful than hearing a description of it.

Ethnographies have become popular and as with any other approach they can be rich in their product or a waste of time. That is why the choice of an experienced and culturally contexted individual can be of great importance to the success of the project. There is a definite allure and value added in sharing experiences with consumers while listening to their stories, passions, and perspectives. This is an approach that is likely to continue to grow in its use.

Scrapbooks and Photographs

As part of ethnographic interviews or as part of most other qualitative approaches, the use of scrapbooks can be very useful in eliciting stories, metaphors, and documenting behavior. If the consumer is given the homework of preparing a scrapbook telling the story of how they use a particular type of product, or their personal history in coming and becoming settled in the United States, the researcher can obtain important insights. These scrapbooks can be used as stimuli for further discussion and for interpretation along with the data obtained in the qualitative research session.

Similarly, disposable cameras can be sent to consumers who have been recruited for qualitative research. Then these consumers may be asked to take photographs of their activities, their homes, and their product usage and bring these to the research setting. They may either come with the developed photographs for stimuli for the research session, or turn their cameras in for the researcher to develop and use for analysis.

Quantitative Approaches

Selection of Approach

A typical first question is "Should I conduct my quantitative study with Hispanics via mail, phone, door-to-door, intercepts, or perhaps online?" All approaches work and have severe limitations. Many times the choice of approach or method of administration will depend on the objectives, the desired rate of return, and the representativeness of the approach.

Mail

Generally, mail administration of a quantitative instrument to Hispanics is not advisable. Again, the success of this approach is related to consumer level of acculturation and socio-economic status. The better educated, more acculturated, and more affluent consumer, if properly motivated, will reply to a mail survey. Those who are more dominant in Spanish, more recent immigrants, and less affluent are less likely to reply to a mail survey.

Overall, mail has been shown to have the lowest rate of return of all methods of administration. The conditions under which mail surveys do somewhat better include:

- The survey comes from a known and trusted source.
- The completion and return of the survey provides a reward to the consumer that is seen as compensating for the effort.
- The survey is very simple to answer with no complex matrixes and no small type.
- The survey is bilingual, back and front, so that language ability or preference is not a deterrent.
- The survey questions are interesting to the respondents.
- The survey is conducted among a group of people with an affiliation to a respected organization.

Response rates to mail questionnaires, as we have observed, have been as low as one percent and as high as 80 percent. The 80 percent return has been very rare and achieved only when the respondents are affiliated with an organization and the president of that organization requests that the instrument be completed and returned for the sake of some organizational goal.

The self-selection of mail surveys among Hispanics tends to favor responses by more formally educated consumers. This, of course, can strongly bias the perception of the marketer studying the results.

Phone

Phone surveys tend to generate the largest amount of cooperation and completion among Hispanics. Although the phone telephone interviewing industry is declining in general, Hispanics still tend to answer their phone and cooperate. This is probably because Hispanic consumers tend to be less jaded than non-Hispanics and enjoy sharing their opinions. This is true in general, although there are markets that have proved to be increasingly difficult. Miami, for example, is one of the markets with the lowest cooperation rate among Hispanics. This is probably because the more acculturated population of Miami has been more extensively studied than others, and this is likely to have generated fatigue and cynicism.

One of the biases in phone research is that more affluent and educated respondents are more impatient and less likely to cooperate than their counterparts are. Respondents to phone surveys, then, are likely to over-represent the newer immigrants who are more dominant in Spanish and who have lower levels of formal education. Still, it seems that phone surveys are the most representative of all approaches. Clearly the sampling approach will largely influence the degree to which the final sample represents the population. So, for example, if the marketer wishes to reach an overall sample of Hispanics in the United States, he or she may want to have a couple of sampling approaches combined. First, he or she may want to have a component by which Hispanics who live in areas of high Hispanic concentration are included.

For example, this could be a random sample of Hispanics in exchanges that have a minimum of 30 percent concentration of Hispanics. This would capture those who are more likely to live in concentrated areas and who tend to be less acculturated for being newer immigrants. Another sample could be a random sample of Hispanic surnames or name-surname combination in areas of low concentration of Hispanics. This would account for those who are more affluent and who do not live anymore in high Hispanic density areas. It is clear that those who do not have a Hispanic surname or name-surname combination may be excluded, particularly from the more affluent segments. Unfortunately, there is no perfection. Research consists of a series of compromises. A fully random sample of Hispanics in areas of low Hispanic concentration could be extremely expensive.

The requirements for interviewers and supervisors are very similar to those expected from recruiters and their supervisors for focus groups. Contracting with research field services for Hispanic quantitative research needs to take into account the importance of having a firm with documented, successful experience in the Hispanic market. A shop that is not specialized in Hispanic survey research is likely to experience setbacks resulting in the cost of the project being higher than anticipated. The best approach in establishing parameters for conducting Hispanic quantitative research is to specify the anticipated incidence and cooperation rate up front in the contract, both with research suppliers and clients. This way, if the incidence or cooperation rates turn out to be very different from expectations, then the costs or the approach can be revised.

Door-to-Door

This used to be a preferred way of interviewing Hispanic respondents. The claim was that Hispanics would be more cooperative and sincere in a face-to-face situation. In the abstract that is probably true. Nevertheless the interviewing situation in door-to-door research is much less glamorous than one would like to imagine.

First of all, more and more consumers refuse to open their doors to strangers due to rampant criminality in certain areas that happen to have high concentrations of Hispanics. Further, the supervision of door-to-door research is much more difficult than in any other approach. Nightmare situations include supervisors and interviewers in collusion making up answers to questionnaires in order to achieve quotas faster. It happens.

The other issue that has largely discouraged the door-to-door approach is the liability exposure of the company doing the interviewing and the company sponsoring the research. There have been cases of interviewers being held at gunpoint in homes of potential interviewees. And this is just one of the liabilities that could be incurred. We recall the stressful time when an interviewer called from the field indicating that drug dealers in East Palo Alto, California, were chasing the interviewer to get him out of their territory.

In this day and age, door-to-door does not seem to be a good approach for data collection.

Intercepts

Intercepts of Hispanic consumers in malls, strip malls, and other public places is common. This is a good approach, particularly if the marketer needs to show them a stimulus to react to. Generally, this approach works well. Cooperation tends to be good, and the data obtained can be verified efficiently.

A main drawback to intercept type of research is its generalizability. A key requirement for being able to generalize from a sample to a population is that the probability of selection of the respondents be known. When randomly selecting from populations, the marketer knows the probability of selection. In intercept research the selection of respondents is by convenience and you can never be sure that the sample represents the population. Still, this is a popular method of data collection, particularly when stimuli need to be presented to respondents.

Online

Online research is becoming increasingly popular. It allows the marketer to present stimuli and obtain responses very quickly. Current estimates are that about 60 percent of Hispanic adults, 18 years of age and older, are at least minimally online. This is a restriction but for certain topics this may be an acceptable limitation. For example, for research on software or online services, this is the right target population. Online research can be very practical if it can be effectively self-administered, the stimuli lend themselves to be shown on the Internet, and the target population is likely to be well represented online. Also, when the research targets younger Hispanics they tend to be more likely than their adult counterparts to use the Internet.

The representativeness of online research tends to be less than that of phone research because respondents for online research generally are recruited via pop-up ads or e-mails that go to affinity groups that may exclude substantive segments of the population. Still, some online panels are very large and contain the profile of the target audience. The marketer may decide to compromise some representativeness for the convenience and speed of online research.

Adrien Lanusse Lopez,[13] a Strategic Director at Cheskin, a research and consulting firm, reports the following characteristics associated with Hispanic adults online compared with those offline based on a Cheskin study conducted in 2004. The study was conducted for the magazine "People en Español," in September 2004, and the subsample used for this analysis consisted of 586 Hispanic adults that came from a random listed sample of Hispanic surnames. According to that study, Hispanics online are more significantly than those offline to:

- Be male (59% of those online vs. 47% of those offline)
- Be younger (average 39.6 yrs vs. 42.6 yrs)
- Be born in the United States (42% vs. 19%) or have lived in the United States longer (19.6 yrs vs. 17 yrs)
- Have a smaller household (3.8 people vs. 4.2 people)
- Be more educated (14.1 yrs vs. 9.6 yrs)
- Be single or divorced (20% vs. 13% single, 7% vs. 4% divorced)
- Be more likely to be employed full-time (68% vs. 50%)
- Be more likely to own a home (81% vs. 62%)
- Not be married to a Hispanic (30% vs. 5%)
- Not have kids under 18 in the household (65% vs. 55%)

- Have household incomes of $50K or more (49% vs. 13%)
- Have a wireless phone (91% vs. 65%)
- Speak English at home most often (48% vs. 20%)
- Speak English most often with friends (65% vs. 21%)
- Prefer speaking English (49% vs. 20%)
- Speak English well or very well (84% vs. 37%)

These contrasts highlight the need to consider carefully who needs to be reached by the online research before using this approach. The Internet likely will be one of the most cost effective ways of reaching Hispanics in the future. Hispanics have been embracing the Web at a fast pace because, as they state, it gives them an advantage educationally and professionally. There is little doubt that in the next few years the Internet will be as pervasive as the phone is now among Hispanics.

Common Types of Quantitative Studies

The most common types of quantitative studies conducted routinely with Hispanics are "Usage and Attitude" and "Tracking" studies. Usage and attitude studies should be really called "Awareness, Usage, and Attitude" studies because product and advertising awareness typically are included as part of those studies. These types of studies tend to concentrate on understanding how a brand fares in terms of awareness, usage, and attitude as compared with key competitors. These are very useful studies because there are few syndicated studies that center on the Hispanic consumer. More and more syndicated studies are appearing in the marketplace, but few can measure all the specific aspects that brand managers are likely to want to know. These studies can provide excellent strategic insights.

Tracking studies tend to concentrate on following consumer behavior over time in order to capture changes in awareness, attitudes, and purchase regarding a brand that is being advertised and distributed in specific markets. These types of studies are very useful to evaluate the effectiveness of a marketing program. Some marketers prefer to do before-and-after tracking studies. Others prefer to do continuous tracking. Each approach has its own advantages and disadvantages. Continuous tracking over time, if the sample size is large enough so that every month there are a couple hundred completed interviews, can be particularly useful. This continuous tracking can serve as a barometer of variations in consumer behavior. If the marketer varies the marketing efforts over time he or she can see variations that can be attributed to his or her actions and discern which are more effective. Clearly, this is not as simple as it sounds, but it tends to be better than just looking at one point in time before a campaign and another point of time after the campaign.

Specific Hispanic Issues in Quantitative Research

Generally, key issues that need to be thought about when conducting or commissioning a quantitative research project with Hispanics include the following.

It is tempting to give the general market supplier the Hispanic part of a quantitative study if they are already familiar with the type of study. The logic appears to be sound. In practice, however, the glitches overwhelm the benefits of the simplicity and synergy of having one supplier. Although many so-called general market suppliers have been incorporating Hispanic research capabilities, that is more the exception than the rule. Even when some suppliers claim to have a Hispanic capability, it could be that they have a supervisor who speaks Spanish, or a couple of interviewers who happen to speak Spanish. As indicated in several parts of this book, having some people who speak Spanish on board does not mean that either the supplier or the Spanish speakers understand the issues that arise in doing research with Spanish- and English-speaking Hispanics. The marketer needs to go out of his or her way to determine the Hispanic proficiency and capabilities the research supplier has. The many issues of translation, cultural adaptation, supervision, and even word order, need to be understood ahead of time. Many times the cultural input that should be included in the formulation of the questionnaire is nonexistent to the detriment of the marketing effort.

Though not foolproof, suppliers who specialize in the Hispanic market are more likely to understand some of the issues. At a minimum they will have had the experience so that the effort is not a waste of time and money. Sometimes it works well to have a specialized company collaborate with a general market company. The key to this is not to give absolute power over the study to the general market company. This way the specialized Hispanic company should have the discretion to make changes that are likely to improve the product.

Still, in our opinion, there are very few companies, even among those who specialize, that understand the market in a way that the research will be enriched by cultural input.

The way in which questions are worded and located in the flow of the questionnaire can make an important difference in the results. One simple example, in which wording and the order of possible choices made a difference, illustrates this point. Interviewers were having a difficult time with a beer study. They could not find very many beer drinkers to interview. Their suspicion was that among Hispanics, particularly Mexicans, to admit that one drinks alcohol can be a strong taboo. When, in the screener for the interview a question read, "do you drink beer," respondents generally said no, and thus they did not qualify for the study. The researchers reasoned that the question should be placed in a context. The question was reformulated as follows:

"Please tell us whether or not you eat or drink each of the following:

READ
a. Soft drinks
b. Coffee
c. Mexican food
d. beer"

Placing "beer" after "Mexican food" dramatically increased the number of people who said they drink beer. The cultural reasoning behind this reformulation was that Mexican food and beer are strongly associated in the culture, thus after admitting to eating Mexican food, respondents would not have difficulties admitting they drink beer. After this relatively simple example, you can see how any study could produce different results just by the researchers' knowing some of the issues associated with the intended questions and products.

Obtaining cooperation from respondents on the phone, or via other administration methods, is difficult. With Hispanics, one key to getting their cooperation is knowing what is important to them and talking with them in a way that they feel the interviewer is empathic and *amable*. The concept of *amabilidad* is not directly translatable. It is related to the concept of kindness, but saying someone is *amable* means the person has a good disposition and treats the consumer with warmth. Approaching an interviewing situation with Hispanics in a machinelike fashion and just reading the interview protocol is likely to result in a rejection. The interviewer has to engage the consumer. We have witnessed the differences between interviewers that for the same study could interview six people in one evening compared with others who could barely get one or two completed interviews. The key difference was not the Spanish language, nor the professionalism; it was the *amabilidad* in engaging the interviewee from the very beginning.

Although interviewers cannot deviate from the way the questions are worded, when conducting surveys with Hispanics, particularly Spanish-preferred Hispanics, some latitude needs to be provided. This latitude should be homogenous and rehearsed before the actual interviewing takes place, however. This means that if the interviewer detects that the interviewee is not understanding a question, or is responding in a rote way, the interviewer should have "ready to go" alternatives right on their computer screen or questionnaire. Clearly, it is better to modify the questions after a problem is detected, but given ample variations in the level of education of Hispanics, some may understand the original question perfectly well, and others may not understand it at all. The provision of alternatives is a way to make the study more valid, as long as all interviewers are trained to do the exact same thing when required.

The interpretation of data is difficult in qualitative and quantitative studies. In quantitative studies the interpretation is particularly difficult when the analyst is not part of the culture. For example, finding out that Hispanics spend over $100 a month in long distance calls compared with a much smaller figure for non-Hispanics is interesting but not terribly illuminating. Digging further into the data with hypotheses in mind can highlight issues that clarify the phenomenon, but for that we need to know more to begin with. For example someone who understands the market would ask for an analysis by years of residence in the United States. Other analyses could be by composition of the family, composition of the local friendship network, and other cultural factors that go beyond income and other demographics.

These are examples of issues that the marketer and researcher need to consider when conducting Hispanic research. Definitely, this is not an exhaustive list, but it should point to the sensitivities that need to be addressed.

The Account Planner

Ultimately, an "account planner"[14] with Hispanic sensitivity is the ideal person for guiding the process of cultural market research. This type of account planner should be a person contexted in Hispanic culture who understands cross-cultural research issues and the logic of scientific inquiry.

The role of the account planner was initially defined within the confines of an advertising agency. More recently that role has been expanded and there are now independent account planners who work with ad agencies and their clients, and sometimes they work directly with marketers in companies. It is an evolution of the role of the researcher in the typical ad agency environment.

The account planner is a strategist that has at the core of his or her thinking the consumer as opposed to the product. The account planner is the representative of the consumer who orchestrates resources to create a successful advertising/marketing effort. The consumer-centric aspect of this role makes it ideal for cross-cultural marketing, assuming the planner is well qualified.

Conclusions

Throughout this book you have heard the importance of understanding culture as key to developing successful Hispanic marketing strategy. Again and again, the emphasis in the book has been on listening to the Hispanic consumer through research. Now, in this chapter the theme is that the research itself must be constructed, implemented, and analyzed with a cultural underpinning.

Whether the marketing researcher is adapting an existing questionnaire for the non-Hispanic consumer, writing a questionnaire in English and then translating it into Spanish, constructing a research instrument, deciding on the advantages of qualitative vs. quantitative, or whether and when to do both, there are cultural nuances to think through. Basic to useful and successful research is the inclusion of well-trained researchers and account planners who are contexted in the culture being studied. With their sensitivity regarding what research questions to ask, how to ask them, and how to interpret them, and a thoughtful, culturally sensitive research process, marketers will be en route to a better understanding of his or her Hispanic marketing target.

This chapter has provided the researcher with broad concepts for understanding the difference between research as it is conducted in the mainstream market and research conducted in the Hispanic market. The marketer now understands the importance of cultural adaptation in translation of an English instrument, the paradox of striving for cultural equivalence, emic and etic theories on cross-cultural research, and common problems with scales as well as other biases in questionnaires. The marketer also has been provided with detailed guidance and suggestions concerning both qualitative and quantitative research. He or she has basic tools to guide research, this critical means for becoming closer to the Hispanic consumer.

This information will also arm the culturally enlightened marketer to lobby for the resources to conduct this all-important research. An important part of those resources are trained Hispanic professionals on the team. As stated in the beginning of this chapter, the subjective parts of cultures are hidden and must be discovered through research. Unfortunately, in the past when Hispanic research did not have the prominence it is now demanding, resources for Hispanic marketing were meager compared to the non-Hispanic market. When conducting research within a culture, marketers intuitively know what makes sense and what doesn't. However, when conducting research with another culture marketers need to practice well-conceived and professionally guided approaches as suggested in this chapter, to its conceptualization, implementation, and analysis.

Implications for Marketers

- The first step in Hispanic marketing research is to consider, in a culturally enlightened way, what you need to learn about these consumers in order to make essential marketing decisions. The various segments of this book as well as this particular chapter have alerted you to the hidden, subjective culture and the psycho-socio-cultural aspects that may lie beneath the observable surface. Taking these into consideration, and working with a trained researcher and account planner, think through what approaches will be best suited to answer your research question.

- Your research question will lead you to deciding whether you need to conduct qualitative or quantitative research, or both, in finding out information about the Hispanic market. Qualitative research will prove particularly useful in developing insights into how Hispanics within your target group think, feel, and make decisions about your product or service. Quantitative research will guide you in understanding what awareness, attitudes, and usage patterns are generalizable to your target and in tracking these over time.

- For qualitative research, make sure to work with a firm that is experienced in Hispanic research. Every step of the way, from the development of bilingual screeners, to recruitment by a well-supervised bilingual team, to moderation by an *amable* (warm or kind) Hispanic qualitative researcher, to simultaneous interpretation by an experienced qualitative research interpreter, needs to be undertaken with cultural guidance such as you find in this chapter. You will need the "right" Hispanics selected, to be interviewing/moderating with them in the appropriate language, a comfortable and culturally sensitive research environment, a Spanish-English interpretation (if conducting in-language research), and a researcher who can debrief with you to help make sense of what has transpired.

- For quantitative research, again select a firm that is experienced working in the Hispanic market and that has a Hispanic research team to lead and implement the project. This chapter has provided very specific guidance on aspects of quantitative research that must have cultural consideration from the development of the instrument, through data collection and interpretation. If the marketer asks the wrong questions, asks them in a way that biases the data, speaks to the wrong respondents, uses the wrong data collection procedures, and other potential pitfalls listed in this chapter, the quantitative research you conduct can end up being worthless or misleading. This could mean a tremendous waste of resources and a marketing failure with your Hispanic initiative.

- On the positive side, the marketer can learn from culturally sensitive qualitative and quantitative research in the Hispanic market, which has brought tremendous benefits to numerous clients in their marketing campaigns. For example, Nissan, working with its advertising agency, Acento, implemented a highly successful campaign in Southern California to bring Hispanic business into Nissan dealerships. This was based on a combination of qualitative and quantitative research in which they developed insights as to what would draw Hispanics into the environment of Nissan's dealerships, and then tested their hypotheses with quantitative research (see Acento Nissan Case Study at the end of Chapter 3).

- Marketers frequently find themselves in the position of being asked to find out the difference between Hispanic and non-Hispanic consumers by testing the Hispanic market using the questionnaire developed for the U.S. general market. The assumption generally is that translating the questionnaire into Spanish will make it suitable for the Hispanic market, and that those who already speak English can use the existing English language instrument. It will be important for the researcher to discuss the potential problems with this approach with those who are requesting it. Among these problems are:
  - The concepts regarding the product or service in the non-Hispanic market may differ for the Hispanic market, while Hispanic concepts, interests, issues, and barriers may not be present in the instrument.

○ Translations present strong challenges as it is almost impossible to reach equivalence between two languages. Actually, often the harder you try for equivalence the less you achieve it, a phenomenon known as the Cultural Research Paradox. Revisit the initial sections in this chapter for more details.

○ Interpretation of findings on items that do not make sense culturally can be misleading and lead to costly marketing decisions. For example, understanding why Hispanics give higher ratings than non-Hispanics requires informed consideration.

• Should you need to move ahead with a translated questionnaire, make sure to use the translation suggestions in this and other chapters, or "cultural adaptation" in order to clarify potentially confusing items for the Spanish-speaking consumer. In addition, work with a culturally trained researcher on the interpretation of the data. Should research findings still prove mystifying, then it will be to your great benefit to conduct qualitative research to develop insights into the rationale.

References

1 Sechrest, Lee, Todd L. Fay, and S.M. Hafeez Zaidi. "Problems of translation in cross-cultural research." *Journal of cross-cultural psychology* 3.1, 1972: 41–56.

2 Pike, Kenneth L. *Language in relation to a unified theory of the structure of human behavior*, 1st ed. Vol. 1. Glendale, CA: Summer Institute of linguistics, 1954.

3 Hofstede, Geert. "A case for comparing apples with oranges: International differences in values," *International journal of comparative sociology* 39.1 (1998): 16+.

4 Van Hemert, Dianne A., Chris Baerveldt, and Marjolijn Vermande. "Assessing cross-cultural item bias in questionnaires: Acculturation and the measurement of social support and family cohesion for adolescents." *Journal of cross cultural psychology* 32.4: 381–396, 2001.

5 Ibidem

6 Osgood, Charles E. and Oliver C. S. Tzeng, eds. *Language, meaning, and culture: The selected papers of C.E. Osgood.* New York: Praeger Publishers, 1990.

7 Argyle, Michael. *The scientific study of social behaviour.* London: Methuen, 1957.

8 Nevaer, Louis E. V. *The rise of the Hispanic market in the United States: Challenges, dilemmas, and opportunities for corporate management.* Armonk, NY: M.E. Sharpe, 2004.

9 A typical focus group facility has a meeting room with a one-way mirror behind the back of the moderator. The clients and observers sit behind the mirror where they take notes and sometimes discuss the conversation of the focus group.

10 Now, this is the U.S. Department of Homeland Security.

11 Zaltman, Gerald. *How customers think*. Boston, Mass: Harvard Business School Press, 2003.

12 Newman, Isadore and Carolyn R. Benz. *Qualitative-quantitative research methodology: Exploring the interactive continuum*. Carbondale, IL: Southern Illinois University Press, 1998.

13 Personal communication.

14 Cooper, Alan, ed. *How to plan advertising*, 2nd ed. London: Cassell in association with the Account Planning Group, 1997.

U.S. Hispanic Media Environment and Strategy

8

Until recently, talking about Hispanic media tended to be associated with Spanish-language media. That differentiated the media environment with which Hispanics have been associated for a long time. The common sense in the industry was that Spanish-language media should logically be the media for Hispanics. That was the logic of the rise and success of the Hispanic advertising industry until recently.

Television

Hispanic-targeted television has been the medium into which most advertising money has been poured. According to Advertising Age, ad spending on network/national and local television in 2003 was approximately $1.8 billion[1] an amount that surpasses expenditures on any other type of media. For many years television has been the gold standard for creating awareness and forming first impressions in the minds of consumers. That role continues to be valid. The evolution of media and consumer preferences is likely to modify the prevalence of this medium. Interactivity and a multiplicity of channels will shape the future of advertising. For the time being the television marketplace is being shaken by competition. This is a very welcome development that should enhance the quality and diversity of content targeted to Hispanics.

Poor quality has characterized the offerings of television, in general. Many viewers, instead of watching what they like, seem to navigate in selecting the least objectionable option.[2] When it comes to television directed to Hispanics, these complaints are exacerbated, but Hispanics have faithfully watched their least objectionable options. For some it has been because of their affinity and need for the Spanish language. For others, favoring television targeted to Hispanics has been because of the cultural affinity it provides. We have heard, over the years, huge amounts of complaints against the programming and the advertising offered in Hispanic-targeted media. These consumers have been complaining about poor quality particularly in comparison with English-language media. The television scene started to change at an accelerated pace right around the year 2000.

Univision Grew with the Market

Univision is one of the most representative media outlets characterizing media thinking from the 1960s to the turn of this century. Emilio Azcarraga Vidaurreta was the pioneer of radio broadcasting in Mexico in 1930, and then became the pioneer of television broadcasting in 1952. As a visionary he purchased television stations in San Antonio and in Los Angeles in the early 1960s. That became the foundation of Spanish International Network in the United States. The rules of the Federal Communications Commission limit the amount of foreign ownership that broadcast organizations can have. That led to the sale of Spanish International Network to Hallmark in 1986, at which point the network acquired its present name of Univision. Hallmark, however, did not seem to know how to manage and organize a Spanish-language network, and their expectations for return on their investment were not realized.[3]

Visionary investors Jerrold Perenchio (United States), Gustavo Cisneros (Venezuela), and again Televisa (Mexico) organized the purchase of Spanish International Network from Hallmark in 1992. These investors were content providers and largely contributed to the success of the revitalized organization that, soon after the purchase from Hallmark, became a publicly traded company. Univision has been a dramatic success in the past few years and has seen profit growth when general market companies experienced losses, particularly during the 2001–2003 recession.

Univision's success was correlated with the dynamic growth of the U.S. Hispanic market over the past quarter century. As we detailed earlier in this book, according to official figures there were 10 million Hispanics in the United States in 1980 and almost 40 million in 2004. The rush of marketers to sell products and services to Hispanics was a major contributor to the success of Univision, who had almost undisputed dominance in Spanish-language broadcasting in the United States until recently. Univision is now a media conglomerate of very large proportions and includes multiple television, cable, print, and Internet outlets.

Telemundo Trying Harder

Telemundo for a long time was a distant second to Univision in the Spanish-language television domain. This network originated in New York in 1986 and had a Puerto Rican orientation at first, and later tried to compete for the much larger Mexican origin audience that Univision had claimed for itself.[4] A group of investors led by SONY purchased Telemundo in 1992. The fortunes of Telemundo were mixed in trying to catch up with Univision for years. In 2002 the Federal Communications Commission ruled in favor of a merger between NBC and Telemundo.[5] Clearly it was General Electric's NBC that acquired Telemundo. This change of fortunes appears to have made Telemundo a much more competitive entity.

Upon inspection of the programming of Univision and Telemundo, you will likely come up with one general conclusion: Both networks offer very similar fare. An abundance of telenovelas is one of the most prevalent features of Spanish-language television and seems to be deeply rooted. The rest of the programming is heavily concentrated on news and entertainment shows. Entertainment shows appear to thrive on beautiful and scantily clothed women, and on very down-to-earth humor. Talk shows are similar to those on Anglo television but have a Latin American slant that make them culturally unique. Reality shows and "candid camera/funny videos" type shows occupy a chunk of the programming. Sports are, of course, a very important part of the offerings of these networks. It is not a stereotype that soccer and boxing are very important to Hispanic consumers. In addition, NBA and American football games have become increasingly attractive to Hispanics.

The Acceleration of Change

Mun2

Telemundo, in its pursuit of a competitive edge, has investigated avenues for strategic advantage. Something that no television enterprise had ever done was to cater to young Hispanics who use English as their main language. No specialized television outlet had tried to reach this segment with cultural relevance. Soon after joining NBC, Telemundo launched mun2 (www.mun2tv.com) as a cable channel directed to Hispanics 18 to 34, with 90 percent original programming in English. Since the median Hispanic age is about 10 years younger than that of the U.S. population at about 26 years of age, targeting Hispanic youth makes sense.

Mun2 has shows that break molds and still target young Hispanics, specifically. For example *Adrenalina* is for x-gamers with adventure, fast action, and outrageous women. *Loco Comedy Jam*, with Mike Robles, searches the United States for the funniest stand-up comedians. *L.A. Streets* is about inner city music including Spanish alternative and Hip Hop. The physical, stylistic, and cultural features of these shows reflect a strong Hispanic profile but lean toward the tastes of youth, particularly urban youth.

The emergence of Mun2 seems to be a symptom of change in direction in the U.S. Hispanic media industry. The emergence of Mun2 has accelerated the rate of change in the industry. It represents a change in assumptions and target. It represents a break with tradition. Their own media had typecast Hispanics for many years. The assumption was that Hispanics would adhere to their Latin American roots and tastes even when living in the United States. Thus the storyline of masters and servants in telenovelas continues. But for young Hispanics, being 50 percent under the age of 26, the story of the maid that aspires to marry the rich master is irrelevant. That story is aspirational in Latin America, but in the United States it breaks down. It is true that rich Anglos and Hispanics have Hispanic maids and nannies, but these are very few. In Mexico having a maid is common and mainstream, thus the relevance diminishes when crossing borders. The weeping and tragic communication style of women on telenovelas can be hardly relevant to young Hispanic women who are growing up in Los Angeles, Miami, New York, Dallas, Houston, and so many other places.

As stated earlier in this book, the Spanish language will continue to be important for U.S. Hispanics on many dimensions for many years to come. Young Hispanics, however, are living in a dual world and their choices and preferences need to reflect their lives. Mun2 is one of those attempts.

Even in the case of those above the median, 26 and older, the relevance of many of the offerings on Spanish language television can be questioned. It is not necessarily that the quality of the shows is questionable, but that the lives of Hispanics in the United States, regardless of how attached they are to their culture, are different here. Their problems, their hopes, dreams, aspirations, and fears, are not the same here as they were "there."

This is partly why Hispanic media is changing, albeit slowly. This is why the competition is increasing. In January 2002, Univision created its own competition with Telefutura. Telefutura programs against Univision to capture viewers that would otherwise be going to English-language TV or alternative Spanish-language stations. Sales materials on Univision.net take pride in announcing that in 15 markets Univision and Telefutura have a duopoly position.[6] Telefutura provides a vast array of movies, reality and talk shows, news, and other programming geared to Hispanics 18–34, very much like Mun2, except that Telefutura is in Spanish. The key strategy of Telefutura is counterprogramming.

Azteca America

Television Azteca from Mexico also has been interested in the U.S. Hispanic market. Azteca America commenced operations in the United States in mid-2001 in Los Angeles and with affiliate stations in several Hispanic markets.[7] Their programming is very much influenced by their Mexican production capabilities and talent. They seem to be gaining momentum among U.S. Mexicans. Still, their programming approach is not radically different from that of Univision and Telemundo, although their slant is more focused on Mexico as opposed to the U.S. Hispanic.

Hispanic Television Network

As part of the transformation of the industry, a new network emerged in 1999 with the name Hispanic Television Network. This was a failed effort that resulted in a filing for bankruptcy in 2002.

Cable and Satellite Options

Cable and satellite companies, besides carrying established networks, have embarked in a competitive campaign to acquire Hispanic subscribers. Their efforts have been successful. According to Nielsen Media Research, by 2000, the penetration of cable among Hispanics was 61 percent compared with 76 percent for the total U.S. population.[8] Data from Nielsen Media Research as well shows that in 2004 16.8 percent of Hispanic TV households have satellite television access compared with 17.5 percent of the total population.[9]

The relatively small differences between cable and satellite TV access for Hispanics and the total population is important. Given that Hispanics are less affluent than the population at large makes their willingness to spend their money on access to entertainment that is relevant to them revealing. Hispanics tend to allocate resources to the consumer products that are important to them in amounts that are disproportionate to their income. Horowitz Associates Inc.[10] report that in their 2004 FOCUS: Latino III study they found that about a quarter of all urban Hispanics subscribe to digital cable compared with an almost identical figure for overall urban markets. This further substantiates the importance that Hispanics place on obtaining the entertainment and information services they want regardless of cost.

Liberation Technologies

Hispanics generally have acquired technology in ways that are disproportionate to their incomes compared with the overall population.[11] This tendency can be attributed to a desire of not being left behind. Thinking about the many U.S. Hispanics that come from underprivileged backgrounds in Latin America elucidates the issue. Many of these consumers did not have a phone line in their homes in Latin America; for them a mobile phone became a technology of liberation. Similarly, the access that cable and satellite television provide to culturally relevant programming and simply more varied and interesting programming becomes aspirational. These technologies allow Hispanic consumers to skip the stages of technological development many of them did not have access to until now.

DirecTV and Dish-Network for satellite television and players like Comcast, Cox Communications, Time Warner Cable, and others are multiplying their Hispanic offerings beyond the offerings of the large networks. Some offerings are directly from Latin America. The availability of movies originally in Spanish or dubbed into Spanish is increasing dramatically via these services. Hispanic targeted programming seems to have had an impact on the adoption of digital services[12] even though not all programming watched is in Spanish.

Time Warner Cable Houston initiated a campaign to increase their number of Hispanic viewers. They found through research that Hispanics were not satisfied with the television content available and wanted more entertainment and sports programming similar to what they enjoyed in Latin America. They also learned that Hispanic households contain members with diverse language preferences. Some family members prefer Spanish, others English, and others switch back and forth. Time Warner Cable Houston addressed these programming interests and provided access to both Spanish- and English-language programming to these consumers. Time Warner Cable initiated a campaign to appeal to them through targeted direct mail. The campaign was made possible by using predictive modeling provided by Geoscape. Since then, Time Warner Cable Houston has experienced significant growth in their Hispanic market. They were particularly successful in attracting bilingual Hispanic households (see the Time Warner Houston Case Study at the end of this chapter).

What Hispanics Watch

A study conducted by Cheskin[13] in 2000 with 4000 randomly selected Hispanics throughout the United States provided interesting data that shows how Hispanics watch television. The response of these consumers to the question, "Approximately how many hours of TV in [Spanish/English] do you watch per week?" provided the breakdown shown in Figure 8.1.

The approximate number of total hours watched per week was found to be about 23. Spanish-language exposure was slightly higher than that to English-language television, with some variation between genders. It is surprising that Hispanics reported they watch as much Spanish as they do English television. The surprise is not because they watch about as much English as Spanish, but that they watch so much in Spanish. Given the availability of literally dozens or even hundreds of English-language channels in almost any location, it is surprising that Hispanics make a special effort to watch television in Spanish. This seems to reveal that the cultural appeal of Spanish-language tele-

Figure 8.1

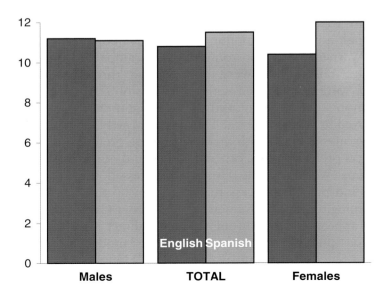

Approximate number of TV hours watched in English/Spanish per week

vision has a strong hold on Hispanic preferences. Clearly, this has given impetus to Hispanic media entrepreneurs to increase the competition in the Hispanic targeted media market. Among the most popular network Spanish shows are the Latin American soap-operas called *telenovelas*. On Spanish cable the most popular shows are comedies like *El Chavo* and *El Chapulin Colorado*, which can be watched by the entire family. Soccer programs are also very popular on cable.

Hispanics are also watching a large amount of English-language television, however. Exposure to English-language media is just logical given the ubiquity of it. On one hand there are popular programs among Hispanics that are available only in English network television like "American Idol," "Friends," "The Apprentice," "The Simpsons," and "Fear Factor." On English cable, programs popular among Hispanics include "Raw Zone," "Sponge Bob," "Scooby Doo," "MTV's Punk'd," and "Fairly Odd Parents."[14]

The division of time exposure to Spanish and English television seems to be driven by gender, age, and acculturation. Adult women largely drive exposure to *telenovelas*, whereas young people and adult men drive exposure to most of the other programs. Because of the collectivistic orientation of Hispanic consumers, different members of the family influence many consumer decisions. This information on programming preferences by family members within a household has important implications for Hispanic marketers who choose to advertise in this medium. They should consider using both Spanish and English television when attempting to reach Hispanic consumers. In this way they will reach family members who prefer to watch in one language or the other, as well as have overlapping coverage when family members watch the same programs in English and in Spanish together.

Radio

Radio is a very culturally relevant Hispanic medium that has experienced rapid growth and consolidation in the past few years. The chart shown in Figure 8.2 is from the 2000 national study of Hispanics by Cheskin.

According to that study Hispanics listen to about 15 hours of radio per week, with slightly over half of that exposure being to Spanish radio. Hispanic radio is mostly in Spanish with the exceptions of the *Tejano* format found largely in Texas, and a few new youth-oriented formats in major metropolitan areas. These formats mix Spanish and English.

Figure 8.2

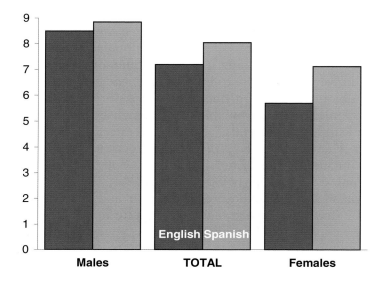

Approximate number of hours Hispanics listen to radio in English/Spanish per week

Given that Hispanic consumers tend to be largely concentrated in the service and labor occupations of the U.S. economy, their jobs lend themselves to radio listening. Hispanic workers with outdoor occupations in construction, landscaping, transportation, and agriculture can have the radio on while working. Others in service-related occupations in food service, hospitality, and housekeeping jobs have similar opportunities for radio exposure. Hispanic radio provides companionship and information while driving to and from work, and while at work. In fact, Hispanic radio exposure peaks early in the morning, in the middle of the day, and during the afternoon commute, and 66 to 75 percent of radio exposure between 8 A.M. and 6 P.M. occurs outside of the home.[15]

Hispanic radio offers the music that reminds the listener of home and the joy of being culturally connected. Many very successful Hispanic radio talk shows in several parts of the country deliver humor that touches these consumers in ways that English radio cannot. *El Vacilón de la Mañana* is an example of this very culturally contexted humor and entertainment show. These programs have been so successful that they have been expanded to different regions in the country. In this format, a host with a team of talent orchestrate short sketches and tell jokes, tell about rare and unusual events, and inform the audience about items of relevance to their jobs, immigration status, education, and so on. Radio, in the Hispanic community, plays the role of the town crier evocative of medieval times.

Hispanic radio shows provide education about finance, cooking, children's education, consumer issues, health, and many other topics of relevance to the community. Hispanic radio in many communities still provides community service announcements so people can locate each other, ask for and get advice, and provide a sense of community.

The success of Hispanic radio has been such that in 10 of the 12 largest Hispanic markets, a Hispanic radio station has the largest rating not just among Hispanic stations but among all radio stations.[16]

The Culture of Radio Listening

The heritage of radio listening comes from a long-term tradition from Latin America. Latin America has over 4000 radio stations that serve everywhere from the small communities with local stations to the large metropolitan areas.[17] Local radio stations act as voices of the community to entertain, to locate people and services, and even to disseminate agricultural prices.

Although Latin Americans watch much television, access to good signals is still not universal. This is particularly true for less affluent consumers. Given the limitation of television availability and the relatively low levels of literacy impacting print media usage, radio is a media mainstay for many. This Latin American tradition of radio exposure is then carried to the United States through migration.

Radio stations in the United States have been, in many ways, the folk carriers of Hispanic culture. Hispanic radio stations in the United States have been able to serve the small communities and the needs of workers and farmers. Loyalty to radio appears to be persistent. Radio listenership has increasingly carved a niche in Hispanic media plans due to its pervasive use.

Hispanic Radio's Growth and Consolidation in the United States

Several Hispanic radio networks have been created as the result of consolidation over the past few years. Hispanic Radio Networks include:

- CNN en Español Radio
- Entravision Communication

- Hispanic Radio Network, now Univision Radio
- Katz Dimensions
- Lotus Entravision Network
- OM Media Networks
- Salsoul Network
- Spanish Beisbol Network

Radio Unica Networks was one of the larger competitors in recent years. It would have figured in this list but its investors decided to sell the properties and recover their investment. Radio Unica is perhaps the most notable example of a failure in Hispanic radio. Most other consolidations and acquisitions have enjoyed relative success in recent years.

One of the most salient acquisitions in 2004 was Univision's purchase of Hispanic Radio Network, with over 150 stations. Univision Radio, as it now is known, has added to the multimedia platform of Univision, further enhancing Univision's capacity to offer media packages to advertisers. This acquisition reflects the importance of radio as a powerful medium in the Hispanic community.

Other media conglomerates are now eager to make a Hispanic radio play. Viacom has recently entered into a strategic alliance with Spanish Broadcasting System to build a Hispanic multimedia aggregate of offerings. In addition, Spanish Broadcasting system has also entered into a five-year agreement with ABC radio to syndicate the three most popular morning Hispanic talk shows.

Spanish-language radio was an assortment of properties in Hispanic markets in the United States. The current trend of consolidation is leaving fewer but powerful players that are likely to both limit competition on one hand, but enhance the stature of Hispanic radio through multimedia alliances on the other.

Underestimating Radio

Many who advertise to Hispanic consumers choose radio as a secondary option. Sometimes the main reason for using radio is because it is much less expensive than television. As stated earlier, from a cultural perspective, Hispanics have a strong tradition of radio listenership.

Many marketers do not seem to understand the usefulness of radio. As a medium, radio has great potential in delivering the stimuli that consumers embody in their heads. Radio, if used properly, should be used to stimulate the consumer's imagination. It should be used in an integrated communication plan in which the different brand touch-points are included. The strengths of each medium should be exploit-ed in a cohesive planning approach.

Marketers sometimes let inaccurate consumer observations drive their media decision making. Hispanic consumers, almost invariably, will say they learned about a brand mostly from television, even if for that specific brand there has not been any television weight. The abil-ity of the marketer to judge information and discriminate consumer input is crucial. It is even more crucial in the case in which the mar-keter crosses cultural boundaries.

The successful use of radio is by engaging the imagination of the consumer with story-telling and stimuli that spark creative thoughts. Consumers remember engaging stories. If these stories have strong brand relevance and pairing, radio can be more powerful than most other media. A key obstacle is to come up with the creative talent that knows how to write ad copy for radio. Radio is not television without pictures. Once this is understood the power of radio can be unleashed. The success of talk shows like *El Cucuy de la Mañana* in Los Angeles, and now in other markets, demonstrates that radio is unique and pow-erful in delivering entertainment and commercial messages. Renan Almendarez Coello *El Cucuy de la Mañana* has created a very suc-cessful artistic career by understanding how to create great radio and the cultural background of his listeners.

Still, It Is Not Only Spanish Radio

Although Spanish-language radio is very successful, and increasing-ly so, as seen in the chart in Figure 8.2, Hispanics also listen to English-language radio. Clearly, those who are more acculturated are more likely to listen to English language radio, but on average, radio expo-sure is about equally divided between English and Spanish. As with other media, the conclusion here is similar. The marketer needs to look at the media mix to reach different Hispanic constituencies with an open mind. English language radio also attracts the attention of Hispanics and should be considered in media plans.

Print

Print has been an underdeveloped category of media in the U.S. Hispanic market. This underdevelopment has been due to three major issues:

- Functional literacy
- Distribution
- Content

Functional Literacy

Since the vast majority of Hispanics in the United States trace their roots to humble backgrounds in Mexico and other parts of Latin America, their access to formal education before coming to the United States was limited. Although Mexico and most of Latin America claim low illiteracy rates, functional literacy has been the key problem. Workers from farm backgrounds and other labor-related occupations do not have much opportunity to rehearse their literacy skills. These skills tend to atrophy and actual readership of materials has tended to be relatively low. Data from the Cheskin study of 2000 quoted earlier produced the results shown in Figure 8.3 regarding newspaper and magazine readership.

Hispanic consumers in that study read newspapers approximately two to three times a week, in English somewhat more than in Spanish. They also claimed reading newspapers and magazines for a total of close to five hours per week. English-language publications were favored to some extent over Spanish-language options. Clearly, the

Figure 8.3

Approximate weekly time spent reading English/Spanish newspapers and magazines

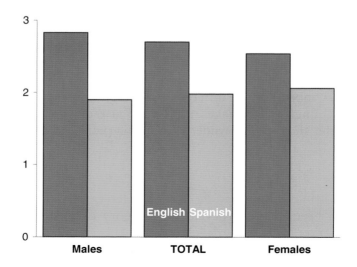

amount of time spent on print is dwarfed by the time these consumers spend on television and radio.

A lack of a reading tradition in the cultures these consumers come from is reinforced by the functional illiteracy of many of these consumers. These authors have estimated that about 30 percent of Hispanics studied over the years are functionally illiterate.[18] That does not mean that they cannot read simple materials. It means that they face severe obstacles reading at the level in which most publications are written, be it Spanish or English.

Some marketers assume that by advertising in Spanish-language print they will reach Spanish-dominant Hispanics. Marketers can reach some readers in Spanish, but many Spanish-dependent Hispanics have serious difficulties reading in Spanish as well as in English. Preference for Spanish-language publications is for one or a combination of the following reasons:

- The consumer cannot understand the content in English, thus Spanish is his or her only option. Publications like *Nuestra Gente* from Sears are specifically geared to this audience. Clearly, any Spanish-language publication works for this consumer with the caveat that functional illiteracy can be a constraint. As discussed earlier, just the fact that a publication is in Spanish does not mean it can reach all Spanish-dominant consumers. The readability level of a publication should be considered here. Consumers who can read at the third grade level or lower need a style of writing different from those who can read at the ninth grade level. Thus print directed to less literate Hispanics needs to have an approach that is very different from that needed to reach Hispanics who are fully literate.

- The consumer can understand some English but feels reassured by reading the material in Spanish, or having a bilingual publication for comparison and learning purposes. Most Spanish-language or bilingual publications can satisfy this consumer.

- The consumer can understand English well, but the content is more available in Spanish. There are publications like *El Nuevo Herald* or *La Opinion*, which have news from Latin America and U.S. Hispanics that cannot be easily found in other publications. Also, publications like *People en Español* and *Latina* satisfy this type of consumer.

There are cultures that are more oral than they are literate.[19] The United States has traditionally been a literate culture. The circulation of the daily edition of Los Angeles Times on September 2004 was over 900,000 copies.[20] In contrast, the circulation of *La Opinion*, the Hispanic newspaper with the largest circulation, also based in Los Angeles, has slightly over 125,000 copies.[21] Considering that there are now over seven million Hispanics in the Los Angeles DMA, representing 41 percent of the DMA,[22] the contrast is impressive.

Another illustrative contrast would be to compare the daily circulation of the New York Times of 1.1 million[23] to the circulation of Mexico's *Reforma*, which could be considered a comparable paper, of 150,000.[24] No other serious news-oriented papers in Mexico have higher circulation, and Mexico now has over one hundred million people. To put it in a different perspective, the New York and Mexico City DMAs have approximately the same official population of about 20 million people. Each of the two newspapers is a leading paper in their DMA and that makes the contrast even more striking. A lesser orientation toward literacy has been part of the obstacles associated with lack of readership. This obstacle is slowly subsiding as U.S. Hispanics become more educated.

Distribution

Distribution has been another major obstacle to readership. The observation that Hispanics spend some more time per week with English-language publications can be partly explained by the ubiquity of general market English-language publications. It is still very difficult to find Hispanic- or Spanish-language magazines or newspapers in major outlets, with the exception of stores in areas of very high Hispanic concentration. As with other media, English-language print is part of the omnipresent environment of Hispanics and non-Hispanics. But even English-language Hispanic-targeted publications are hard to find.

Magazine racks at checkout stands in supermarkets generally do not feature Hispanic titles because they try to maximize their sales to the demographic of the specific geographic area. Still, not having Spanish-language publications available in areas of relatively low Hispanic concentration contributes to a self-fulfilling prophecy. If the publications are not available they are not purchased, and if they are not purchased marketers do not make them available. For example, a city like Redwood City, California has Hispanic traffic but not as high as the other areas of neighboring Menlo Park. Hispanic publications are more available in small outlets in the Menlo Park areas where density is high. However, supermarkets in Redwood City are unlikely to carry any Hispanic-targeted or Spanish-language publications, and even less likely to display them at checkout stands.

Marketers should take note of the importance of distribution as they attempt to target Hispanics. Hispanic publications will prosper to the benefit of advertisers when consumers can easily find them.

Print Media Content

Magazines that are considered successful in Latin America, like *Vanidades*, have relatively small circulations in the United States. Vanidades has paid circulation of over 95,000 copies and attracts the largest amount of advertising[25] of any paid circulation magazine directed to Hispanics. Still, magazines like this tend to be directed to middle class, literate types of consumers. This type of publication does not seem to target the less educated consumer or the more U.S. acculturated consumer.

Few magazines in the past 20 years have made a concerted effort to understand the U.S. Hispanic consumer until recently. The advent of magazines like *People en Español* and others like *Latina* magazine have come to fill the gaps that have existed for a long time. These two are very successful paid circulation magazines. *People en Español* has over 425,000 paid circulation copies and *Latina* has almost 310,000.[26] These are unprecedented numbers for Hispanic targeted magazines. An interesting exception is the legendary *Selecciones del Reader's Digest* that has a tradition tracing back to Mexico and other parts of Latin America. Its circulation is over 330,000 copies.[27]

Now, in 2004, there is a proliferation of periodicals attempting to fill Hispanic content voids. These voids have been largely due to the lack of understanding of the consumer, and the lack of financial interest in the market. Prior to the current explosion in Hispanic print, content was generally translated and outdated by the time it made it to Hispanic publications. The key is the identification of audiences and their needs and preferences.

Hispanic print is now experiencing a renaissance in the United States. *El Diario La Prensa* of New York, and *La Opinion* of Los Angeles joined forces in 2004 to create a Hispanic print consortium of great magnitude. Recently they announced the acquisition of the number one Hispanic newspaper of Chicago, *La Raza*. The years 2003 and 2004 have seen the launch and enhancement of several newspapers and magazines serving the Hispanic market. Newspapers like *Hoy* in Chicago and Los Angeles have been sprouting and commanding attention. Magazines like *Catalina* are attempting to attract new women readers by catering to "mind, body, and soul." The list is extensive and very encouraging.

There is a print transformation in the U.S. Hispanic market. Marketers should now start to capitalize on their Hispanic print investment. It is like other self-fulfilling prophecies. The more interesting and appealing print outlets there are, the more Hispanics will pay attention to them, and the more these publications will find a place at retail and through subscription. There is no question that, as in any gold rush, there will be winners and losers. Overall, consumers and marketers will benefit from this surge.

The Movie Theater

According to the Motion Picture Association of America, in 2002 Hispanics spent $1.5 billion at the box office. According to figures from this organization, Hispanics account for 55 percent of the opening weekend audience.[28] Movies are one of the least expensive entertainment options in Latin America and there is an established movie-going tradition. Also, the social aspect of movie-going makes this custom culturally compatible.

At the same time that Hispanic culture is becoming increasingly popular in the United States, Latin American cinematography has experienced a renaissance. Titles like *Y tu Mama también*, *Amores perros*, *Frida*, *Women at the verge of a nervous breakdown*, and many others have brought added cultural reinforcement to U.S. Hispanics and also have created a new respect for Hispanic culture among the overall U.S. public. More recently there is a new current of movie titles that attempt to appeal to both Hispanics and non-Hispanics with a cultural or social message. The movie *A Day without a Mexican* is the dramatization of the hypothetical situation in which all Mexicans leave Los Angeles for one day. The importance of the work that Mexicans do becomes painfully apparent when they disappear from the social and economic sphere, even for one day.

Another recent movie, *Spanglish*, brings to the fore the drama of Mexican immigrants that come to the United States to serve the needs of better-off Americans. This is a story that resembles the typical Latin American *telenovela* or soap-opera in which the humble maid falls in love with the master. Although the title *Spanglish* does not have much to do with what the movie is about, it conveys the culture clash that the movie portrays. This movie dramatizes the cultural encounter of American middle class with illegal working class immigrants from Mexico. The aim of this movie is to appeal to both Hispanic and non-Hispanic audiences, and it has elements of attraction and interest for both. More of these type of productions are expected in the near future; that is, movies that address the circumstances of Hispanics in the United States.

The Internet

Studies of Hispanic use of the Internet have proliferated. The accuracy of those studies vary depending on sampling approaches and the ability of the researchers to properly design studies to understand online consumer behavior. Some of these studies are done by asking about how many people in the household use the Internet. Others are samples of individuals who are asked about their own individual online behavior. Studies of the latter type usually are conducted with adults. The discrepancy of existing estimates is quite large. For example, the Pew Hispanic Center estimated that 59 percent of Hispanic adults were online in 2003,[29] but ComScore Media Metrix estimated that the same year a third of all Hispanics were online.[30] You can see that there is ample uncertainty about the actual number of Hispanics online.

An educated estimate based on the different available studies and our experience is that about 65 percent of all Hispanics use the Internet in 2005 in some way. That would include the young person who uses the Internet at school, the worker who uses it at work, and the adult consumer who has access at home. Clearly, many individuals have access at home, at work, or at school. And, of course, the levels of use vary dramatically from sending and receiving a few e-mails to surfing and using the Internet for shopping, banking, and so forth. Those who are more acculturated tend to use the Internet more than those who are less acculturated. Increasingly, however, those who are still dependent on the Spanish language are becoming involved in online activities.

Portals like AOL Latino, Univision.com, Terra, Yahoo en Español, and others are increasingly attracting the attention of those who prefer to communicate in Spanish. Still, most online browsing is in English. That is not surprising because there are so many more options in English. Nevertheless, sites in countries of origin, and the increasing quality and depth of Spanish-language sites, will continue to drive the Spanish-language Internet experience.

The Customization of Culture

The Internet has provided Hispanic consumers with unique tools to customize the culture of the different environments in which they live. With the advent of the Internet and other digital technologies, Hispanic consumers have been able to escape the forceful immersion into the Anglo world that their predecessors experienced. The Hispanic consumer can communicate with friends and relatives in countries of origin with unparalleled ease and economy. Via e-mail, and now Internet telephony (VOIP), Hispanic consumers can be in constant touch with others who may live in Latin America or in other Hispanic communities in the United States. This is something that has never been possible before.

The Internet makes it also possible for Hispanic consumers to learn about news in their countries of origin via web sites. It allows them to be exposed to streaming media of their cultural preference. Innovative music sites such as Batanga.com make a very large assortment of Latin American and Spanish music available online, in addition to English-language genres that appeal to young Hispanics, like Hip Hop.

One of the main complaints of Hispanic media consumers of local news broadcasts and newspaper coverage is their parochialism. The Internet does away with parochialism by definition. International and Latin American news are now available all the time to those who care to seek them out.

The Hispanic consumer can watch shows with Hispanic cultural flavor, listen to Latin music, learn about developments in Latin America, learn about Latin American history and traditions, communicate with significant others who share their cultural orientation, and in sum, can customize the cultural environment of the home to their liking. The exact degree to which the customization of the home environment is a mix of Hispanic and non-Hispanic traditions constitutes a very important empirical question worth pursuing. At a minimum now Hispanic consumers can decide what to keep and what to abandon from their original culture. Thus the home culture can be quite different from the culture at work, and at other social settings.

Customization is the key to the freedom that the Internet provides. The Internet makes the need to assimilate much less pressing than ever before. That is why biculturalism is the most likely Hispanic trend. Hispanics can increasingly navigate between the two cultures and behave in ways relevant to each.

Marketing and the Internet

Different studies have shown that Hispanics shop online. A 2002 study conducted by Cheskin for *People en Español*, the HOT study, showed that 50 percent of Hispanic adults, 18 years of age and older, had purchased something on the Internet in the past year. This is an outstanding finding because the proportion of Hispanics purchasing online, if at least sporadically, seemed very high. Many Hispanics had indicated in qualitative studies that they distrusted the Internet for purchases due to potential fraud and other hazards. This finding should encourage marketers to find ways to serve Hispanic customers online.

Reinforcing that finding, as reported on March 2004, the second AOL Roper ASW Hispanic Cyberstudy found that in 2004, 43 percent of Hispanic adults shop regularly or occasionally online, and 52 percent indicated that shopping online was one of the reasons they obtained Internet access.[31] The Internet, as an empowering technology, shows great promise in expanding the potential of marketers to establish relationships with Hispanic customers.

Grassroots, Networks, Promotions

Marketers have started to realize something that has been a cultural trademark of Hispanic consumer behavior. Approaching Hispanic consumers where they live and socialize had been the secret of just a few marketers. Almost a third of Hispanic women in the United States have at some point in their lives been associated with a network marketing effort.[32] Avon, Tupperware, Shaklee, Jafra, Home Interiors, and others have been extremely successful by capitalizing on the affinity that Hispanics have to be approached via social networks for commercial purposes. These are household brands that have grown because of the great word-of-mouth power of network marketing.

Network marketing is particularly compatible with the ways in which people buy and sell in Latin America. The notion of buying from relatives and friends is traditional and well accepted. This is a form of grassroots marketing. These companies stimulate informal networks to build brand equity and excitement for products.

There are product categories that have not exploited this potential. Technologies, and particularly computer companies, have been notably slow to realize that Hispanics are more likely to buy if approached via a social network. We have argued for many years that the penetration of computers in Hispanic homes could be accelerated dramatically by going out of the store and into the homes of consumers.

If computer retailers were to stimulate computer parties at the homes of Hispanic consumers that do not yet have the technology, the diffusion of computer adoption could be accelerated quickly. It is very unlikely that a Hispanic consumer, after seeing a culturally appropriate demonstration of a computer at home, would fail to make a purchase on the spot. Once the consumer witnesses at home, in a social group situation, the communication, entertainment, and informational strengths of the Internet, the benefits become undeniable. Further, if the group sees the virtue of the technology, individuals are very likely to make a commitment.[33] Getting out of the store and into the places where consumers are has shown to be a powerful marketing approach among populations of developing countries.[34] U.S. marketers generally are not used to the idea of going out to the streets and homes in the pursuit of consumers. Those who know the secret have done very well.

There are companies that have specialized in Hispanic grassroots approaches. Alternative & Innovative Marketing LLC (AIM) led by Jeff Symon is one such company. AIM conducts grassroots experiential marketing to Hispanics. One such approach has been to send vans to promote consumer products. They have also organized concerts in which specific products are promoted. Several other companies of this type are emerging. In other cases, traditional Hispanic advertising agencies are now including grassroots marketing approaches in integrated marketing communication campaigns.

A New Way of Thinking

The marketer and his or her media planner seeking to reach Hispanic consumers these days need to start with a media-neutral planning approach. They cannot assume anymore that Hispanic marketing is done only via Spanish language media; they cannot even assume that they should use conventional media.

Media-neutral planning starts with few assumptions. A profitable starting point is to begin with a matrix of touchpoints, which include conventional media, by objectives. Each cell in the matrix is then filled out with the action needed for each objective and for each touch point. Clearly, the emphasis placed on each touchpoint will depend on the likelihood that a particular touchpoint will reach the target consumer. Media, or rather touchpoint, weights need to be assigned according to the anticipated impact of each touchpoint.

One of the weaknesses in traditional media planning has been the assumption that if a medium or touchpoint is capable of reaching a certain number of consumers, that number will correspond to the effectiveness of the touchpoint. That has been a fallacy promulgated by traditional media for a long time. Eventually media and touchpoints in general will be evaluated not for how many people they can reach, but for how many people they actually have an impact on or engage. This is similar to the notion of charging for "clicks" on web sites. The click is a good indicator of effectiveness because it means the person actually did something to get more information or take an action. Just knowing that a person receives a newspaper does not mean he or she will see the ads or even read the paper at all.

Hispanic media-neutral planning means to look at Hispanics in their complexity in the light of marketing objectives without prejudging the effectiveness of any touchpoint. Cross language, cross media/touchpoint approaches can always be a consideration. A message in Spanish in Spanish-language media can be complemented by a message in Spanish in an English-language medium in order to better capture the interest of an audience. Similarly, an English-language message in Spanish-language media may deserve consideration under specific circumstances.

Conclusions

The evolution of the Hispanic media in the United States mirrors the story of the discovery of Hispanic consumer identity. In each medium—television, radio, print, movies, and the Internet—there has been an historical awakening to the existence of the Hispanic audience and its interests. At first, pioneers brought limited Spanish-language programming to a grateful audience longing to hear the Spanish language, view images from their home countries, and learn the news from Latin America. But, over time, as their numbers grew, Hispanics felt discontent with the paucity of media offerings for them, and the lack of fit in the content to the reality of their lives in their adopted country. The media began to attune to the newly identified Hispanic consumer in the 1980s, and wake up to the market's growth in the 1990s; but it took off in new directions like a Roman Candle with the explosion of Hispanic consumer identity in the 2000s.

Each medium has its own story with accomplishments and future challenges. However, competition is stiffer from within each medium and across platforms, and Hispanic consumers are more demanding and have more options to customize their own media environment. Television for Hispanic audiences has emerged from one to two networks mainly in Spanish, and now includes a variety of cable and satellite options to appeal to Hispanic consumers. The greatest innovations have occurred since the beginning of the millennium. Some of these include English-language programming to address the diverse language segments of the Hispanic population. Still, the available programming does not meet the needs of Hispanic viewers, and they do watch about as much non-Hispanic English TV as Spanish.

Radio perhaps has been a medium for U.S. Hispanics with the keenest awareness of their cultural identity. Radio stations have brought humor tuned to the reality of Hispanics' existence within their adopted country. The medium has recognized their information needs for news from the United States and from their countries of origin. It is also a very important companion medium for Hispanic listeners who can tune in during their work hours. Hispanic radio stations have enjoyed enormous popularity compared to their English-language competitors, and are top stations in 10 of the largest Hispanic markets. There has been enormous growth and consolidation of Hispanic radio networks since 2000, attesting to its importance in Hispanic media. Radio will need to continue to diversify in order to maintain its salience with the Hispanic market, particularly as bilingual and English-language Hispanics will be looking for entertaining, culturally relevant programming.

The print medium has been the least popular of all media with the Hispanic market. Potential reasons for that are numerous: Print media is less important in their countries of origin, Hispanics tend to have more of an oral vs. a literate culture, functional literacy is relatively low for Hispanic immigrants to the United States, newspapers and magazines have been fewer in number and less available, and finally content has not been tuned to the Hispanic identity. Only recently have such magazines as *People en Español* and *Latina* caught the interest of Hispanic readers with stories they can relate to and images of popular Hispanic stars. These magazines have been highly successful, and the message behind their success is clear. There is no success without cultural awareness of Hispanic readers.

The Internet usage by Hispanics, again a phenomenon of the 2000s, is the story of using a medium to reflect unique cultural interests. Hispanics are on the Internet, across generations in the household, across languages, and across platforms. Their rate of adoption of the Internet is outstripping the general market. Their use of the Internet is versatile—e-mail, telephony, video streaming, tuning into music, playing games, shopping, and so on. With the Internet, they are satisfying their cultural longings in a way that has never been available to them before.

Marketers need to understand the media options available for communicating to the Hispanic market. Each medium continues to evolve in response to the demands of the Hispanic market; and Hispanic consumers are customizing their use of each to fit their own unique cultural requirements.

In previous chapters, the current complexity of the Hispanic market has been discussed from a variety of perspectives. In order to communicate advertising messages to this complex culture, Hispanic marketers must be clear in their marketing objectives and then select the medium or combination of media that will best carry their message to Hispanic consumers. These decisions need to be made in a culturally informed, systematic way in order to reach the Hispanic target market in the most effective way. The history of Hispanic media, its success and shortcomings, has taught that lesson.

Implications for Marketers

- Marketers have a new range of media at hand to target the complex, segmented Hispanic market of the 2000s.

- Marketers have the traditional Spanish-language television networks for access to Spanish-dominant Hispanics, and TV continues to be a persuasive and informative medium for a large segment of the market.

- Marketers should be aware of the potential of evolving English-language television options such as Mun2 for younger English-speaking Hispanic consumers.

- English-language media has become a viable option for communicating with Hispanic consumers and media plans now call for starting with a blank slate.

- Spanish speakers have branched out to a range of cable and satellite options to get more variety in programming; take these into consideration when advertising to the Spanish-speaking audience.

- Radio is an excellent, local medium for reaching a large swath of Spanish speakers, depending on the specific objectives of your campaign. It can serve as a more intimate complement to wider campaigns as well as give attention to other local grass roots advertising.

- Be aware of the limitations of print advertising in reaching the Hispanic market. Tailor content to the reading levels of the target. Be mindful of the newspapers and magazines that are actually relevant to the cultural needs of Hispanics.

- Keep in mind that the Internet is achieving wide usage in the Hispanic market with both Spanish and English speakers, with more than half of Hispanics shopping online. Using the Internet as a medium can provide versatility in reaching Hispanics across language segments, and should be taken into consideration depending on marketing objectives.

- Overall, marketers have the chance to think in a new way about media planning and to use a wide variety of media options from traditional television to the Internet to grass roots strategies to reach Hispanic consumers. Carefully planned, cross language, cross media/touchpoint advertising can create powerful outcomes for Hispanic marketing campaigns.

Case Study: *Time Warner Cable – Houston*

Company/Organization: Time Warner Cable–Houston
Geodemographic Research Company: Geoscape
Campaign: Increase Hispanic Adoption of Time Warner Cable Television in its Houston metropolitan service area
Intended customers/clients: Hispanic households in the Houston area

Background:

Time Warner Cable set out to increase market share in its Houston service area and to fulfill its FCC obligation for making cable television service accessible for the entire community. The company understood the potential of the Hispanic market segment in Houston, which, as of 2003 according Geoscape data,* had the fifth largest Hispanic population in the United States, with 405 thousand Hispanic households and 1.6 million individuals in the metropolitan area. Yet, Hispanics appeared to have a lower adoption rate of cable than the non-Hispanic market, which meant that noncable subscribers had either direct-to-satellite service or no service at all.

Time Warner Cable decided to appeal to the Hispanic segment of the Houston population through a targeted direct mail campaign. However, they had only addresses of those who did not have cable in the area, which did not help to identify which of these addresses were households of Hispanic origin. Their challenge then was two fold: 1) To craft a culturally relevant message for their multimedia campaign which included television, radio, and direct mail that would increase the appeal of their cable service, and 2) to reach Hispanic noncable subscriber households in the Houston area with their direct mail campaign.

---

* Geoscape, *American Marketscape DataStream: 2003 Series*

Discovery Process/Research:

To address these challenges Time Warner Cable Houston conducted qualitative research to understand the reasons why their cable services were not attracting larger portions of the Hispanic population. They also used Geoscape, targeting specialists in the Hispanic market, to create a multivariate statistical model for predicting noncable subscriber Hispanic households' likelihood to subscribe to cable television.

Cultural Insights:

Time Warner Cable recognized that to create a culturally relevant and persuasive message for Hispanics, they needed to think both about the campaign itself and the programming and service that were the heart of the content. They learned that the Hispanic market wanted mainly entertainment and sports, basically similar programming to that which they had in Mexico or other areas of Latin America. These consumers were used to Mexican networks, which brought them news from Mexico and Latin America. However, Time Warner Cable also knew from their research that they had a challenge since programming with the broadest Hispanic appeal was not available due to contractual restrictions.

They learned that they should not stereotype Hispanic households regarding language preference. These households had various language preferences within them with some family members preferring Spanish, others English, and others switching back and forth. Overall, regarding language, they understood from Hispanics in the area that they did not want to be consigned to a Spanish-only world, they wanted options of watching relevant Spanish language programming and then being able to switch to English programs as well. They particularly disliked watching English language movies which were dubbed in Spanish, and often badly translated. They preferred to watch a movie in English rather than to have it ruined with bad Spanish coming out of the mouth of a movie star they were familiar with as an English speaker. They objected to badly translated subtitles and to poor translations overall.

They also learned from the research that television-watching was a social activity, in which family members gathered within their own home, or joined other families in their homes for particular programs of interest. Once they understood this, they could interpret statistics from quantitative studies which showed more households watching HBO than subscribing to it. This meant that households joined together to view programming particularly that which may have been too expensive for some to purchase on their own.

To create their predictive model, Geoscape made use of existing data sources including transaction data items of Time Warner Cable's existing customers, household level information from Geoscape's existing household level database, and from its geo-demographic database. They used CASS standards of the US Postal service to ensure that compound names were appropriately formatted. After all of this preparatory targeting, they directed mail to likely households with culturally appropriate messages for these Houston Hispanic potential subscribers.

Expression of Insights in the Campaign:

The main guideline for Houston Time Warner Cable's communication campaign was that Hispanics needed to be invited to be customers, with culturally relevant messages and visuals. They wanted the product explained clearly and to have the reasons why the cable service was relevant to their lives. They didn't want to be consigned to a Spanish language world, but to have options that fit with their cultural interests. Time Warner Cable learned that they had a strong challenge in making their campaign a success since Mexicans were more used to having satellite than cable; they needed to change perceptions with a message on what could satisfy these consumers' interest. Houston Time Warner Cable runs continuous back-to-back acquisition campaigns utilizing TV, radio, and Direct Mail.

Effect of the Campaign:

Time Warner Houston Cable has experienced significant growth in the Houston Hispanic market since the introduction of their Hispanic-focused campaign. In particular, they have been successful in attracting bilingual Hispanic households with higher incomes.

Figure 8.4a

Time Warner Houston Cable mailer (front)

Figure 8.4b

Time Warner Houston Cable mailer (back)

References

1 *Hispanic Fact-Pack*. New York: Advertising Age, 2004 edition.
2 http://www.iek-akmi.gr/corpus/tvsched_concepts.htm
3 http://www.ketupa.net/televisa.htm
4 Dávila, Arlene M. *Latinos, Inc.: The marketing and making of a people*. Berkeley, Calif.: University of California Press, 2001.
5 http://www.fcc.gov/transaction/nbc-telemundo.html
6 http://www.univision.net/corp/en/utg.jsp
7 http://www.aztecaamerica.com/corporate/what/history.shtml
8 http://www.nielsenmedia.com/hispanicsvs/hisp/n_p_4.html
9 *Hispanic Fact-Pack*. New York: Advertising Age, 2004 edition.
10 http://www.horowitzassociates.com/stories_templates_67.htm
11 *The digital world of the US Hispanic II*. Redwood Shores, CA: Cheskin, 2001.
12 http://www.horowitzassociates.com/stories_templates_67.htm
13 *The digital world of the US Hispanic II*. Redwood Shores, CA: Cheskin, 2001.
14 Information on program preferences was derived from the *Hispanic Fact-Pack*. New York: Advertising Age, 2004 edition. These are based in ratings by Nielsen Media Research data.
15 *Hispanic radio today*. New York: Arbitron, 2004 edition.
16 Tichenor Jr., McHenry T. "Don't sell Univision short," *AdWeek marketing y medios*. December 2004: 27.
17 http://www.zonalatina.com/Radio.htm
18 Interestingly, Mexico recognizes that about 30 percent of its population is illiterate. See http://www.esmas.com/noticierostelevisa/mexico/393825.html.
19 Biakolo, Emevwo. "On the theoretical foundations of orality and literacy," Research in African literatures, a.2: 42–65, 1999.
20 http://www.latimes.com/services/newspaper/mediacenter/la-mediacenter-2004-1028,0,4741715.story
21 http://www.laopinion.com/corporate/company_information/circulation/index.phtml?lang=en
22 SRDS. *Hispanic media and market source*. Coconut Grove, Florida: SRDS, 16, 2, June 2003.
23 http://www.nytadvertising.com/was/circulation/pages/contentCirculation/0,1013,,00.html?l1Id=5
24 http://www.elasesor.com.mx/listas/lista287.html
25 *Hispanic Fact-Pack*. New York: Advertising Age, 2004 edition.
26 Ibidem
27 Ibidem
28 http://www.ahorre.com/archives/2004/08/hispanics_spend.html
29 Spooner, Tom. *Regional variations in Internet use mirror differences in educational and income levels*. Washington, D.C.: Pew Internet & American Life Project, August 2003.

30 Morrissey, Brian. *US Hispanics are biggest share of Spanish speakers online*. Internetnews.com, March 17, 2003. http://www.internetnews.com/stats/article.php/2110451

31 http://www.timewarner.com/corp/newsroom/pr/0,20812,670346,00.html

32 This is an estimate based on observations in several hundred qualitative sessions.

33 Schramm, Wilbur Lang. *Big media, little media: Tools and technologies for instruction*. People and communication; 2. Beverly Hills: Sage Publications, 1977.

34 Rogers, Everett M. Communication strategies for family planning. New York: Free Press, 1973.

The Evolution of Hispanic Marketing

9

Introduction

There are three main sections of this chapter. The first is a historical overview of the market—where it came from, how it got its name, and the evidence of its growing importance. The second section is the story of the Hispanic market based on the interviews of six professionals who share their perspectives as those who dedicated years of their lives to its development. The final section concludes with a discussion of what the Hispanic market has achieved and its meaning for Hispanics and the United States overall, as well as implications for marketers.

The Origin of a Market

The Hispanic market is perhaps one of the greatest marketing creations of recent times. It exists because marketers have been saying it does for over 30 years. The Hispanic market can be thought about as a gigantic culturally identifiable segment of the U.S. population. However, the Hispanic market did not always exist as such in the United States. The term Hispanic first became a reality from the need of government entities to enumerate and classify types of U.S. residents.

Local and regional marketing efforts to reach pockets of Hispanics in the United States have been around since the origins of the U.S. as a nation. Prior to the 1980s these targets were identified as Spanish speakers or those from certain Spanish-speaking countries rather than

Hispanics. Small- and medium-sized businesses in Texas, California, Florida, and New York, where there were relatively large concentrations of Spanish speakers, have been addressing the needs of aggregates of Hispanics for a relatively long time.

The origin of the term Hispanic goes back to the U.S. government's awareness of an uncounted population segment that warranted being included in the census. In 1977, the director of the U.S. Office of Management and Budget, Bert Lance, issued a document entitled "Race and Ethnic Standards for Federal Statistics and Administrative Reporting."[1] The document emphasized that the classifications were not scientific or anthropological, but of practical importance to the different branches of the government. That taxonomy is still in use with some modifications.

In that document Hispanics were defined as "A person of Mexican, Puerto Rican, Cuban, Central or South American or other Spanish culture of origin, regardless of race." The specification of the term "Hispanic" resulted from much discussion and compromise. The classification scheme created controversy but appeared to serve the purpose of counting and clustering those people living in the United States who traced their roots to Spanish-speaking countries.

The 1980 Census, which included statistics on this new Hispanic classification, gave rise to major news stories. These stories generated debates about the implication of there being approximately 10 million Hispanics in the United States. This aggregate term now provided a way to think about this market and to consider its business potential. This was, after all, an issue of labels.

The 1980 Census, then, with its ability to aggregate Hispanics, brought about a major shift in the way in which American companies looked at this emerging population. It was the magic of language that influenced the social cognition of companies, and of Hispanics themselves.[2] The Hispanic market was now on the scene.

An Explosion of Identity

Organizations like LULAC,[3] The American GI Forum, ASPIRA,[4] The Congressional Hispanic Caucus, The Cuban American National Council, MALDEF,[5] The National Council of La Raza, The National Puerto Rican Coalition, and other Hispanic organizations had been established before 1980. The impetus of the 1980 Census stimulated the creation of many more organizations at the national, regional, and local levels. The Hispanic Yearbook of 2004 lists approximately 4000[6] Hispanic organizations compared with just a few in its first year of publication in 1986. Interestingly, the new Hispanic label in 1980 has been utilized by many of the new organizations that have emerged in the United States since then. Not only have organizations adopted the label Hispanic, but also two of the most established magazines carry the name Hispanic; that is, *Hispanic Business Magazine* and *Hispanic Magazine.*

Similarly, the number of national and multinational marketers who started paying attention to the Hispanic market experienced a surge after the release of the 1980 U.S. Census. Soon after the 1980 proclamation that the 1980s was to be the decade of the Hispanic, Hispanic businesses, and Hispanic units within businesses emerged or consolidated. This decade set in motion the rise in the influence of the Hispanic market, an up-curve that not only has continued but increased its incline into the new millennium.

The label Hispanic, as if it were a brand, became the symbolic handle by which everyone could refer to a population that had been seen as disparate before. This became an interesting illustration of how a name creates the reality it is supposed to represent. The social identity of Hispanics started to become salient not only to organizations, the media, and marketers, but to Hispanics themselves. All of a sudden a new identity had been created.

Understand that this identity did not come about without controversy. Soon after the Census launched the label Hispanic, academics and social organizers protested and attempted to create alternative labels. Latino was the label that came about as a protest to being labeled by the bureaucrats in Washington. Still, as noted earlier in this book, the label Hispanic has been more widely accepted.

The new construction of the Hispanic social and consumer reality has become a major phenomenon in U.S. business circles. All major businesses have increasingly paid attention to Hispanics in most regions of the United States. Hispanic consumers, on the other hand, have largely accepted this pursuit. U.S. Hispanics have enjoyed the recognition and the attention.

In an interesting turn of events, the labeling has strengthened Hispanic identity and pride. Many Hispanic consumers in the many surveys that we have conducted have stated that they feel good and important because marketers are after them. They have also stated that they reciprocate to the importance that has been conferred upon them. They have stated routinely that they become loyal to those who cater to them.

In a consumer society, the recognition of the consumer contributes to the strengthening of identity. The next pages contain the story of Hispanic ad agencies and Hispanic marketing units in companies that have been the architects of this market.

The Story of the Hispanic Market

For this chapter, six professionals[7] have shared their perspective of the U.S. Hispanic market based on their experience across the years they have dedicated to its growth. They have created a composite story of the Hispanic market as those who have participated in shaping it. Like other leaders who drive the development of a culture, they and their organizations in turn have been changed by Hispanic consumers who feel their identity in a new way. Hispanic consumers have grown not only to understand themselves through Hispanic marketing, but also to demand the recognition and attention they deserve from those who serve it—as individuals, agencies, companies, and the government. As Dolores Kunda from Lápiz-Integrated Hispanic Marketing said: "When you have John Kerry and George Bush on the campaign trail trying to speak Spanish, people are getting it."

There are common characteristics that define these six Hispanic marketing professionals that are evident in this chapter: unstoppable perseverance, supportiveness for their colleagues, courage in the face of obstacles, creativity in confronting the uncharted, and devotion to increasing personal and organizational professionalism. They have acted as change agents within their own organizations as well as those of the client companies they serve. Consummately, they have displayed the devotion and care to the Hispanic consumers that they ultimately serve. The culture they have created within Hispanic marketing is similar to the overall Hispanic market—it's personal, highly interactive, and laced with a great sense of humor.

Five of these six professionals have operated within the context of Hispanic advertising agencies, and one as a marketing professional in a large corporation. Most have been in Hispanic marketing since the 1980s, with two entering in the 1990s. The stories they told of their careers are typical of the history of this market. Several worked within organizations with evolutionary name changes from the companies and partners that merged and separated over the decades. Others founded their own companies or moved from one company to another as they pursued Hispanic marketing. Another has worked in key marketing positions within a large corporate structure with a focus on diversity marketing.

Ernest Bromley of Bromley Communications has been managing Bromley for over 20 years. He joked that sometimes changes in ownership resulted in company names as long as some law firms, which created tongue twisters for the telephone receptionist. Bromley states that over all these changes the philosophy and management of the company have stayed constant. Now the company he heads carries only his name.

Ray Celaya of Allstate had a strong intuition in the 1980s that there was enormous potential in the Hispanic segment of the population for Allstate. He worked within the corporate structure of Allstate on the creation of their Diversity Action Team in 1989 and the eventual sophisticated company-wide Hispanic marketing strategy of the 1990s described in the Allstate Case Study (at the end of Chapter 5).

Dolores Kunda of Lapíz Integrated Marketing began her work in the U.S. Hispanic market with a four-person service department within Leo Burnett. She tells of her drive to create an independent entity for Hispanic marketing, and after seven years of pressing her vision, Lapíz became a reality in 1999.

Hector Orcí, of La Agencia de Orcí & Asociados, and Rochelle Newman-Carrasco of Enlace Communications began their careers as professionals within different Hispanic agencies, and eventually ended up heading their own. Mr. Orcí began at La Agencia de McCann Erickson, McCann's Hispanic Division, in the 1980s and founded La Agencia de Orcí in 1986.

Rochelle Newman-Carrasco started her Hispanic marketing career 25 years ago with a newly formed agency in New York, Font Vaamonde. She ended up founding her own company, Enlace Communications, in California, 10 years ago.

In contrast, Montse Barrena of Grupo Gallegos has worked across several major agencies in California and Texas since the early 1990s, eventually becoming associated with Grupo Gallegos. This latter company was formed by a colleague, John Gallegos, with whom she had collaborated at Noble y Asociados before it merged with Bromley.

These marketing professionals and their organizations seem like the interlocking genealogy of an extended family. Indeed many, many professionals within Hispanic marketing have known each other over the years, and are well aware of their indebtedness to common early-generation "ancestors" of the Hispanic market from the 1970s.

These six Hispanic marketers described their perceptions of the history of the Hispanic market with emphasis on the struggle in the early days of the 1960s and 1970s for recognition, and followed by three decades of increasing clout and professionalism in the industry. Their story falls in four major segments: The Early Days of the 1970s; The 1980s' "Decade of the Hispanic"; The Take-off Years of the 1990s; The 2000s "Latin Boom" with Hispanics now, according to the census, the largest U.S. minority. The story of the media is told in more detail in Chapter 8. However, these six marketers include its evolution as part of the history of the Hispanic market, so it will be alluded to in this chapter as well.

The Early Days of the Hispanic Market

Mr. Orcí described the early days of the market in the 1970s as the beginning of an infrastructure on which the Hispanic market of the 1980s based its take-off. Spanish-language media in the early days of this decade and even back to the 1950s and 1960s was already devoted to Hispanic consumers. It included SIN, Spanish International Network, with roots in Mexico's Televisa, founded by Emilio Azcarraga Vidaurreta, which eventually became Univision; Caballero Radio Network in New York; and La Opinion on the West Coast.

Telemundo, founded in 1986 and now part of NBC, created a nostalgic video, "Hispanic Marketing: Yesterday, Today, and Tomorrow"[8] with comments from some of the early pioneers in the Hispanic market, such as Danny Villanueva, Alicia Conill, Paul Casanova, Norma Orcí, Hector Orcí, and Lionel Sosa. The stories told in the video show an early understanding of the growing Hispanic consumer dynamic in this country and the pride in the pioneers who addressed it.

In this video, Danny Villanueva of SIN (Spanish International Network) described the struggles in these early days of the Hispanic market as doing "missionary work." He recalled a time when he made an impassioned pitch in Milwaukee to a beer client. "When I finished they asked—why don't they just speak English?" Alicia Conill, founder of Conill Advertising in New York, described the first major national campaigns in the 1970s, such as Colgate, McDonald's, and Coca Cola. Regarding those early days, she described their struggles: "Young people should know what we went through."

These are a few examples of the pioneering feel of these early days. These are the times when the market did not yet have a name and when marketers worked on regional projects in relative isolation. The ensuing decades give evidence to the growing solidarity of professionals who serve the market, and its increasing influence on business and Hispanics themselves.

The 1980s' "Decade of the Hispanic"

The 1980s got branded as the "Decade of the Hispanic" by Lionel Sosa in a late 1970s' campaign for Coors, according to Ernest Bromley. Although the name for this decade stuck, several of the marketers interviewed feel that the term better applies to the following two decades in which wider awareness of the Hispanic market grew among advertisers, the general population, and Hispanics themselves.

The greatest boost of the decade to the Hispanic market was the 1980 Census, which counted Hispanics as a category for the first time and established this as an important segment in the United States with a population of about 10 million. Large corporations began to take notice and got into the Hispanic market in the 1980s in the beer, tobacco, fast food, soft drinks, and package goods categories. Mr. Orcí mentioned La Agencia de McCann worked in the early days with Coca-Cola, Disneyland California, Delmonte, Buick, and the California Milk Advisory Board.

Mr. Bromley noted that big companies in these categories had sales teams out in the stores where Hispanics were making purchases. These sales representatives were the ones that brought the message back to their corporations on the potential of this previously unacknowledged market. Procter & Gamble, which has always been consumer oriented, took early initiative to reach these consumers. Interestingly, for P&G Hispanics have now become the dominant moms of 18–24 years in their diaper category in the United States.

Prior to the 1980s, data on the U.S. Hispanic market from reputable research companies either did not exist, or had to be obtained through expensive studies conducted for an individual client. This was a sales barrier for Hispanic agencies. Hector Orcí mentioned that one of the important happenings in the 1980s was that SIN sponsored the Yankelovich study on the Hispanic market. This research was conducted twice in the 1980s, yielding trusted findings for companies to base decisions about entering this market.

Still, expanding into ethnic segments was an innovation, and companies were reticent to take risks. When they did decide to enter the Hispanic market in the 1980s they kept their Hispanic agencies on a tight leash. In those days, according to Mr. Orcí, Hispanic agencies had to offer to take very small budgets and return profits on that budget within the quarter.

Ms. Newman-Carrasco characterizes the 1980s as "the sleeping giant" years. Although the Census was a big deal, worthy of a Time Magazine cover, it wasn't until the 1990s that the Hispanic market came into its own decade. In those earlier years, she noted, you had to sell the Hispanic market through "belief and vision" because there wasn't yet sufficient data to support its relevance to companies' products and services. Those large companies who had already opted into the Hispanic market were beginning to see results in the 1980s. In fact, it was in 1987 that Procter & Gamble, according to Ms. Newman-Carrasco, told all their general market agencies that they needed to have Hispanic market capabilities. This launched intense activity in the advertising world with purchases, mergers, and growth of agencies that were focused on the Hispanic market.

The Take-off Years of the 1990s

The 1990s brought a new sophistication to U.S. Hispanic marketing from client companies that had early commitment to it from the 1980s. These companies now institutionalized that commitment throughout their organizations with the support of the highest levels of management. Allstate provides an excellent example of a company that developed a diversity marketing plan with a carefully considered integrated initiative, that permeated the way they do business with the Hispanic market, and eventually with other diversity markets as well.

According to Ray Celaya of Allstate, Allstate formed a small team of high-level managers to clarify the meaning of diversity for the company in 1989–1990. Subsequently, a Diversity Change team developed the strategy for the U.S. Hispanic market that was implemented in the 1990s and later. The Allstate Case Study at the end of Chapter 5 describes their 800# campaign in detail. This campaign was integrated through all parts of the company that touched the Hispanic market, from corporate entities to insurance agents in the field, as well as the advertising agencies and other involved vendors. It is important to recognize in this chapter that Allstate's commitment to the Hispanic market resulted in extraordinary measured results for the company.

In the 1990s, other large companies that had marketed to Hispanics began to be rewarded for their "investments in segmented markets," according to Mr. Bromley. These were companies like Allstate and Honda, which integrated Hispanic marketing into the way they do business, from strategic planning from the top of the organization down through the implementation of advertising and delivery in the marketplace. Ms. Newman-Carrasco, Ms. Kunda, and Mr. Orcí all spoke of the need for Hispanic marketing to be brought into initial planning and budgeting stages, rather than tacked on as an afterthought. The ad hoc treatment of the Hispanic market as if it weren't part of the overall marketing of a company, has often meant that available funds have not been allocated to it. This was a strong challenge to Hispanic marketers in the 1990s, and still continues to be so with many advertising investors today.

Ms. Barena explained that in the 1990s "the category" drove which companies were early investors in advertising to the Hispanic market. Although packaged goods companies like P&G readily saw relevance of their categories to Hispanics, for example, automotive companies saw more restricted opportunities. Although they had a long-term interest in the market for the future, they didn't recognize broad immediate importance across their makes. For example, stereotypes of Hispanics, in the absence of hard data, influenced some companies. Ms. Barena mentioned one consumer stereotype she was exposed to in the automotive industry: Hispanics buy used cars and don't have enough money for new ones. This over-generalization to the market is an illustration of what Hispanic marketers had to battle in this period.

Ms. Kunda noted that in the early days of her work with Lapíz in 1992–1999, the Hispanic market was almost like a "stealth bomber" for companies: "It was there and it was growing but nobody really new about it." Even though those in industry knew the demographics and many were contending with saturation of their product/service in the general market place, they did not see the Hispanic market as a potential for addressing their problem. Ms. Kunda commented, "I remember in the early days, I would know that they wanted to grow their business . . . that they can grow their business if they pay attention to the U.S. Hispanic market in their backyard, so I would go and sell my heart out and present the loyalty and growth of the market."

Near the end of the 1990s Hispanic advertising agencies formed AHAA (Association of Hispanic Advertising Agencies),[9] an association that would consolidate Hispanic Ad Agency mutual interests and concerns, and increase the professionalism of Hispanic marketing. Hector Orcí was the first president, one of the founders, and its historian. He said that Eduardo Caballero of Caballero Radio Network called a meeting eight years ago in Dallas, which resulted in the creation of the charter and its first 15 members. Mr. Orcí said that there had been talk over the years about doing something like this, but that Eduardo took the initiative to organize the event and invite about 40 agencies. According to Mr. Orcí, Mr. Caballero opened the meeting by saying, "I'm going to leave you guys and check on you at the end of the day . . . to see what you have done." By the end of the day, 15 agencies signed the charter and there were many others who had interest.

In the first year AHAA achieved its objective to get 20 Hispanic agencies to join. Its next objective was to have every one of the Hispanic agencies that qualified become a member. This more ambitious objective took several years to accomplish. Currently, AHAA has over 70 members. AHAA has become a vital organization, which has shaped the focus, standards, ethics, and professionalism of Hispanic marketing.

AHAA has become a visible entity known to advertisers, the government, and the press. Internally, according to Orcí, AHAA is well-managed both from an organizational and financial perspective. This has allowed the organization to increase its services to members. Its web site, www.ahaa.org has information on many of these member benefits including AHAA's semi-annual conferences, media university, research reports, and facts about the Hispanic market.

Mr. Orcí says that AHAA starts from a very Latino basis, that members share information and support one another. He said that the reason people go to meetings is because they really like each other. Hispanic agencies face the same kinds of problems, and people who have met and solved such problems are willing to share. He believes that the power of sharing has made individual Hispanic agencies and AHAA as a group very successful.

The 2000s' "Latin Boom"

Ms. Newman-Carrasco refers to this last decade as the "Latin Boom." The 2000 Census figures kicked it off with the Hispanic market for the first time emerging as the largest minority group in the United States, making up almost 14 percent of its population. It is a time when Hispanic performers like Jennifer Lopez, Salma Hayek, and Ricky Martin are known across the spectrum of the U.S. population; when Hispanics, Anglos, and other ethnic groups are dancing salsa; when being Hispanic is something to be proud of; and when speaking Spanish is considered an asset. About 45 million Hispanics are now a market force, spending over $700 billion annually in the United States. No longer is Hispanic marketing driven by a few categories like milk, diapers, and beer, but opened wide not only to the staples of the 1990s but to a full range of products including luxury items.

In the 1990s, Hispanic agencies formed around large major clients such as Procter & Gamble, AT&T, Bank of America, and Coca-Cola. They needed these major corporate clients to survive. Some clients, as previously mentioned, were dedicated to the Hispanic market as part of their marketing strategy; other large and small clients were hot or cold on the Hispanic market depending on which marketing manager was in place. Hispanic clients and their agencies marketed mainly to the large bulk of the Hispanic population who were Spanish dominant. They reached them through the limited Spanish-language media available. Client companies who were committed developed loyal Hispanic customers and received a substantial return on their investment.

In the 2000s, Hispanic marketers are turning their attention to a different, more segmented Hispanic population than the previous decade. Given the increase in the overall number of Hispanics in the United

States, there are now sizeable new segments of the market of interest to Hispanic agencies and their clients. These are clearly in addition to the huge Spanish-dominant part of the market, which is continuously refreshed through immigration.

One of these areas of segmentation is according to languages spoken: Spanish, English, or both. Mr. Bromley emphasizes that Hispanic agencies must take ownership of the whole language spectrum of the Hispanic market including the English dominant and bilinguals, as well as the Spanish dominant. The expertise of Hispanic agencies needs to focus on the cultural commonalities of the Hispanic market, rather than be limited to the Spanish language. He considers that the bilinguals will be the battleground for Hispanic agencies and for Hispanic media content providers in the future.

"We're all after Hispanic eyeballs," Mr. Bromley contends, and bilinguals can turn to Spanish or English programming, depending on what's of interest to them. This means that network TV, and all mainstream English language programming, can now compete for a large sector of the Hispanic market. Already the more sophisticated companies take into account the various language segments of the Hispanic market, and Hispanic agencies develop campaigns to address them. However, more companies in this decade are asking about marketing to specific language segments and the rationale for targeting them.

According to Ms. Barrena, it is now a challenge to explain to clients why the English-speaking segment of the Hispanic market cannot be addressed through the English media campaigns from the general market. Her research for one client indicated that more acculturated English-speaking Hispanics had more in common in product usage and attitudes with less acculturated Spanish-speaking Hispanics, than with the general market. Her client had assumed that they could speak to English-speaking Hispanics in the same way as the general market. Although it would depend on the product, Ms. Barrena said, "you just cannot make that assumption."

The bicultural segment is becoming increasingly salient in the Hispanic culture. Ms. Kunda believes that the Hispanic teen segment will spawn the next wave of trends in the United States. She feels that the teen capacity to flip back and forth between English and Spanish, selecting from various aspects of both cultures, lends itself to creativity. She also mentioned that an important related trend toward biculturalism is "retroacculturation." This is the tendency of Hispanics to reclaim their roots. Hispanic adults who gave up speaking Spanish in the United States, perhaps in their teens, are going back and studying the language of their heritage to recapture their Hispanic identity.

Also, Hispanic parents, motivated by renewed pride in their culture, urge their English-speaking children to learn Spanish. This retroacculturation trend is occurring as part of the more open and accepting environment in the United States toward the Hispanic culture.

Another way segmentation is discussed more frequently in this decade between marketers and clients is by generations in the United States, according to Ms. Barrena. This adds to the complexity of the conversation because it becomes confounded with language and acculturation. Should a client target more recent immigrants who are first generation for a product that may hold considerable equity from their country of origin? Or, should that client expand and include second-generation Hispanics who may still hold a cultural affinity to the product, but speak primarily English? These kinds of questions are among those that Hispanic agencies need to address.

One clear trend mentioned by Hispanic marketers is that the Hispanic market itself is more demanding. Hispanics in the 2000s expect to be addressed by advertisers. Their expectations frequently include having bilingual materials with well-translated Spanish, having marketers come to them in appropriate venues such as the supermarkets where they shop, having retail environments that are culturally friendly, having Spanish speakers who explain products and services, and having advertisers who are involved in their communities in culturally relevant ways.

Companies that target this market in culturally relevant ways tend to be successful. Those who don't turn these self-aware Hispanics away from their business. In addition, there's a little bit of mistrust from Hispanics toward advertisers. They are more sophisticated and recognize when campaigns include less Spanish language coverage than English, according to Ms. Barrena.

Mr. Orcí also mentioned that now in the 2000s, the Latino community itself has become a lot stronger. Various Hispanic organizations served the Hispanic community across the 1990s such as LULAC and MALDEF. However, what has happened in this decade is that Hispanics are more visible outside Hispanic circles as well. They participate on boards of directors and serve in prominent government positions. For example, Mel Martínez was elected a U.S. Senator from Florida and Alberto González has become the U.S. Attorney General in the second Bush administration. Hispanics are also much more involved in the business world now, graduating MBAs and achieving the kind of success in corporations that is noted not only in Hispanic business but in mainstream business magazines as well.

The Hispanic market is also gaining tremendous stature from its influence on the general market. Latin influence is everywhere: in music, dance, movies, food, fashion, and movie and TV programming, as mentioned by these professionals. Speaking Spanish is "cool" and can be heard often and sometimes exclusively in U.S. cities. Spanish words are being absorbed into English. Eating salsa instead of ketchup is the norm. Hispanics are also seen in advertising both in English and Spanish with greater frequency. This influence of Hispanics seeing and hearing themselves in the wider society has brought pride to the Hispanic community. The efforts of Hispanic marketers have strongly contributed to making this happen.

The Hispanic media has grown tremendously in the 2000s. Still, the breadth of options does not approximate what is available in the Anglo-English language media. Univision has grown, and Telemundo, now part of NBC, is competing more strongly and has launched Mun2 for English speaking 18–34 year olds. Other options now include Azteca America, Telefutura, and many cable and satellite offerings. Radio, print, and the movies have also increased their targeting of Hispanics, and Spanish-language Internet options are available. All this, of course, opens up avenues of marketing to Hispanics, including the new segments already discussed. (A fuller description of Hispanic media is presented in Chapter 8.)

Despite all this change in Hispanic marketing, Ms. Newman-Carrasco, Mr. Orcí, and Ms. Barrena all mentioned that there are still old themes that persist. There are still companies who have not yet considered the Hispanic market, and the Hispanic market is underrepresented in overall U.S. advertising dollars compared to the general market, documented in the AHAA web site. Building new clients' knowledge about the Hispanic market and keeping them from dropping out will require the same patient effort already offered over the years by Hispanic marketers. In addition, Ms. Newman-Carrasco maintains that working with CEOs to set Hispanic strategy seems to be harder these days. They seem to delegate more, have ROI pressures, and staff cut backs.

Ms. Barrena says that she has clients at various stages in marketing to Hispanics: those whose main target is the Hispanic market, those who have advertised before in the Hispanic market and are coming back, and those who are just starting. A mix of clients at various levels of commitment to the Hispanic market seems to be common to advertising agencies. This means that they need to explain the market to those who are unfamiliar with the culture and guide their entry, as well as respond capably to the marketing expectations of those who are more sophisticated. The overall versatility of Hispanic agencies as the market booms, requires cultural expertise, the capacity to be articulate about a complex market, and the persistence that has brought the

Hispanic marketing culture so far in the last three decades. As Ms. Newman-Carrasco says: "The more things change, the more they stay the same!"

According to the Hispanic marketing professionals interviewed for this chapter, these are some of the key trends for the future of Hispanic advertising.

- Hispanic agencies need to exert dominance over the total Hispanic market, not just the Spanish-dominant segment. Cultural relevance needs to be the supporting rationale for their claim. Bilingual Hispanics will be a key segment of influence.

- English-language media and advertisers will offer much stiffer competition given the growth of the Hispanic market relative to the diminishing size of the Anglo market. The Anglo media will increasingly compete for access to bilingual Hispanics, who can switch between Hispanic and Anglo media according to program preference.

- Hispanic marketers must work toward client liaisons that include them in strategic planning for the marketing of their products and services to the Hispanic market. High-level support within client companies is needed for driving Hispanic marketing efforts.

- Integrated marketing is essential to build lasting relationships with Hispanic consumers. Hispanic advertising agencies and marketers need to team with clients to make this happen. No longer is it acceptable to Hispanics that companies advertise in Spanish but do not have Spanish-speaking service to support their claims.

- Agencies must have well-trained culturally astute Hispanic planners who can work with clients on the increasing complexity of Hispanic marketing. These planners need to understand the diverse segments of the market and the changes that are continually occurring within it.

- Overall, Hispanic agencies must become increasingly sophisticated to address the challenges of marketing to Hispanics in a highly competitive period of history.

- Organizations such as AHAA will only become more important as the competitive pressure on Hispanic advertising continues to mount. AHAA should continue to support the cultural knowledge and relevance of its members, promote a forum for mutual learning among its members, and provide an outside face to the country on key Hispanic marketing issues.

Conclusions

Across the 1980s, 1990s, and 2000s, the Census has counted the population swell of Hispanics in the United States. But the surge of awareness, influence, and power of the Hispanic market has come from another source—Hispanic marketers and the media through which they reach consumers. The enormity of their achievement in shaping the identity of the Hispanic market was built client by client: informing companies about the culture, explaining its needs, and communicating to Hispanic consumers.

The marketers we interviewed for this chapter described the challenge of developing the Hispanic market. Hispanic advertising agencies grew up in the 1980s, serving large corporate clients who took notice of the size of the Hispanic population and saw its relevance to their products. Yet, these companies were skeptical, Hispanic marketing budgets were small, and data was scarce. Hispanic marketers had to prove their effectiveness in the short term, and client commitments to the Hispanic market ebbed and flowed.

More companies took notice of the Hispanic market in the 1990s as the population grew. Hispanic agencies multiplied and transformed themselves to meet client opportunities across the decade. Hispanic marketers increased in professionalism as they served mainly the Spanish-dominant segment of the market. But, they were always knocking on potential clients' doors, repeating the story of how Hispanics differed from the general market, and how Hispanic consumers could make a difference to their bottom line. Hispanic agencies recognized their common struggles, and in the latter part of the decade formed a professional organization, AHAA, for professional support and growth.

Nobody quite anticipated the impact of the Hispanic market in the 2000s. The 2000 Census provided the shock of larger than expected growth of the Hispanic population to over 40 million people. However, what was really different was the undeniable presence of the Hispanic market as a force in the overall U.S. culture. Hispanic marketers had expressed to their clients and communicated in their advertising who Hispanics are, what touches their hearts, how they live, how they celebrate, and how they contribute to this country. They had defined this market over and over across three decades. Now, even Hispanic consumers had recognized themselves in these advertising communications. Hispanics had increased in their pride, and demanded the attention of U.S. companies. As Ms. Barrena said, "before you (as a Hispanic) were a stepchild . . . but now you are part of the family."

The challenge of building the Hispanic market is not over. The market is more complex now, and deserves increasingly professional attention by Hispanic marketers. Integrated marketing to the Hispanic market is still in its early stages. This concept needs to be spread to committed companies that do not yet understand its importance for building long-term Hispanic customer relationships. There are not enough trained professionals available in Hispanic agencies to fill critical roles such as account planning. And, U.S. companies are still not allocating marketing dollars to the Hispanic market in proportion to its presence in the population. Hispanic marketers still have the primary role to spread the message of the U.S. Hispanic market, and to keep on discovering and defining it for themselves, their clients, and the consumers they serve.

Implications for Marketers

- Celebrate and recognize the enormous contribution of Hispanic agencies and marketers to the creation of the identity of the U.S. Hispanic market.

- Set clear goals for Hispanic marketing within your agency or company, understanding that the market is growing, changing, and demanding.

- Segmentation of the market is a reality of 2000 and beyond. Prepare to address this through thorough understanding of the data at hand, and conducting the research necessary to advise your clients and target your communication.

- Communicate the benefits of Integrated marketing to your clients and underscore that the trust of a more demanding Hispanic market is earned through consistent communication of your brand message. Emphasize that this trust is a prize worth winning for a loyal Hispanic customer base.

- Be clear that Hispanic marketers need to own the whole spectrum of the Hispanic market—Spanish dominant, bilinguals, and English dominant. Communicate clearly that your expertise in this market is a cultural expertise, and back it up with culturally grounded advertising.

- Remember that the often-heard question, "Why don't they just speak English?" requires a fuller explanation now. In fact, many Hispanics do, and communication in English may be the most appropriate way to reach your target.

- Be ready for competition from the Anglo market for Hispanic bilingual consumers. With the demographic power shift from a declining Anglo market to a growing Hispanic market, it's bound to come.

- Hispanic marketers and agencies need to have a clear message as to why they are the most capable for communicating to Hispanic consumers. They need to be in front of the competitive curve for Hispanic consumers in promoting their image.

- Join and support AHAA. Marketers need the personal support and combined wisdom of a professional organization to address the enormous challenges of the demanding 2000s and beyond.

- Encourage training and education programs aimed at developing culturally astute, professionally competent, bilingual Hispanic marketing professionals. The growth of Hispanic agencies, Hispanic and multicultural marketing departments within large companies, and demand from Anglo marketing organizations indicate that these human marketing resources will be increasingly scarce.

References

1 Forbes, Jack D., "The Hispanic spin: Party politics and governmental manipulation of ethnic identity," *Latin American perspectives.* Autumn: 59–78, 1992. August 30, 2004 <http://links.jstor.org/sici?sici=0094-X%28199223%2919%3A4%3C59%3ATHSPPA%3E2.0.CO%3B2W0094582x>

2 Padilla, Amado M. and William Pérez. "Acculturation, social identity, and social cognition: A new perspective," *Hispanic journal of behavioral sciences* 25: 35–55, 2003.

3 League of United Latin American Citizens.

4 Not an acronym, this organization derives its name from the Spanish verb *aspirar*, to aspire.

5 Mexican American Legal Defense Fund.

6 http://www.hispanicyearbook.com/

7 Montse Barrena, Account Director, Grupo Gallegos; Ernest W. Bromley, Chairman & CEO, Bromley Communications; Ray Celaya, AVP Emerging Markets, Allstate; Dolores Kunda, President & CEO, Lápiz-Integrated Hispanic Marketing; Rochelle Newman-Carrasco, CEO & Principal, Enlace Communications; Hector Orcí, Co-Chairman, CEO, Founder, La Agencia de Orcí & Asociados.

8 *Yesterday, today, and tomorrow* video produced by Telemundo with special content direction by Hispanic Business, Inc, no date specified, circa 1999.

9 www.ahaa.org

The Future

10

This chapter concludes our examination of a cultural perspective on Hispanic marketing. There has been a proliferation of writing and attention dedicated to U.S. Hispanics in recent years. This attention has been bestowed on U.S. Hispanics first by marketers and second by politicians. Hispanics have become a recognized force in this country. They have changed the panorama of how business is conducted.

These days the question is not so much whether or not you should market to Hispanics, but rather, how to do it. This book has been dedicated to answering that question. Our main mission has not been to provide the vast array of statistics that are routinely talked about. It has been to better equip marketers of any service or product by understanding the humanity of the Hispanic culture. The Hispanic culture encompasses the pride, excitement, pain, and despair of many waves of people who trace their origins to a Spanish-speaking country.

Hispanic culture has gained the acceptance that permits it to flourish in the United States, and non-Hispanics appear to be enjoying the cultural encounter and the plurality. Hispanics feel proud that Americans covet Corona Extra. Just a few years ago nobody would have thought that Americans would pay a premium for a Mexican beer, which is obviously made with Mexican water. Hispanics have experienced the pride of seeing their artistic performers on the cover of prestigious publications, on TV, and in the movies. All this positive recognition has contributed to reinforcing Hispanic self-esteem.

The United States is experiencing a cultural renaissance that no one could have predicted 20 years ago. The large scale encounter between Hispanic and Anglo cultures has produced both rich developments as well as struggle. However, demographic trends and economic realities indicate there is no going back. Although some in the United States may still think that this country can remain isolated and powerful on its own, reality contradicts this belief. Quite simply, the forces that propel this cross-cultural phenomenon of U.S. Hispanization are too strong.

Size and Futurism

Estimates about the size of the Hispanic market in the future are all over the place. Most predictions up to now have been underestimates. The mid-range estimate of the U.S. Census Bureau is that by 2050 there will be 100 million Hispanics in the United States, comprising about 25 percent of the U.S. population at that time. Other estimates are that Hispanics are likely to be close to 50 percent of the U.S. population by that time. No one can predict that far ahead because there are too many variables to consider.

Still, futurism is important. Paraphrasing Edward Cornish[1] of the World Future Society, futurism is not about predicting the future but about preparing for it. Marketers and politicians woke the sleeping giant, and now the United States has to get ready for it. Now that the United States is aware of the importance of Hispanics, education for this population segment and sound, rational migration policies are crucial. Attention to this large segment is critical for the United States to continue being the most powerful country in the world. In essence, the United States needs the labor from Latin American immigrants, but that labor force needs to be educated so it can enact its destiny.

Taking Hispanics into account in education within the United States will have language implications. It is likely that by 2050, both the Spanish and the English languages will be required in American schools. Not only will Hispanics speak Spanish but non-Hispanics will want to as well. On the other hand, more and more Hispanics will become increasingly proficient in English.

With increased language capabilities, both in English and Spanish, the United States will be a cosmopolite bilingual nation. English will continue to be the language of business but everyone will enjoy the satisfaction of speaking the Spanish language as well. As we in the United States rehearse other languages, our way of enjoying life changes. We are indeed uncovering parts of our hidden selves and, as discussed in earlier parts of the book, we are participating in the fundamental part of another culture.

Removing Obstacles

What a surprise when Banamex was acquired by Citibank in the early 2000s. Banamex, the pride and joy of Mexican banking, was purchased by an American bank. Mexican economists and politicians would have considered that action to be anathema just a few years earlier. But the forces of free enterprise seem to have prevailed.

Borders have served important purposes at different times in history. As populations grow and as economic activity expands, many of the rules associated with those borders become obsolete. Americans and Mexicans need each other for different reasons. Many politicians, however, have been reluctant to acknowledge that need openly. At the time of this writing, President George W. Bush is trying to implement measures that recognize a more orderly and realistic approach to the common border with Mexico. The relationship between Mexico, the largest exporter of Hispanics to the United States by far, and the United States will be strongly affected if President Bush succeeds in this effort.

Making border flows more orderly and to the benefit of both countries should spell increased economic growth and prosperity. In our opinion, it also will reflect the unavoidable trend toward the elimination of artificial national obstacles. The European Union has provided an example of this.

Lifestyle and Economic Borders Replace National Borders

Stephen Palacios and Maria Flores Letelier, both senior personnel at Cheskin, contributed to this section. Cheskin is a market research and consulting firm with one of its practices dedicated to the U.S. Hispanic market.

Cross-border lives are now a reality. We can see this most clearly with folks who go back and forth between the United States and Mexico, or those who manage to have commitments in both places. These commitments encompass family, friends, homes, and finances. Many Latin American immigrants to the United States come here to work, but find themselves having children and establishing roots here.

U.S. communities are increasingly experiencing the inflow of immigrants they did not expect. This phenomenon is happening all over the United States in varying degrees. North Carolina, for example, saw a nearly 400 percent increase in its Hispanic population between 1990 and 2000, according to the U.S. Census Bureau. But we also find people from the United States living in Mexico full or part time, 2.2 million in 2003.[2] Both groups perceive economic and lifestyle benefits in living cross-border lives. Years of research have taught us that Latin American immigrants obtain more than economic rewards when settling in the United States. Synergistically they acquire parts of American culture and export them to their countries of origin through the various communication channels they use. Simultaneously, many U.S. baby boomers are finding that they cannot afford to retire in the United States, and that Mexico provides higher quality of life, both because of their increased purchasing power there and also because of the charm of the culture.

The large-scale relocation of Latin American immigrants in the United States has positive and negative consequences. The most positive consequence for the United States is the availability of young workers willing to do jobs that Americans are not interested in doing. Negative impacts include strains on community services from illegal immigrants, who tax schools, hospitals, and housing communities. But this flow is very likely to continue unabated and create a dynamic that involves cross-border, transnational lives. This new dynamic will impact both the United States and the countries of origin of these Hispanics, and in the process create new opportunities for businesses and marketers seeking to serve them. Here we explore who these new transnational citizens are, and the implications of their cross-border lives for businesses.

Twin Small Towns: Small Town USA and Small Town Latin America

As Hispanic immigration now moves beyond urban centers such as Los Angeles and Chicago to locations where Hispanics were not previously common, smaller towns in the United States are being redefined. Take for example, the recent Salvadorian immigration explosion in Long Island, New York. In 2004, Suffolk County experienced the largest parade in its history. The Central American Independence Day Parade in Brentwood attracted 50,000 people. As reported in Newsday, the parade was large enough to attract four cabinet members from El Salvador's government, including Foreign Minister Francisco Lainez. For its part, Honduras was represented by its ambassador to the United States, Mario Canahuati, and its foreign minister, Leonidas Rosa Bautista. Many small towns and communities have seen their populations swell by as much as 25 percent in five years due to Hispanic migration, most of which is from one country, if not one town within that country.

It is estimated that the amount of money sent back by immigrants has nearly tripled since 1992. In the case of El Salvador these remittances from the United States now account for approximately 15 percent of its gross domestic product. Mexico has seen a similar rise in remittances, and has become reliant on this inflow of dollars estimated at the time of this writing at nearly $20 billion. Several small towns in Mexico, like Matehuala, Parral, and Atlixco, depend on these inflows for the well-being of the community.

In smaller rural towns, the dependence is extreme. Two thousand of the 3500 inhabitants of General Treviño, Mexico work in the United States. According to the local mayor, Raquel Villareal, the workers in the United States not only support their local families, but they also play an important role as citizens. They donate money for parks and school buses, among other causes. Doctor Aroyo, another small town in the south of the Mexican state of Nuevo Leon, with an aging population and little infrastructure, continues to exist only because of the $400,000 the town receives in remittances each week.[3]

The Consequences of Self Exportation

When towns export themselves, and 8,000 residents relocate from a small town in El Salvador to a small town in Long Island, cultures are exported as well. The effects are widespread:

> "From *pupusas* (meat and cheese stuffed corn tortillas) to *sopa de gallina* (hen soup) and other childhood treats that I can remember savoring when I was in El Salvador, I no longer have to wonder where or how far I have to travel to get them. From Hempstead to Brentwood to Riverhead, with restaurants, specialty stores and packed soccer games, the Central American population has brought not only its food but its culture, flavor, beliefs and dreams to a new land."[4]

Indeed, immigration has been transforming U.S. American culture for some time now. These immigrants have loosened up a stern Protestant culture and turned it into a culture where informality and intimacy are becoming the norm. These cultural shifts are felt on both sides, on both small town counterparts.

El Otro Lado *or The Other Side*

In Mexico, *El Otro Lado* is the code name for the United States used by millions of Mexicans who live with mixed feelings regarding "The

Other Side." People residing in small towns in Mexico live with *El Otro Lado* as part of their daily lives, with hope, wonder, curiosity, fear, and resentment. On *El Otro Lado*, everything is unusual. The streets seem more organized, the cemeteries more dignified, the homes look bigger, and the clothing and cars are flashier. The fancy lives of *telenovelas* appear accessible there to Mexicans who used to think that they were only an illusion, *una ilusión*.

On the other hand, one woman who had given up any hopes for that lifestyle stated that *El Otro Lado* is also a *prision*, or prison. The communication style she uses for establishing relationships does not work in *El Otro Lado*. Gestures lose their meaning and reality becomes transformed. The smile that means respect and recognition for a neighbor has no effect. Exchanging favors as if they were currency has different meanings. Expressions of emotion are misunderstood. That is what happens in *El Otro Lado*. El Otro Lado is the place that has absorbed her son. She asks, "Where is he during the day? Is he safe? What if he becomes ill? How will I cross the border to go take care of him?"

In the course of conducting an ethnographic research project we met with a woman in Matehuala, Mexico. This was a working mother supporting a family of five. Her thoughts were with her son, who had been away for two years and had not returned yet, even once. While the study was taking place, a neighbor came to her running and yelling, "Doña Celia, he is on the phone," and they both ran to the barber shop to take the call. They spoke for one hour. She returned with her eyes full of tears. He had promised to take care of her one day. But for her the important question was, "Will he be here for the festivities in December?" The younger daughter of this woman said that she had seen pictures of the United States. She was amazed at how orderly and big it all looked. She said she spent many days learning everything she could about *El Otro Lado*. She said she watches the Discovery Channel in her eagerness to learn. Her mother may be heartbroken, but her daughter cannot escape the influence of *El Otro Lado*.

El Otro Lado has become part of Matehuala. The streets are ordered. People stop at the stop signs. People driving give others the right of way. These actions are in sharp contrast to what most Mexicans experience. They are proud of these U.S. customs. In Matehuala cars with U.S. license plates are everywhere. Some ride bikes and the really lucky ones ride a scooter. Fashion is in fast forward in Matehuala. Young girls wear hip hugger jeans with tops that reveal their bellies, à la Britney Spears. In addition to the *telenovelas*, people in Matehuala watch self-help shows such as *Lo Que Callamos Las Mujeres*, or "What We Women Keep Silent About." This is an

Oprah type show in Mexican style. They also watch the Mexican version of "Who Wants to Be a Millionaire." Even the traditional *Rosticerias*, or places to eat roasted chicken that exist throughout all of Mexico, have become *Rosticerias* "Fried Chicken" in these towns. This is part of the Americanization of Mexico.

In another ethnographic study in Atlixco, Mexico, we observed the influence of Queens, New York on the region. While studying eating and meal preparation practices a young man talked about his aspirations of importing what he learned in the United States:

> "I was in New York, working at a deli. Now that is my dream. I want to start a deli here in Atlixco, like the kind that they have in New York, but with a Mexican touch. I have seen how some people do it. Some people go to the U.S., come back, and spend all of their money on parties. But some do very well. There is a family who started a pizza place. It is the best pizza in the world. They use local cheese. Domino's has been trying to get our attention here, but they cannot, because this family makes the best pizza. The family picked up skills about running a pizzeria in *El Otro Lado*, in Queens, New York."[5]

During the celebrations of Christmas and *Semana Santa* or Easter, folks from *El Otro Lado* return with all kinds of gifts, and throw a huge party for the entire town. The young man interviewed has noticed this Mexican practice, and he now divides the world into those that spend all the money on parties, and those that become entrepreneurs.

Technology Enables Cross Border Lives

As we have seen earlier in this book, technology now facilitates a dual cultural and national lifestyle. Technology allows for satellite and cable reception of Spanish language programming from both Latin America and the United States. The boom of Hispanic media and technological infrastructure enables linguistic and cultural experience on a scale that other immigrant groups never experienced.

As an extreme in borderless experience, now people use Motorola phones in Monterrey, Mexico, to communicate with others in Houston using push-to-talk features. Nextel is also enabling Mexican companies, such as Sigma Foods, to stay in touch on a daily basis with employees in the United States as they embark on opening new markets. As these technologies become more affordable, more and more people will be using them also for personal purposes. One can envision an "always on" communication flow across-borders. There is not much that politicians can do to stop that. Someone recently complained to me, "my wife IMs (Instant Messages) her mother everyday in Venezuela. They [those in Venezuela] are involved in everything . . . where we were going to live . . . what we ate . . . even our personal finances . . . enough is enough!"

There are other examples of technology that shape the ways in which people live and think. Salvadorians from Metapan in northern New Jersey today can go to http://www.tumetapan.com/ to send e-mails, chat with others, and even see an online video called *Tu País*. They also listen to the radio station in Metapan, and even conduct a variety of commercial activities that vary from cellular phone plan purchases to travel plans. The online and offline lives of these peoples are melding.

To assist the community of Metapan, the parish in New Jersey is working on a twinning project with the church there. As a first step, the English- and Spanish-speaking parishioners of St. John's in New Jersey sent a gift of 200 Bibles, with handwritten notes, to the Church of El Señor Domingo de Ostua.

In less formal ways, the New Jersey parish helps those in need. After a Salvadoran construction worker died in a fall in June 2001, the church in New Jersey raised money to return the man's body to Metapan and arrange for his burial. They held a wake at the church, and organized a party for his son's second birthday."[6] These exchanges appear to have made the Salvadorians in New Jersey and in El Savador part of one community, with the more affluent partner in New Jersey sharing resources and extending a helping hand, as if these geographical and political boundaries did not exist.

Mutual Cultural Influence and Consumer Behavior

According to Louis Nevaer, Mexicans are being influenced by Americans to adopt Protestant ways of life.[7] Qualitative research on both sides of the border shows that the hybridization of culture tends to result in each side taking the more appealing aspects of the other side while struggling to maintain those they treasure of their own. Mexicans in Mexico regret the routine imposed by U.S. influence; they yearn for the freer life of the past. To improve their economic situation they give up some of the more spontaneous and festive aspect of their native Hispanic culture.

Consumer research has repeatedly shown that U.S. Hispanics experience tension between a festive, spontaneous life and a routine, disciplined lifestyle. These consumers struggle with their desire to prosper and their conflicting wish to enjoy the present. For example, the cultural value for celebration persists for Hispanics. These consumers get together to party as often as they can. They do this to compensate for the rigor of the disciplined routine they experience in the United States.

This cultural ambivalence between a strict regimen and enjoying life generates opportunities for products and services that legitimize the possibility for taking a break during the day and savoring the moment. No one would have been able to anticipate the success of Starbucks in Mexico. Starbucks, despite its high prices, legitimizes the festive custom of the social break. People in Mexico get together in commercial venues such as Sanborns and VIPS (popular chains for eating out in Mexico) at all hours for a social break. Women routinely get together for breakfasts and *meriendas* (evening tea/coffee) with other women, thus adding social festivities to an otherwise routine calendar. In this way Hispanics yield to the stricter lifestyle demands of their adopted culture, but interweave the pleasures of their own.

Brands Transcend Nations

U.S. brands are increasingly being taught to Hispanics in their own countries. Upon arrival in the United States they have established brand preferences. Indeed, one reason why Colgate has remained the number-one brand with U.S. Hispanics is because of its prevalence in Mexico and other Latin American countries. The same holds true for Kellogg's, McCormick, and Knorr. Knorr has learned to address the U.S. Hispanic market in the same way they address the Mexican market. They use the name *Knorr Suisa*, a name that is more Spanish friendly, and they offer the product in bottles in addition to cubes. U.S. Mexicans prefer McCormick mayonnaise because of its popularity in Mexico (see the K. Fernandez McCormick Case Study at the end of Chapter 5).

When consumers of Mexican origin have been asked about brands from Mexico that they purchase in the United States, they mention brands such as Pam cooking spray, Aunt Jemima pancakes, and Coke at the top of the list. Another example is that the well-known Texas retailer H.E.B. is now considered to be Mexican by those who come from the north of Mexico. H.E.B. has made important inroads in northern Mexico and has become a Mexican brand for consumers. In a parallel fashion, Mexican companies like *Sigma Alimentos*, notice that there is an opportunity for their brand in the United States because their cold meats products are very well liked in Mexico.

Economic Behavior Changes

The growing interaction between two cultures creates new economic needs and business potential. The mutual flow of economic influence requires increased financial structures in the United States and in Latin America. One of the most significant examples of current developments in financial services is the spate of banking acquisitions and joint ventures between international banks and banks in Mexico. Between 2001 and 2003, three major banking developments took place: Citibank acquired Banamex, HSBC acquired Bital, and Bank of America took a 24 percent stake in Banco Santander. They all want a part of the estimated 20 billion dollars that went from the United States to Mexico in 2004. A notable example is the combination of the real estate footprint of Household, HSBC, in the United States with that of Bital in Mexico, to form a vast network that can service both sides of the border. These aggressive institutions will use remittances as baseline revenue, and from there they will create new cross-border products and services for U.S. Hispanic consumers.

Other financial services companies have also responded to cross-border needs of U.S. Hispanics. For example, MasterCard and Visa have been working on products such as the family card, which consists of issuing cards for relatives without credit in Mexico. Also, retailers like Sears, who have for years innovated in extending credit to previously underserved consumers, are also creating credit facilities that introduce U.S. Hispanics to formal credit and have also introduced cross-border services. A U.S. Mexican can now purchase a washer/dryer in Texas to be delivered to his mother in Mexico.

At this point we can visualize the day when the Bank of America local community centers in Brentwood, Long Island, and San Miguel, El Salvador, provide a TV simulcast of the local Salvadoran soccer in El Salvador to be shown on a large plasma screen in the United States. The community center could be equipped with video phone booths, banking services that move beyond remittances, and include cross-border mortgages and even cross-border health and property insurance. The center would serve traditional foods and celebrate traditional events, but the brands represented would come from the United States as well as El Salvador. The cultural exchange would result in a new type of cross-cultural consumer.

There are also implications for the kinds of products and services that banks can offer to Hispanics. Fatalism is an archetypal tendency among Hispanics; that is, "you never know what the future holds." This archetype is in sharp contrast with the values for planning that the United States cherishes. In many studies we have found that Hispanics are reluctant to commit to a vocation or a particular goal because they wish to "keep all doors open," since no one knows what the future will bring. Furthermore, planning too far in advance is seen as arrogant;

only higher powers can really determine what the future holds. Hence, folks resist planning too far in advance so as to respect fate.

Indeed, in conducting work for the financial services sector, we have learned that respondents of Hispanic origin have a difficult time expressing what their financial goals are for the long term. They cannot describe their planning process. However, when asked about concrete savings and spending goals, many respondents describe savings for family festivities and vacations. These include cultural celebrations, yearly trips to their country of origin, and weekend get-togethers with extended family.

As Hispanic consumers acculturate, they begin to engage in planning for both career and financial goals. When marketers understand the progression that Hispanic consumers go through, they can plan the offering of services to match the steps in this acculturation trajectory. This gives attention to the changing perspectives of Hispanic consumers as opposed to imposing ill-timed planning concepts that are alien to their lives.

The Right and the Wrong—Ethics in Hispanic Marketing

Good Hispanic marketing establishes relationships with consumers. The ethics of modern marketing call for attention to the needs and wishes of consumers as opposed to imposing on them. It just makes business sense to create and reinforce consumer relationships that are based on respect. Cultural sensitivity as addressed in this book is part of that respect.

Hispanic marketing done well should be ethical by definition. Good Hispanic marketing seeks to enhance the lives of consumers. An attempt to better understand the Hispanic consumers shows respect for them.

When marketers conduct market research to understand consumers better, and specifically Hispanic consumers in this case, they get closer to them. Qualitative research is particularly productive in creating closeness. We have heard marketers conducting Hispanic research become emotional in the back room of a focus group facility many times. This emotion is associated with a deeper human understanding of the consumer. A marketer who understands the consumer is more likely to do a good communication job, and to think more carefully of the benefits that his or her products offer to the consumer.

Opportunities to observe and live with Hispanic consumers are great vehicles for understanding and for good marketing. Market immersion experiences allow the marketer to see, smell, touch, hear, and taste Hispanic culture. These experiences typically include home visits, observation of food preparation, talks with the family, consuming meals at restaurants, and store observations and checks where Hispanic consumers live. There is no better way to prepare the marketer to do a good marketing job and to also do good while marketing.

Another approach to getting the marketer closer to the Hispanic consumer is to create video documentaries based on home and community explorations. These documentaries have great impact on upper management. These audiovisual tools also help create a deeper commitment to a marketing effort.

In sum, the more the modern marketer metaphorically goes back to the idyllic village of the past that gave rise to marketing, the better the marketing and the more good accomplished. In that old village the marketer and the consumer interacted as part of a community. Now the village is too large but new communication technologies and research tools allow for that closeness to be reestablished.

Conclusion

This book has been about Hispanic culture with the intent of bringing the marketer closer to the Hispanic consumer. This book is about empowering marketers to know how to think about Hispanic marketing. Even though statistics were used, they were only props to allow for the ideas to flourish. One thing is to tell the marketer what to do and another is to enable the marketer to think about what to do. The latter has been our intent.

To make the concepts come alive the book has been laced with examples, case studies, stories from Hispanic marketers themselves, and excerpts from research reports. Our hope is that you are empowered to do a better job in marketing to U.S. Hispanics. The corollary to this hope is that Hispanic consumers will benefit from better marketing efforts directed to improve their lives. Hispanics and other consumers will increasingly influence how and what is communicated to them. Interaction between consumers and marketers is at the core of the future of marketing.

References

1 Cornish, Edward. *Futuring: The exploration of the future.* Bethesda, MD: The World Future Society, 2004.

2 Nevaer, Louis E.V. *The rise of the Hispanic market in the United States.* New York: M.E. Sharpe, Inc, 2004, p. 109.

3 "Sobrevive la zona rural con paisanos," *El Norte*, 01 January, 2005.

4 Mendez, Luis F. "From pupusas to pizzas: Central Americans become part of Long Island's fabric," *Newsday* (New York), Monday September 13, 2004: A41.

5 From ethnographic notes in Atlixco Puebla, June 2004.

6 Rae, Leah. "Immigrants in suburbia," *The journal news*, October 9, 2004. http://thejournalnews.com/immigrants/.

7 Nevaer, Louis E.V. *The rise of the Hispanic market in the United States.* New York: M.E. Sharpe, Inc. pp. 127–129, 2004.

About the Authors

Felipe Korzenny was born in Mexico City where he studied advertising and television production at the Universidad Iberoamericana. He worked in advertising in Mexico for several years until he decided to pursue a Ph.D. at Michigan State University in the 1970s. At that time he initiated his interest in Hispanic research and published several papers on Hispanic media behaviors. When the 1980 Census focused the attention of U.S. marketers on the Hispanic market, which at the time was about 10 million people, Felipe had moved to California where he developed one of the first specialized Hispanic marketing and consulting firms in the United States. That company, Hispanic & Asian Marketing Communication Research, established the foundation of much of the market understanding of today, when the market is about 4.5 times larger than it was in 1980.

H&AMCR merged with Cheskin in 1999 to capitalize on talent and economies of scale and continues to be a premier provider of Hispanic marketing intelligence. Felipe has worked with a very large number of Fortune 1000 companies and their advertising agencies, to provide insights, understanding, and data for marketing decisions. He has helped launch many products and line extensions, and has contributed to numerous Hispanic marketing strategies and initiatives. He has published a large number of articles and several books, and has made many professional presentations on Hispanic marketing. He is known as one of the leaders of the field.

Felipe received a Distinguished Alumni Award from Michigan State University in 2003. This is the highest award bestowed by the MSU Alumni Association and is presented to MSU graduates who have demonstrated the highest level of professional accomplishment. He also received an Outstanding Alumni Award from the College of Communication Arts and Sciences, Michigan State University, in 1997. In April 2005 he received the first HispanSource Award for Achievement in Hispanic Marketing Research.

In 2004 he established the foundation at Florida State University of what is now the first Center for the Study of Hispanic Marketing Communication in the United States. This center provides an undergraduate minor, a graduate certificate, education, research, and other activities to train Hispanic marketing professionals. Besides his academic activities Felipe continues his involvement with industry, providing research and consulting. For further information and to contact him visit http://www.korzenny.com.

Betty Ann Korzenny's international experience and passion for cultural understanding have shaped her personal and professional life. She is a native of Troy, New York, and has spent more than 17 years living and working in other cultures outside of the United States. She has pursued her interests in intercultural communication, education, and research in Germany, Nigeria, Italy, and Mexico, and has worked in the U.S. Hispanic market beginning with her early research at Michigan State University in the 1970s.

She received her undergraduate degree from Vassar College, and her Masters and Ph.D. from Michigan State University, all in education. While pursuing doctoral studies at Michigan State University, she expanded her cultural interests to include the role of management in bringing about cultural change and innovation in organizations. She lived and worked as a director of research and development in the communication research wing of one of the largest advertising companies in Mexico.

Returning to the United States in the 1980s, she held key management responsibilities in major corporations for organizational and management development, employee education, and internal communications. She provided leadership in the introduction of organizational innovations, particularly those concerned with customer orientation, for large national companies, including two owned by Ford Motor Company.

In the early 1990s Betty Ann became COO of Hispanic & Asian Marketing Research, where she collaborated with Felipe Korzenny to grow the company into one of the leading multicultural research companies in the United States. Her responsibilities at H&AMCR included managing the company on a daily basis and working with managers of major Fortune 1000 companies and their ad agencies to shape their approach for developing a deeper cultural understanding of the Hispanic market. As an owner of Cheskin from 1999 through 2003, she continued to play a lead role working with clients in the Hispanic market.

Currently, Betty Ann is teaching at Florida State University in the Department of Communication and pursuing her own writing interests. She continues to maintain strong contacts with key players in Hispanic marketing. Her collaboration in writing this book is the result of her long commitment to culturally sensitive customer-oriented marketing.

Index